T0286903

Praise for
ANCESTRAL MINDSET

"UNDERSTANDING OTHERS is the name of the game in today's world, business and personal. John Daniel synthesizes decades of research in psychology and behavioral neuroscience into easy-to-understand terms that gives us the knowledge to become better professionals, leaders, and people. His stories from his personal and professional lives bring the content to life and provide examples on how to apply our newly found understanding and insights to our everyday situations."

—Bill Burch
SPHR, SHRM-SCP, PCC, EXECUTIVE COACH,
FORMER HR LEADER AND PRESIDENT OF
HARMONY COACHING AND CONSULTING

"WITH *ANCESTRAL MINDSET*, John Daniel provides a concise framework for understanding how leaders and those they lead process everyday interactions and events. With his thirty-plus years of experience in HR, he translates his framework into understandable and actionable steps to improve individual and organizational performance. I consider this a must-read for any new or emerging leader."

—Bryan Jordan
CHAIRMAN, PRESIDENT AND
CHIEF EXECUTIVE OFFICER OF
FIRST HORIZON BANK

"ANYONE WHO has served in a leadership role knows that while strategy, financial management, and other traditional disciplines are important, understanding and managing people effectively is what truly makes the difference. John Daniel's insightful, important, and must-read new book will help current and aspiring leaders understand human behavior at a deep level by explaining the evolutionary and neurological underpinnings of what makes us all tick. John's own extensive leadership experience allows him to add practical advice and firsthand examples to drive home his lessons."

—*Bill Burke*
FORMER CEO OF THE WEATHER CHANNEL COMPANIES
AND FOUNDER OF THE OPTIMISM INSTITUTE

"*ANCESTRAL MINDSET* is a fascinating compilation of John Daniel's decades-long study of human behavior and leadership development. Packed with research on brain evolution, behavioral neuroscience, psychology, and leadership theory, Daniel delivers an engaging, insightful, and applicable guide for leaders who want to better understand and lead their teams. His valuable, time-tested insights woven together with heartfelt stories and case studies make this a valuable resource for leaders."

—*Cindy Cleveland*
CHIEF TALENT OFFICER,
DIVERSIFIED TRUST

ANCESTRAL MINDSET

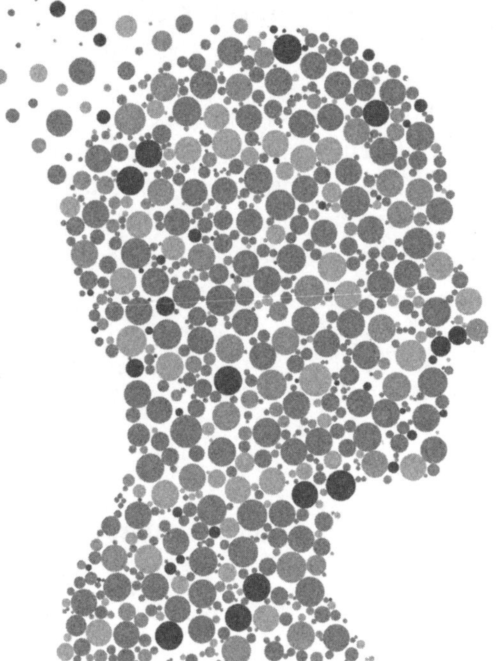

Adopting an Evolutionary Framework to Lead, Influence, and Collaborate

John Daniel

ANCESTRAL MINDSET: Adopting an Evolutionary Framework to Lead, Influence, and Collaborate

Published by Forefront Books.
Distributed by Simon & Schuster.

Library of Congress Control Number: 2024919460

Print ISBN: 978-1-63763-358-8
E-book ISBN: 978-1-63763-359-5

Cover Design by Faceout Studio, Elisha Zepeda
Interior Design by Mary Susan Oleson, Blu Design Concepts

For Leslie. Your unwavering love,
endless support, and beautiful smile
have been the guiding light in my life.
I dedicate this work to you with all my heart.

Contents

Introduction

> Everyone has a theory of human nature.
> Everyone has to anticipate the behavior of others,
> and that means we all need theories
> about what makes people tick.
> —Steven Pinker

My First Ten Thousand Hours

John Melvin Daniel was born on February 2, 1909, in what is now the Brookline neighborhood of Pittsburgh. Pap, as he was known to me, was a quiet, caring, but stubborn man. He had little education. His father, a miner, died in a freak accident digging a well at the age of thirty-eight, and Pap had to quit elementary school to help his mother. Pap's family and friends all called him Mel, no doubt a nickname derived from his middle name, to avoid confusion with his father who was also named John. This served our family well; Pap named his first son John Melvin Jr., and in 1954 I joined the long string of John Melvin Daniels with a III attached at the end.

As a teenager Pap worked at a department store as a wrapper. He married my grandmother, Ruth, at the age of nineteen and—with little education and few job skills—spent most of the Depression era doing odd jobs to survive. In his rare reflective moments, he would talk about the challenges of the Great Depression. Pap and Ruth had two sons in the first years of their marriage, adding to their struggle. My dad arrived in 1930 and his brother less than two years later. A third son, a big surprise as the family story goes, was born thirteen years later in 1944. Uncle Ed, who was only ten years older than me, became a banker and, early in my career, a mentor.

World War II opened opportunities for low-skilled men. Pap got a job working as a truck driver for the Atlantic Richfield Company. With young sons at home and now working in the critical oil industry, Pap received a deferment and was not called up to serve in the war. But he served the Atlantic Richfield Company for over thirty-five years. He wore his company baseball cap, adorned with his many loyalty and safe-driving pins, with great pride.

Still, Pap had mixed views about the company. He sometimes spoke disparagingly about the "big bosses," and I listened attentively as he told stories about how he subtly undermined his supervisor's directives. Yet he spoke with pride about his long years of service and the recognition he received for his driving record. I got the sense that he loved the independence and responsibility that comes with driving a big rig truck. One of my fondest memories as a child was the annual union picnic held for all the workers and their families. I was fascinated by the way Pap interacted with his coworkers. The fellowship was marked by loud, boastful conversations and much teasing. I enjoyed the rides and games of skill, but I was enthralled with the stories, the conversations, and the interactions.

When he was fifty-six, Pap received a cash settlement from an insurance company over an automobile accident caused by another driver. He decided to use the money to fulfill a dream to become a small business owner. A local filling station franchised by Atlantic Richfield was up for sale. The details behind the transaction are long lost to history, but I remember Pap and my dad putting together plans to run the station. They agreed to run the business as equal partners, but both would keep their full-time jobs. At the time Dad was a police officer on the third shift, so he would watch over the business during the day. Pap would continue to drive his fuel truck and work at the station on the weekends. The latter was under one condition: that I would be his apprentice. So at the tender age of thirteen, clearly skating child labor laws, I started a new phase of my life as a worker. The gas station would become my laboratory for observing people. While I learned how to pump gas, change a flat tire, and replace an alternator, I learned way more about the idiosyncrasies of human behavior.

Pap rarely shared his feelings and emotions with me, but I could tell he was proud of the grandson who shared his name. As I washed customers' windows or filled their gas tanks, he would proudly point out that I was his grandson. During those few years we worked closely together we developed a special bond. He was not a man filled with wisdom and eager to share erudite lessons. But I learned by watching him. He always showed up to work early. He was respectful of everyone. And he did every job well. He insisted that I wash the windows to the edge, that every gas cap be checked twice to make sure it was tightly secured, that oil spills were wiped clean before closing the hood of the customer's car. There were to be no shortcuts. These lessons stuck with me throughout my work life.

The employees at the gas station were a motley crew. One key employee was a man who worked part-time to augment his full-time job. Hardworking and dependable, he could be relied upon to do his job without much supervision. The rest were unfocused and unreliable. Pap would ignore the workers he didn't like or act in passive-aggressive ways. He would grumble to me about so-and-so being lazy or a "dumbass," but he never addressed his concerns directly. He left the supervision to my dad, whose main management lever was to burst into a screaming rage and watch his employees scramble to do something, anything, that would make him stop. Once he cooled, he would explain his complaints and things would return to some semblance of normal. I kept a low profile during those heated moments. But I remember thinking that neither Pap's nor Dad's strategies seemed very effective. The station's employees always drifted back to their old behaviors—lots of sitting, talking, and cursing while customers' cars sat waiting to be fixed—until Dad showed up and they scurried back to work again.

I was not privy to the financial details of Dad and Pap's entrepreneurial venture, but cracks emerged not long after the family took over the business. Many conversations took place behind closed doors, but I could see the strain of the business taking a toll on everyone. Pap and Dad must have disagreed about important decisions, which resulted in Pap's stubbornness kicking in. He and Dad would not talk when they were in the same room, and eventually Pap stopped working at the station altogether. I do not remember the details of how it all ended, but Daniel's Atlantic Station was swept up in the shift from small, family-owned neighborhood stations to the multibay convenience store combinations we have now. At fifteen, my career as a gas station attendant ended. But the experience left an indelible mark on me. Years later I remembered how Dad and Pap treated the customers. They knew most of them by name, having lived in the community all their lives. They greeted them like close friends, and the conversations included questions about life, the goings on in the neighborhood, and lots of storytelling.

But I also remember how they treated the local bank manager and other men in suits and big cars differently. They welcomed them more formally and deferentially and referred to them as *Mr.* rather than using their first name. I remember thinking, *I want to be one of those guys.*

My period of unemployment did not last long. While school was a priority, Daniel children learned that work was important. Dad's police salary did not stretch very far, and there were eleven mouths to feed in the Daniel family. I first earned money delivering the local newspaper. That paper route, secured at age twelve, would later pass down to three brothers and three sisters. When the gas station closed, I got a work permit and began my employment at the Crafton-Ingram Speedy Carwash. The job at the car wash would change my life in several ways. It was there that I met a beautiful girl with long brown hair, a cute dimple on her left cheek, and a warm, welcoming smile. I fell head over heels in love. She was the cashier, and I remember racing to work after school not just to be on time but to see her smile. I asked her to the high school prom and over the next few years we spent every moment we could together. We got engaged at the age of twenty and married less than a year later. We were together for over thirty-seven years, until she lost her long and courageous battle with cancer at the all-too-youthful age of fifty-six.

The car wash was my second laboratory in the study of human behavior. My work ethic and the leadership skills I had learned in the Boy Scouts impressed the owner. He took me under his wing and treated me like a son. Under his tutelage I learned to balance the books at the end of the day, make bank deposits, order supplies, and manage the payroll. Frank trusted me and gave me a great deal of autonomy. Unlike my dad, he was calm and collected. He coached me when I made a mistake, mostly by needling me in a kind way, and never raised his voice.

Frank appointed me supervisor of the rest of the staff when he was away. At seventeen, I felt a great burden of responsibility but took on the challenge with enthusiasm. Without formal leadership training I had no idea how to lead. At first, my directives were ignored by the high school students and low-skilled, hourly wage employees. But over time, and with reinforcement from Frank, they grudgingly accepted me as a boss. The staff knew I understood how the place worked, and they came to me for answers. I gained confidence as I slowly won them over.

While working at the car wash, I was also attending college. I had only vague ideas about a career, but marriage caused me to think more deeply about my future. Working as a car wash attendant didn't seem like the path to career and financial stability. My soon-to-be father-in-law, concerned about his daughter (as he later admitted), introduced me to his neighbor who was a vice president at Mellon Bank, one of the most prestigious employers in my hometown. A short while later I started my career in banking as a night shift mail room attendant. My first job was picking up checks from branch banks delivered to the loading dock by courier. I loaded the checks onto carts and raced them to the twentieth floor for processing. I spent a great deal of that first year on elevators. As the old joke goes, my job as a messenger had its ups and downs.

I remember my parents and grandparents congratulating me on landing a job at the bank. They thought it was a big deal, even though I had a slightly better than minimum wage job. "Start at the bottom and work your way up" was a phrase I heard multiple times. From messenger I progressed steadily through several roles: check processor, mail room lead, loan collector, and consumer loan officer to management trainee. The latter role came after my graduation from the University of Pittsburgh with a degree in political science. The management training program at Mellon was highly selective, and I became the first liberal arts graduate and internal candidate to make it into the program. One of my assignments as a trainee was to help design and deliver customer service training to branch staff. I loved the assignment and drew on all my studies in sociology and psychology to create a fun and impactful program. The assignment was serendipitous in that it gave me high visibility to bank executives. It also created a lead into a job in what was then called personnel, now human resources. I quickly discovered I had found my life's work.

My career journey through human resources spanned over thirty-five years, the last twenty as the top HR executive at two banking companies. I worked in recruiting and witnessed first-hand the excitement of people learning about their new jobs—and for many more the disappointment of rejection. I worked in employee relations with employees who were not performing and with others who were looking for help as they struggled with the demands of work or bad bosses. I trained and coached hundreds of leaders, all with different personalities, styles, and strengths. Most were successful, but many desperately wanted the influence, prestige, and pay of a management job but lacked the basic traits and intuitions of successful leaders. I helped facilitate discussions with teams that were looking to enhance teamwork, improve productivity, or transcend differences that impeded their ability to work together. I worked closely with all levels of people, from board members and CEOs to frontline staff. As the chief human resources officer, I had a front row seat to how work life played out for thousands of employees. I have seen people at their best and at their worst. A few of those stories have found their way into this book.

Malcom Gladwell introduced the 10,000-Hour Rule in his book *Outliers: The Story of Success.*[1] The rule is based on the research of K. Anders Ericsson, who studied the development of expertise. The rule suggests that it takes approximately ten thousand hours of dedicated practice to achieve mastery in a particular field or skill. With his skill as a storyteller, Gladwell describes how the Beatles accumulated over ten thousand hours of practice working small clubs in Europe before they had a "burst of success" in 1964. While Gladwell's rule has been subject to some criticism and much debate for ignoring inherent talent, genetic predispositions, and other factors, it underscores an important point about the necessity of practice. I got an early start on my ten thousand hours of becoming an expert on human behavior with my paper route, followed by the gas station, the car wash, and then the bank. Ten thousand hours of engaging and watching others engage. Ten thousand hours of collaborating, listening, storytelling, arguing, negotiating . . . my personal PhD in our social life.

Programmed for Narrative

You will see later in the book that the ability to reflect is traitlike in that it has high levels of heritability and is stable and enduring

....

1 Malcom Gladwell, *Outliers: The Story of Success* (Little, Brown and Company, 2008), 35–38.

over time. I was blessed—or cursed on multiple occasions—with this trait. For as long as I can remember, I have always thought deeply about my behavior and the behavior of the people around me. To the detriment of some of my friends and loved ones, I try to dissect and understand the thoughts, feelings, and motivations that drive behaviors. Reflection can be a source of powerful insights, but at times I came up empty trying to understand what makes people tick. I started reading everything I could find in the fields of psychology, cognitive science, sociology, behavioral economics, political science, and organizational behavior.

Many of the books and papers I read are sources for this book and are documented in the footnotes. Ten thousand hours of doing something badly does not develop expertise. Ten thousand hours of engaging in dysfunctional human behavior just makes one more dysfunctional. What I have learned and am excited to share comes from more than ten thousand hours of observation, reflection, study, and practice. It is a pretty good model for developing expertise. I have also learned that human behavior is amazingly complex, and "experts" need to approach every opportunity to add insight and value with a big dose of humility.

As you will see, my favorite perspective on human behavior comes from evolutionary psychology, a branch of psychology that seeks to understand behavior through the lens of evolutionary biology. One of the first insights I gained from this perspective is why our brains love stories. The best books are the ones with the best stories, and while this is a nonfiction work filled with research, theories, and data, I have tried to add stories as often as I can. Information gained through "stories are far more memorable—22 times more according to one study—because multiple parts of the brain are activated for narratives."[2] Stories that evoke emotions cause an emotional connection that not only improves memory but builds bonds between people. Our ancestors survived and passed on their genes through cooperation, collaboration, and culture. The latter is the store of all knowledge needed to survive in a hostile environment. Before writing, which was invented only five thousand years ago, information was embedded in narratives and thus "our brains evolved with reflexive use of narrative as part of our cognition."[3]

Imagine a hunter-gatherer parent warning her child about wandering too far from the group. An admonition might work, but a story with gruesome details about how a saber-toothed tiger ate another child might have a more powerful and lasting impact. Recent research has shown that effective storytelling, rich with detail and laden with emotion, causes changes in the brain. "Stories put listeners on an equal emotional wavelength, eliciting understanding, trust and sympathy."[4] Evolution shaped our brains to use stories to bind us together as group cohesion and cooperation enhanced group survival. Storytelling did not directly contribute to obtaining food or other resources, but storytelling skills can be considered our equivalent to the speed of a cheetah or the strength and sharp teeth of a lion: important evolutionary adaptations.

Thus, our brains are wired to think in narratives, which help us convey messages, build bonds, and share knowledge. Narratives also help us make sense of the world. We organize random events and

[2] Gaia Vince, *Transcendence: How Humans Evolved Through Fire, Language, Beauty, and Time* (Basic Books, 2020), 85.

[3] Vince, *Transcendence*, 82.

[4] Vince, *Transcendence*, 93.

experiences into a coherent story. Local news organizations do this every night with their evening broadcasts. The anchors do not just announce crime data, new business openings, and economic figures. They weave together information to create narratives like "our city is on the move" or "our city is heading to hell in a handbasket."[5] The choice of defining narrative is guided by the values and biases of the storyteller. Narratives also play an important role in shaping our identity by providing a framework through which we understand and interpret our lives. The stories we tell about ourselves, our experiences, our failures, and our achievements contribute to our concept of self. This concept of self becomes part of our personality, the unique and enduring pattern of thoughts, feelings, and behaviors that others see as us.

Personality is shaped by genetic factors and by early childhood. The former contribute to certain traits and predispositions. The latter is the sum of family dynamics, parenting styles, the level of emotional support, and early life experiences. Both are powerful in shaping who we are, but they are also beyond our control. While traits can change over time, they are relatively stable throughout our lives. An introvert who enjoys quiet time working alone isn't likely to become a gregarious life of the party. And while we cannot change the environment and life experiences that influenced us, we can change the story we have constructed about our lives. In my talks about personality and behavior, I describe how our stories about our lives shape our identity and perspectives about life. After one of my talks, a woman came up to thank me. She recounted how her sister, from whom she is only a few years apart in age and who was raised

[5] This well-known phrase has been linked to the American gold rush of the 1840s, when men were lowered by hand in baskets to set off explosives, which could have deadly consequences.

by the same parents in the same household, has always had a very negative view of her life.

"My sister is always complaining how Mom and Dad were too strict and how we were poor and how we didn't get to go to the best schools. While I thought my parents were tough, I benefited from the discipline. And while we did not have much, we were like most of the people in our neighborhood. I liked my school and had lots of friends and I think I have done well in my life. I have had a good career and have happy family life." She went on to say that her sister has had a rocky career and personal life and blames it all on her upbringing. "My sister has this story in her head that all her setbacks are rooted in our childhood, but I just don't see it that way." There is a lot going on with the sister in this case. She may have certain personality traits or other predispositions that have contributed to her life turning out as it has. But it is clear she has crafted a life story that allows her to make sense of things.

There is a branch of psychology called narrative psychology that focuses on helping people understand and analyze their life stories. The approach starts by helping people understand that their "stories" have been constructed through the ways they interpret the events, experiences, and relationships that have impacted their lives. These stories in turn influence their perceptions, emotions, and behaviors. The narrative method acknowledges that we can't change our past, but we can learn to better understand how our interpretations were constructed and to reframe them in a more positive way. One form of reframing is called transactional analysis, a theory developed by Eric Berne. Berne believed that people adopt certain life scripts to make sense of their experiences and thereby to better navigate the complexities of life. These scripts can guide positive behavior, but they can also contribute to distorted thinking. For example, a person who develops a script that says "I am a loser" will have low self-worth. Perhaps an abusive alcoholic parent caused the development of that script, but that self-perception can be changed through reflection and the development of a new script.

Biology and Personality

A key point you will take away from this book is that there is a lot going on in our brains that we are not consciously aware of and that impacts our thoughts and behaviors in significant ways. Imagine you are on the way to work one day. You feel a little off but can't explain why. Another driver cuts into your lane and nearly causes you to crash. When you arrive at work, your coworkers can sense your mood. When asked if you are OK, you tell the story about the jerk who ruined the start of your day. Imagine another day. On this one you feel on top of the world. On the drive to work someone cuts in front of you. You press the brakes quickly but remain unfazed. When you arrive at work, your coworkers sense that you are in a good mood.

How do we interpret the differences between those two scenarios? The first one may be explained by any number of causes. In one case, you have ignored good sense and eaten lots of trans fats. The trans fats have an impact on your gut microbiota, which in turns causes an increase in the production of stress hormones. Those stress hormones are the explanation for that feeling of being "off." The stress hormones cause heightened sensitivity and alertness. That can be good if you are facing a physical threat, but it also suppresses parts of the brain that control emotional regulation.

In the second example, your brain was not in a heightened state. When the other driver cut in front of you, your brain processed it as a minor irritant, not a major threat, thus it did not impact your positive mental state. That's right, gut bacteria affect your thinking, but your explanation to the world is not, "I ate a big serving of trans fats, which affected my gut bacteria, which triggered stress hormones that are now coloring my mood and thinking." You are more likely to say, "An asshole cut me off on the way to work today and almost caused me to wreck my car." That story is simple, explanatory, and largely made up.

I remember in high school one of my friends falling "head over heels" in love with a girl from another school at a football game. Those were his words; my word was *obsessed*. While he never talked with her, he stared at her all through the game. Over the next few weeks, he talked about her incessantly. I have since learned a great deal about how faces, particularly beautiful faces,[6] trigger strong emotions and feelings. Our brain processes millions of bits of information about faces we've seen in the fusiform face area. When activated it processes powerful subliminal cues. Research shows that "attractive people are judged to be smarter, kinder and more honest. We're more likely to vote for attractive people or hire them, less likely to convict them of crimes, and if they are convicted, more likely to dole out shorter sentences."[7] We think of ourselves as highly rational. We believe we have complete agency over our beliefs and behaviors. Yet lots of stuff is going on in our brains that

---

[6] Beauty standards vary widely across cultures, but there are some universalities that may have evolutionary roots. Clear skin, larger eyes in relation to the face, a prominent limbal ring, and overall facial symmetry are associated with good health and genetic fitness.

[7] Robert Sapolsky, *Behave: The Biology of Humans at Our Best and Worst* (Penguin Press, 2017), 88.

we are not consciously aware of that deeply affects both. Research shows that "the shape of a woman's face changes subtly during the ovulatory cycle, and men prefer faces at the time of ovulation."[8] Viewed from the lens of evolutionary biology, that makes perfect sense and might explain the obsession of my high school friend. The wide pretty eyes, flawless skin, and slightly altered shape triggered a flow of oxytocin that overwhelmed his capacity for clear thinking. He was hooked.

These two examples are the tip of the iceberg. The human brain was "designed by natural selection to guide the individual in making decisions that aid survival and reproduction."[9] That said, the brain was designed to learn, so not everything is innate. But much of human behavior can be traced to predispositions and tendencies wired into our brain because they served an evolutionary adaptive purpose. In his recent book *Determined: A Science of Life without Free Will*, the brilliant professor Robert Sapolsky argues that all human behavior is determined.[10] Once you observe a behavior, your next question is to ask why it occurred. At a biological level it occurred because of the action of neurons in the brain. But why were the neurons triggered? In the example of my lovesick friend, they were triggered by hormones. But the next question is what put the hormones into circulation. Were they triggered by an experience in the past that sprouted neuronic connections outside conscious control? Were they triggered by a comment or behavior from another? If so, why did we interpret these in a particular way? As Sapolsky describes it, the chain

8 Sapolsky, *Behave*, 88.

9 Lance Workman and Will Reader, *Evolutionary Psychology: An Introduction*, 4th ed. (Cambridge University Press, 2021), 1.

10 Robert Sapolsky, *Determined: A Science of Life without Free Will* (Penguin Press, 2023).

of explanation can go all the way back to our ancestors' experiences on the savanna.

Professor Sapolsky argues against the notion of free will because all the variables that influence behavior—from our neonatal and parental environments, hormone levels, and past traumatic experiences to our cultural and socioeconomic environments—are outside our control. I will leave that debate to the philosophers, but Sapolsky's research shows that all the behaviors we encounter are shaped by multiple factors, from seconds ago with a flood of hormones triggered by any number of causes, to millennia ago when brain functions were shaped by evolution to adapt and thrive on the savanna.

The premise of this book is that understanding and adopting an evolutionary framework provides countless insights to help in leading, influencing, and collaborating with the people in our lives.

chapter 1

Carrots and Sticks

Too many people hold a very narrow view
of what motivates us. They believe that the only way
to get us moving is with the jab of a stick
or the promise of a carrot. But if you look
over 50 years of research on motivation,
or simply scrutinize your own behavior, it's pretty clear
human beings are more complicated than that.

—Daniel Pink

Tribute

As I was writing this chapter, my younger brother Marty passed away suddenly from heart failure. I was deeply saddened to lose him; he was a great dad, brother, and citizen who was loved by many. Marty never said no when a friend or family member asked for help. He was kind, quiet, and giving. He was also a bit stubborn, like our Pap. We grew up in a big family of very modest means. Mom had many rules, and the one Marty hated the most was that you had to eat everything on your plate before you were excused from the table. Marty hated cooked carrots, and he hated peas even more. I remember a few times he would sit at the table for hours and Mom would just put his plate in the refrigerator and tell him he would have to eat it for breakfast. I am not sure Mom ever made him eat his peas and carrots for breakfast.

She could be tough, but she was never cruel. I love eating peas today, but I still don't like carrots or the carrot metaphor that expresses a widely held view about human motivation.

Behaviorism

As leaders and colleagues, we are often faced with fascinating questions about people both individually and collectively. Why are people the way they are? Why do they think, feel, and act in often-peculiar ways? Sometimes we are faced with more specific questions: Why do people resist change? Why are some people highly motivated and others less so? Why do some teams get impressive results while other teams flounder in a sea of dysfunction? Why are we tribal, and why do silos spring up so naturally in organizations? The list goes on.

All of us have operating philosophies or models that help us answer these important questions, though we may not be conscious of these models as we developed the beliefs through our experiences. Some of us are behaviorists, although we might not use that label. The essence of behaviorism is captured by the metaphor of the carrot and the stick. If you want someone to do something, you provide a reward (the carrot). If the right behavior is not forthcoming, you use punishment (the stick). Etymologists believe the carrot/stick metaphor can be traced back to the nineteenth century. During those times, people raced on donkeys. One popular technique was to dangle a carrot at the end of a stick to entice the animal to run. Other riders simply used a stick to whack the donkey from left and right repeatedly to get them to run faster.

Behaviorism as a formal school of thought began in 1913 when

John Watson wrote an article titled "Psychology as the Behaviorist Views It." Behaviorism is a theory that states that all behaviors are the product of a reflex evoked by an external antecedent stimulus (a carrot or a stick). Behaviorism was expanded by Harvard psychologist B. F. Skinner, best known for the concept of operant conditioning. You may remember this from your first class in psychology. Operant conditioning is a process during which a desired behavior is induced using a series of positive reinforcements or negative punishments.

Watson and the behaviorists that followed him believed the mind was a blank slate at birth. Watson's views are captured by the following famous quote.

"Give me a dozen healthy infants, well-formed, and my own specified world to bring them up in and I'll guarantee to take anyone at random and train him to become any type of specialist I might select—doctor, lawyer, artist, merchant-chief, and yes even beggar-man, regardless of his talents, penchants, tendencies, abilities, vocations, and race of his ancestors."[1]

In the long-running debate in biology and psychology about nature versus nurture, the behaviorists clearly favor the latter. Their belief is that humans can imprint what they want on others' brains because brains don't come with much prewiring. Behaviorism dominated psychological theory through the early and middle part of the twentieth century and its influence spilled into all aspects of life, including the workplace. Our brain is very good at causal relationships: Behavior + Reward/Punishment = Results. It made sense.

As to the preceding questions, the behaviorist has some answers. Why are people the way they are? Simple. People are

....

[1] John Watson, *Behaviorism*, 1930, cited in multiple articles on behaviorism.

the product of their environment and the conditioning they have experienced. Why do people resist change? Why are some people unmotivated? For the behaviorist, again the answer is simple. There is insufficient reward or punishment. To motivate people to get them to do what we want, design the right combination of incentives and disincentives. Behaviorism seems to have explanatory power. Sometimes the right rewards do lead to desired results . . . but often they don't.

In studies evaluating short-term incentive plans, such as piece-rate plans, financial rewards for higher performance seem to motivate performance. In a piece-rate pay system, employees are paid per unit processed rather than an hourly or annual salary. If the work is highly repetitive, measurable, and simple, the piece-rate system can lead to increased production and efficiency. It also provides its own feedback loop, as the employee and supervisor can easily measure results. This in turn reduces the need for close supervision. The studies seem to confirm one of behaviorism's basic tenets. But add a little complexity to the task being rewarded and things get a lot murkier. If the task involves one or two simple steps, the worker can move quickly and without much thought. But if the task involves multiple steps and some level of real-time decision-making, piecework plans can lead to disaster. The desire of workers to earn higher pay often causes quality to suffer. Studies of piecework plans also show that workers' inner expectations and motivations impact the success of piece-rate plans. For example, a worker's dim view of the fairness of pay can lead to a lower performance than that of someone doing the same work at a rate viewed as more equitable.

I saw firsthand the negative impact of a behaviorist

perspective on management decision-making at my first company. A new manager, David, took over a work unit at the bank that had a reputation for high performance and a desirable culture. Customers rated the business unit's services favorably, employees loved working there, and previous managers had a reputation for developing talent. David, whose bonus plan disproportionately favored revenue growth, decided to change the sales team's bonus plan to an incentive plan that also disproportionately rewarded sales growth. I was called in as an HR consultant when David found himself faced with a disgruntled sales team that was pushing back strongly against the new plan. I suggested to David that he keep the old plan in place and use his first full year for experimentation. I shared with him an example of another manager who had built a system of tracking sales and revenue growth by individual employee for a full year. Once the tracking system was built and the bugs worked out, the manager asked the sales team members to collaborate with him on a new incentive plan. In the case I shared, employee resistance evaporated and after the first full year of the plan's implementation, the plan was deemed a success.

David did not like my suggestion. He wanted the plan in place immediately. I was confident his sense of urgency was driven by the design of his own bonus plan. David said his team was just resisting change. He was determined to forge ahead. Well, to make a long story short, the new plan led to several negative results both immediately and over the long term. A few years later, David was removed from his role, as both morale in his unit and customer service scores had dropped significantly. Rather than a balanced focus on both sales and customer service, team members concentrated on the former. Several high performers who loved the service aspect of the role left for other positions. New team members complained that none of the experienced salespeople would spend time coaching and mentoring. The business unit's strength as a talent developer withered.

In 2009, Daniel Pink published *Drive: The Surprising Truth about What Motivates Us*, which offers a complete indictment of external rewards as a primary source of motivation. In the book, Pink points out the many deadly flaws in the "carrot and stick approach." In addition to the quality of performance mentioned here, Pink shows that external rewards can extinguish intrinsic motivation, crush creativity, foster short-term thinking, and even lead to cheating and bad behavior. The focus on external rewards was highly influenced by the behaviorist movement, and some vestiges of that movement still reside in the minds of leaders and the cultures of many organizations.

Behaviorism has fallen out of favor both in the field of psychology and in business. Its appeal was understandable—the theory is easy to grasp and often works. It is a great way to train a dog and, in the short term, it may be a way to get your children or employees to do something they don't want to do. But in the end, its usefulness as a tool for motivating people or as a framework for understanding them came up woefully short. Pink points out another force that contributed to its end. In the early days of the Industrial Revolution, tasks were mostly repetitive and routine. The word *job* comes from an Old English word meaning piece. Workers were often literally pieces or extensions of steam-powered machines. As Pink describes:

> Workers . . . were like parts in a complicated machine. If they did the right work in the right way at the right time, the machine would function smoothly, and to ensure that happened, you simply rewarded the behavior you sought and punished the behavior you discouraged. People would

> respond rationally to those external forces—these extrinsic motivators—and both they and the system itself would flourish. We tend to think that coal and oil have powered economic development. But in some sense, the engine of commerce has been fueled equally by carrots and sticks . . . It is so deeply embedded in our lives that most of us scarcely recognize that it exists. For as long as we can remember, we've configured our organizations around its bedrock assumptions: The way to improve performance . . . is to reward the good and punish the bad.[2]

So the carrot and stick approach had its day until it didn't. In the latter part of the twentieth century, a more complex world emerged. The Industrial Revolution transitioned into the age of the knowledge worker. The behaviorists' carrot and stick became increasingly problematic and ineffective, but their influence still lingers to this day.

Along with a dramatic change in the nature of work came an explosion of new research from the fields of cognitive psychology and neuroscience about the human brain. It turns out the human mind does come with a whole bunch of prewiring. The behaviorists' view of the mind as a blank slate succumbed to an avalanche of new research and insights. Studies of twins raised apart showed that personality traits were highly influenced by genes. Cognitive psychologists showed that we come into this world with a deep capacity for language and culture. Ethnographers documented hundreds of human universals or patterns of behavior that exist across all human cultures and are seemingly embedded in the structure of the mind.

....

[2] Daniel Pink, *Drive: The Surprising Truth about What Motivates Us* (Riverhead Books, 2009), 19.

A Quick Twelve Thousand Years

Before we dig a little deeper into this inner world of the mind, let's take a brief look at history. Humans started living in large communities about twelve thousand years ago at the beginning of the Agricultural Revolution when crops were first cultivated and animals domesticated. As we will discuss in detail later in the book, prior to this significant transition, humans lived as hunter-gatherers in small groups of a few dozen people. Behavior was mostly influenced by social group processes. With the rise of civilization, a need arose for people to work in the fields and soldiers to provide protection. The former were often slaves and the latter mostly conscripts. As you can probably surmise, neither group gave their efforts voluntarily. A crude form of behaviorism ruled the day as external motivation was needed to force soldiers and field hands to do what was required.

Leadership today is defined in many ways, but through most of post-hunter-gatherer history the best connotation for leader was *ruler*. Power and coercion ruled the day as the Agricultural Revolution created new forms of organization. Social hierarchies, division of power, formal religion, kings, priests, and specialized laborers such as primitive engineers and artisans emerged. Hunter-gatherer society was organized around clan relationships and group norms. These new complex societies resulted in centralized power with an emphasis on bringing order and control.

At the beginning of the Industrial Revolution, the notion of work emerged as we know it today. Jobs were created, and for the first time, outside of the plantation or the military, large numbers of people came together to produce goods for the use and benefit of the larger society. Prior to the Industrial Revolution most people worked as farmers to provide for their families. Others worked as craftsmen producing products by hand, some for personal use and the rest for sale or exchange. Work was a portfolio of activities necessary for survival. Work was fluid. Work was intertwined with life. The first large-scale workforces of the Industrial Revolution were mostly unskilled labor. Those responsible for overseeing these workforces needed a model for how to organize work and define the type of interaction with their workers. They looked no further than the landlord-peasant, military-soldier, even slaveholder-slave models that existed all around them. Like the former, the factory owners, due to the economic and social factors that existed at the time, had significant power, and the individual workers little. The power imbalance led to the first models of worker-boss relationships focusing on hierarchy, control, a few carrots, and a lot of sticks.

The enlightenment and the science that followed it created the steam engine and other technological innovations that allowed for the Industrial Revolution. The social sciences were in their earliest stages of development and played little role in the creation of organizations. The word *leadership* was coined in the early nineteenth century. Its study as a discipline followed much later and was little help to the founders of the first factories. For the educated who looked for insights there were the works of Plato, Sun Tzu, and Machiavelli.[3] But the orientation of all their philosophies centered on military and political leadership and the attendant notions of autocracy, power, and control.

[3] Plato was one of the most important ancient Greek philosophers. He left behind significant writings on governance and politics. Sun Tzu was a Chinese military strategist and philosopher of the sixth century BCE. He is best known for his treatise *The Art of War*. Niccolo Machiavelli was an Italian political philosopher born in 1469. His famous work is *The Prince*. All three were highly influential in the development of Western thinking on leadership.

Scientists considered the human side of the workplace in the early twentieth century. One of the first and most influential was Frederick Winslow Taylor. Taylor was trained as an engineer and was interested in using the tools of science to improve productivity and efficiency. Taylor developed the first time and motion studies. He analyzed steps in the production process and broke them down into smaller tasks, which a worker accomplished in exchange for monetary incentives. Taylor's most famous book, *The Principles of Scientific Management*, was published in 1911 and was highly influential. Taylor was concerned about workers. He specifically discouraged scolding and other negative consequences (sticks) that were common in the workplaces he studied. But his focus on breaking down work to its most menial tasks was dehumanizing and ignored the emotional needs of workers.[4]

With the introduction and refinement of the assembly line as a mode of production, and the application of Taylor's tools for efficiency and productivity, work became faster paced, more rigidly controlled, and increasingly separated from other aspects of life. Factory work took a heavy toll on the people who performed it. Autocratic leadership inherited from the military and plantations, combined with Taylorism and behaviorism, created a combustible period in human history. Worker protests and violence aimed at changing working conditions eventually led to the labor movement, government intervention in the workplace, and a slew of new laws to protect workers rights and improve working conditions.

In the early part of the twentieth century, a new field of industrial and organizational psychology (I-O) emerged. As the core of

[4] Rudi Volti, *An Introduction to the Sociology of Work and Occupations*, 2nd ed. (Sage Publications, 2012), 47–53.

psychology expanded beyond behaviorism to explore the inner mind, industrial psychology followed Taylor into the workplace to better understand human behavior with an eye to increasing worker productivity. The most famous studies of the pre-World War II era were the Hawthorne studies conducted at the Western Electric plant in Chicago by Elton Mayo, a professor at the Harvard Graduate School of Business. Mayo, like most of the researchers of that time, was interested in learning how to increase worker productivity. The original purpose of his studies at the Western Electric plant was to determine the relation between the intensity of illumination and the efficiency of workers, measured in output.[5] The studies resulted in an unexpected insight: the mere fact that the workers knew they were being monitored impacted their output. This reaction was called "the Hawthorne effect."[6]

While Mayo's studies have come under criticism for methodological reasons, they are considered seminal. The Western Electric studies confirmed what researchers were increasingly coming to understand: that productivity and motivation were related to worker satisfaction and other attitudinal factors. Attitude surveys of workers were beginning to be used by researchers in many large companies in the early 1930s. Their expansion was aided by the development of a research tool by the renowned social psychologist Rensis Likert (correctly pronounced "Lick-urt"). His odd-numbered bipolar scale is named for him and is still widely used today.

....

[5] Summary of the Western Electric studies and the human relations movement obtained from Gary P. Latham, *Work Motivation: History, Theory, Research, and Practice* (Sage Publications, 2012).

[6] Researchers found that regardless of the changes made to the lighting, worker productivity improved simply because the workers were aware that they were being observed. The phenomenon has since been generalized to describe any situation in which people change their behavior due to their awareness of being studied.

In the first half of the twentieth century, the management of large organizations and the researchers who studied those organizations were primarily interested in only a few questions focused on worker motivation with the aim to improve worker productivity. While there was concern for employee welfare, it was secondary to the productivity question. The Hawthorne studies as well as the work of scientists interested in worker attitudes laid the foundation for what has come to be called the "human relations movement."[7] The movement encapsulates a wide body of research that focused on the employer-employee relationship and later on the inner needs and wants of workers.

As noted earlier, the behaviorists believed that the mind was a blank slate. They did not acknowledge that the people who entered workplaces came with a bunch of stuff deeply wired into their brains. But by the middle of the twentieth century, greater complexity in the nature of work had entered the picture. Taylor's first factories saw workers as extensions of machines. The ever-evolving workplaces increasingly called for workers with not just strong backs and hands, but also brains.

The 1950s was a period of robust innovation and insight in the fields of social and industrial psychology. Many were highly influenced by Abraham Maslow and his need hierarchy theory. Rather than focus on expressed attitudes, Maslow believed that people were driven by five basic needs, and that those needs followed a sequential hierarchical order.

[7] The human relations movement emerged in the middle of the twentieth century in response to scientific management and its mechanistic view of organizations. The movement recognized the social and psychological factors that impacted the workplace and emphasized the importance of understanding and enhancing employee motivation, the existence of informal organizational systems, the complexity and importance of group dynamics, and the development of leadership theories that challenged traditional hierarchical and authoritarian management styles. The movement led to the development of modern human resources and organizational development functions and the wide use of tools like employee surveys, leadership training, team building, employee participation, and other tactics that are widely used and accepted today.

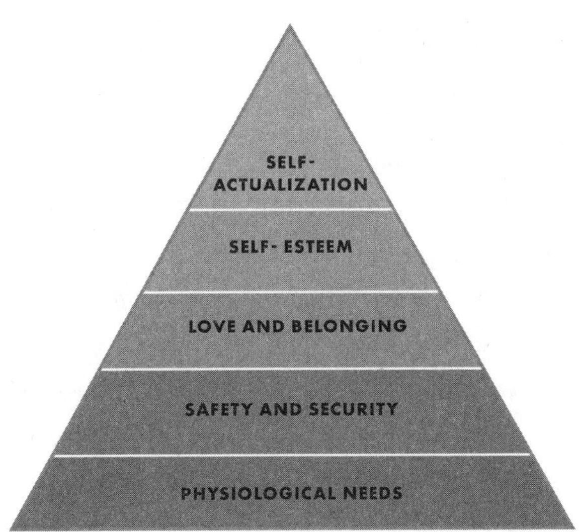

Figure 1: Maslow's Hierarchy of Needs

As depicted in Figure 1, physical needs are at the base of the hierarchy. The needs for food, water, sex, and sleep are primary and necessary for basic survival. If an individual is lacking these basic needs, higher level needs have no power to motivate. The need for safety and security, love and belonging, self-esteem, and self-actualization followed in ascending order.

I remember learning Maslow's hierarchy in one of my first leadership classes in the late 1970s. The facilitator used the model to point out that when employees lack safe and predictable environments (the second tier in Maslow's hierarchy), attempts to build a friendly and collegial environment will be unproductive. The company I worked for at the time employed many managers who believed that the best way to motivate people was to "keep them on their toes." In other words, they would use competition, bullying, and threats to "motivate" their teams. Intuitively, I could see that their methods were counterproductive. Maslow's hierarchy gave me insight as to why.

Theory X, Theory Y, and Human Relations

My first leadership workshops also exposed me to the ideas of other leading thinkers from the human relations movement. Douglas McGregor, another influential Harvard professor, developed two contrasting theories that explained how managers' assumptions about what motivates people significantly impact their management style. He labeled these Theory X and Theory Y. Managers who believe workers are lazy, unmotivated, and not interested in company goals are likely to use a more autocratic, micromanaging management style (Theory X). Those who believe people are self-motivated and want to take pride in their work are more likely to use a participative management style (Theory Y).

My fascination with what I was learning in my leadership classes inspired me to further my studies. I majored in and graduated college with a degree in political science. The study of leadership in a work setting aligned nicely with what I had learned about political leadership. In my first decade in the workplace, I observed management and leadership closely. Many of the first leaders I encountered were part of what is known in generational studies as the Silent Generation. Many had served in the military or were highly influenced in their management style by former military officers. Many of them enacted unapologetically autocratic management practices. Their language and behavior betrayed their Theory X assumptions. Their view of human nature seemed to center on the belief that people were primarily focused on their own interests and thus were passive or even resistant to organizational goals. They didn't think much or care much about their workers' needs or concerns. In fact, it was thought taboo to even delve into such topics. Of course, every generalization is wrong; while I worked for and knew a lot of Theory X managers, there was no pure form. Some seemed more compassionate and caring than others, and I was blessed early on to work for a Theory Y manager who was a master in participative management. He became a role model for my own leadership style.

The human relations movement produced several other theories that were incorporated into management and leadership training. Frederick Herzberg developed the two-factor motivation-hygiene theory.[8] Herzberg believed that the opposite of satisfaction is not *dissatisfaction* but *no dissatisfaction.* He argued that pay, working conditions, policies, and other job elements were hygiene factors. They needed to be seen as reasonable and fair and not as sources of dissatisfaction. Once dissatisfaction is removed, then a manager could use recognition, increased responsibility, a sense of belonging, and so forth, to increase motivation. Said simply, if employees think their pay is unfair and working conditions are terrible, recognition awards and praise will be met with skepticism and even anger.

The human relations movement had a profound impact on workplaces in the latter part of the twentieth century. My exposure to the movement in management and leadership training classes sparked a deep passion in me and propelled me into a career in human resources. My generation of Baby Boomers, those born from 1946–1964, entered the workplace en masse in the late 1960s and 1970s. Influenced by the activism and cultural change of our formative years, we challenged the mores and values of the workplace. Our desire for more autonomy in our work and a preference for participative

[8] Latham, *Work Motivation*, 41.

managers aligned with the growing body of ideas from the human relations movement and leadership studies, which steadily moved management styles from the Silent Generation's more autocratic mode.

As to the answers to our opening questions, the human relations movement introduced a new level of complexity. Motivation is seen largely as a by-product of human needs. For example, workers may resist change because they lack basic safety needs as pointed out by Maslow's hierarchy. The human relations movement was very influential in the workplaces of the subsequent decades. McGregor not only challenged Theory X thinking on the part of managers, but he also ushered in a new era of theory-driven empirical research. Researchers began to look deeply at job design, the social aspects of the work environment, employee satisfaction, goal setting, and other aspects of performance management. Knowledge workers, supported by higher levels of workforce mobility, demanded that employers respond to their needs for autonomy and personal development.

Leadership as a Field of Study

In *The Republic*, Plato describes leadership as a duty that requires wisdom, fairness, temperance, and courage. As noted earlier, Sun Tzu and Machiavelli were influential in describing strategies for engaging in war and politics. While these works were not widely read by the workforce leaders of the twentieth century, their influence endured in the mental models of leadership. Up to that point, leadership was largely framed as a highly directive, autocratic activity. Leaders were at the top of the hierarchy, experienced, wise, and expected to have all the answers. Celebrated leaders were heads of state such as

Abraham Lincoln, Theodore Roosevelt, and Winston Churchill, and generals such as Eisenhower and Patton.

These men—and the ideal models of leadership then were almost always men—were admired for their decisiveness, their courage, and their ability to use power and influence to achieve their objectives. The first formal studies of leadership focused on finding and confirming the qualities of effective leaders. With the development of trait theory, research expanded to the traits of successful leaders. The premise was simple: identify successful leaders, identify similarities across these leaders' competencies and traits, and create a model of the ideal leader. As trait theory and statistical methods advanced, these studies were valued for their scientific rigor and were used heavily in identifying and training leaders.

However, this approach to studying leadership was criticized by many scholars because it neglected the other half of the equation: followers. More recent studies of leadership have considered elements beyond the qualities of the individual in the leadership role. Situational theory suggests that leadership is more than a "great man."[9] It insists that situations produce the person, not the other way around. Situational leadership called for leaders to change their behavior based on the context and the skill and motivation of the people they are leading. Servant leadership combined elements of both preceding theories. Servant leaders were those who had a psychological orientation that allowed them to put the needs of

[9] The "great man" theory is attributed to Thomas Carlyle, a Scottish historian, writer, and leadership theorist of the nineteenth century. According to Carlyle's theory, certain individuals (all men at his time) possess inherent traits and qualities that make them natural leaders, and leadership is manifested because of these inborn attributes. Studies over the past fifty years have discredited the theory. Leadership can be learned through education, experience, training, motivation, and context. See Appendix 2 for an essay on whether leaders are born or made.

employees first by sharing power and focusing on the development of people. Robert Greenleaf, who is credited with developing the concept of the servant leader, emphasized that followers don't exist to serve the leader but that the leader exists to serve the followers. "The servant-leader is a servant first . . . It begins with a natural feeling that one wants to serve first."[10]

There has been an explosion of research and writing on leadership in the last forty years. Adding to situational and servant leadership were a dizzying number of concepts such as transformational leadership, functional leadership theory, expectancy theory, and others. What has emerged from all this study and theorizing is a robust body of research on how to identify, train, coach, and develop leaders. The culmination of this research is seen by many as the clarity that leadership is a complex social phenomenon that takes place in specific contexts between a leader and a unique set of people called followers. Leading one person creates a relationship; once you add another person to the mix, the three brains connect and culture emerges. The concept of culture will be covered extensively later in the book.

While this body of research doesn't answer our opening questions, it does provide a leader with several concepts and tools. When faced with unmotivated, change-resistant workers, a leader can switch to servant mode or experiment with situational leadership styles. As we dig deeper into these questions, I will refer to this brief discussion on leadership by adding insights gained by our deeper understanding of our basic human nature.

Most of us are fascinated by our own and others' behaviors.

[10] Robert Greenleaf, *Servant Leadership: A Journey into the Nature of Legitimate Power and Greatness* (Paulist Press, 1977), 13.

As you will learn in the coming chapters, this interest is deeply imbedded in our nature by natural selection. Figuring out what other people want was necessary for the survival of our ancestors and is very helpful in living a satisfying and productive life today. For leaders, understanding what makes people tick is critical to the success of the role. It is helpful to have some model or framework to anticipate and predict the behavior of others. One of the most famous models is astrology, "a belief system that suggests a connection between celestial phenomena and events on earth including human life and personality."[11] While the system has been debunked by modern science, many major newspapers still include horoscopes that describe personality types by birth date. In 2024, a "YouGov poll found that 32% of Americans at least 'somewhat agree' that someone's astrological sign (e.g., Gemini, Pisces) accurately describes their character and personality traits."[12] Spencer Greenberg, a self-described mathematician-entrepreneur in social sciences, conducted research on the ability of astrology to predict life outcomes and found, as hundreds of research studies before him, that astrology performs "absolutely horribly" when it comes to predictability. Personality traits, which we will describe in a later chapter, do very well.

One framework for understanding human behavior that is also well known and widely appreciated is generational theory. Most generational theorists focus on major events and their impact on generational cohorts, which are, of course, based on birth dates. The idea of categorizing people into generations dates to the early part of the twentieth century but gained prominence in the 1990s with the

....

[11] Definition of *astrology* obtained from ChatGPT 3.5.

[12] Spencer Greenberg (@SpencrGreenberg), X, January 16, 2024.

publication of dozens of books and articles describing the differences between generations based on the "imprint hypothesis." This theory ascribes differences in beliefs, values, and behaviors of a generation based on their shared experiences of major historical events. For example, the Silent Generation, defined as people born between 1928 and 1945, was shaped by the Great Depression and World War II, which caused most of the cohort to trend toward conformity, traditionalism, and thriftiness. Baby boomers (1946–1964) named and influenced by the sheer size of their cohort, were influenced by the Cold War, the war in Vietnam, and the protest movements of the 1960s. Research showed boomers were characterized by idealism, social activism, and a focus on individualism.

As an HR leader and former political science student, I was an enthusiastic reader of generational research. I followed others in introducing the concepts to the workplace, particularly to leaders to help them understand the beliefs, attitudes, and values of their fellow workers. My enthusiasm waned when I saw the application of generational insights translated into overly simplistic generalizations and stereotyping. I saw baby boomer and Gen X (1965–1979) leaders assign broad insights about the millennial generation (also known as Generation Y, 1980–1994) as specific attributes in individuals. The human tendency toward confirmation bias kicked into overdrive, and every anecdote became supporting evidence for the theory that millennials were unmotivated, narcissistic, and indecisive. In the latter part of my career as an HR executive, I discouraged generational training to leaders. I made the case that you can't understand and predict someone's behavior based on a birth date; that's no better than astrology.

While using generational insights to understand an individual's behavior can be counterproductive, the research can be the source of powerful insights to executives, marketing professionals, and HR leaders who are trying to understand large population shifts in attitudes, beliefs, and behaviors. For example, the manager in charge of benefits may want to stay aware of the generational trends in the wants and needs of new workers entering the workforce. Marketing professionals will want to understand shifting customer needs that can be better understood using a generational framework. The most astute generational researcher is Jean Twenge, a professor of psychology at San Diego State University. Professor Twenge discounts the imprint hypothesis and argues that generational differences in attitudes, beliefs, and behaviors are caused by technology. She means technology in its broadest sense, not just computers and phones, but every invention that makes modern life easier, safer, better. This ranges from improvements in medical care to washing machines to new modes of transportation.

Twenge links the generational differences of each cohort and the corresponding technological advancements of each era. Home appliances such as modern washing machines, dryers, and microwaves made domestic chores easier and less time-consuming. The invention and widespread use of the birth control pill changed the lives of women and accelerated the women's movement. Today, social media is dramatically shaping Generation Z (1995–2012)—largely to negative effect, according to Twenge and others, as it minimizes face-to-face social contact, which is a primary human need as we will see in later chapters. Twenge further argues that technology has allowed greater levels of individualism, for better and for worse: "In general, individualism has the advantage of more individual freedom and choice, and the downside of more social disconnection."[13] A second trend that technology fosters is what Twenge calls "slower life." She documents how Gen Y and Gen Z take longer to grow up. They get jobs, leave home, and get married and have children later than previous generations. These dynamics cause myriad generational differences.

I have immersed myself in generational studies and found it has added greatly to my insight into human behavior. But like all the ideas and models introduced in this chapter, I should emphasize one caution: every individual is unique. Our personality, beliefs, attitudes, values, and ways of doing and behaving are the result of complex interactions of biology, environment, and culture. When interacting with another person, we should always try to understand that person at an individual level. However, there is a growing body of research that can help us understand the mysteries of what is going on in our brains and in the brains of all those we meet and engage.

[13] Jean Twenge, *Generations: The Real Differences between Gen Z, Millennials, Gen X, Boomers, and Silents—and What They Mean for America's Future* (Atria Books, 2023), 14.

chapter 2

Raquel Welch, Darwin, and Evolutionary Mismatch

Homo sapiens is primarily a social animal.
Social cohesion is our key for survival and
reproduction. It's not enough for individual men
and women to know the whereabouts of lions and bison.
It's much more important to them to know who
in the band hates whom, who is sleeping with whom,
who is honest, and who is a cheat.

—Yuval Noah Harari

A Long Time Ago . . .

Life on earth began about three and half billion years ago, give or take a few hundred million years. From that first single-celled organism, the forces of evolution created a vast diversity of life, including one incredible species known as *Homo sapiens*. That's us. The story of human evolution has been told by many, but this brief overview will give you some sense of the scope and scale of how evolution by natural selection shaped the bodies and, more importantly, the brains of the people we encounter every day.

The origin of life is much debated. Did life form from a "primordial soup" of chemicals fused together by the energy of a lightning strike? Or was it aided by some extraterrestrial influence? No, I am not talking about ancient astronauts as depicted on the popular TV series *Ancient Aliens*. Some scientists speculate that organic molecules may have hitchhiked on a meteorite and seeded life on earth. In any event, all forms of life on earth depend on the same chemicals (carbon, hydrogen, nitrogen, oxygen, sulfur, and phosphorus). In the right context, add a spark of energy and you get the amino and nucleic acids that form DNA.

All living organisms have DNA within their cells. Furthermore, all forms of life on earth share the same subset of 355 genes and the same cytochrome c.[1] This supports the widely held view that there is a common origin for all life on earth. Over a two-billion-year period these basic chemicals led to more complex forms of life, accelerated by dramatic geological events. The most significant was the Great Oxygenation Event (GOE), which occurred around two and a half billion years ago. While the GOE killed off most of the anaerobic unicellular organisms, it gave rise to multicellular life. We can fast-forward through the evolution of the earliest arthropods and reptiles to species more generally known, our earliest ancestors.

About two hundred million years ago, in the Mesozoic era—better known as the age of the dinosaurs—a new creature emerged. These first mammals were small, furry, nocturnal, and not very smart by modern mammalian standards. Alongside their small brains, these ancient ancestors had biological features we *Homo sapiens*[2] share today: a complex cardiovascular system, oxygen-processing lungs, an internal heat maintenance system, and a four-limbed locomotion system adapted for land mobility.

[1] Cytochrome c is a small heme protein found in the inner mitochondrial membrane of eukaryotic cells, including those in humans. There's no need for deep biochemistry here, but these proteins are crucial for cell functioning.

[2] *Homo sapiens* will be used as the singular and plural forms in keeping with received English usage but eschewing the barbarism *Homo sapien*.

Early mammals shared the planet with dinosaurs whose size and exotic features still fascinate us today. One of my favorite movies as a boy was *One Million Years B.C.*, a 1966 adventure fantasy film about cavemen fighting for survival in a land of dinosaurs. While the stop-motion animation techniques were crude in comparison to the computer-animated creatures of *Jurassic Park*, I remember being mesmerized by the dinosaurs. I suspect my thirteen-year-old adolescent brain was equally captured by the buxom Raquel Welch in her fur-and-hide bikini!

Like many of the dinosaur films of that era, *One Million Years B.C.* was mostly ahistorical as it depicts dinosaurs and humans living at the same point in time. When questioned about that historical era, the film's lead animator commented that he did not make the movie for "professors [who] probably don't go to those kinds of movies anyway."[3] So what do the professors say about the comings and goings of dinosaurs and humans? The scientific consensus is that the era of the dinosaurs ended with a mass extinction event about sixty-six million years ago. The first hominins, our earliest primate ancestors, do not show up until about six million years later.

The last fifty years have produced a vast amount of research across an array of disciplines from evolutionary biology, archeology, paleoanthropology, and paleontology to give us a more robust picture of human evolution. New fields of study such as archaeogenetics, which studies ancient DNA, have provided even more pieces to the puzzle. While many pieces are still missing, enough have been discovered to create a great deal of consensus on how we came to be. And the key to understanding it all is the role of natural selection in the

[3] "Land before Time: 11 Great Prehistoric Flicks," Today.com, Feb. 29, 2008.

evolutionary process. Over one hundred and fifty years ago, Charles Darwin came up with one of the simplest but most profound ideas in the history of scientific inquiry.

In 1831, Darwin, then a very young and well-to-do failed medical student, hitched a ride on the HMS *Beagle*. The royal naval vessel had been chartered to spend two to three years mapping the coast of South America. The British empire was at its peak and the venture could afford the luxury of a naturalist aboard. Darwin had a passion for the natural world and the patience to catalogue dozens of specimens. During the voyage, which extended to almost five years, Darwin studied multiple species, some of which varied significantly depending on location. He took copious notes, which included many keen insights and theories about the natural world.

After returning to England in 1836, Darwin (who was less a professor and more a "gentleman scientist")[4] began writing and speaking about his discoveries. Over the next twenty-three years, he integrated his thinking with the insights and research of other scientists. Eventually, on November 24, 1859, he published his groundbreaking work, *On the Origin of Species by Means of Natural Selection*.[5] In the text he explains how plants and animals change slowly through time via the process of natural selection. The theory

---

[4] A gentleman scientist is a financially independent scientist who pursues study without direct affiliation with a public institution. Other famous gentleman scientists were Benjamin Franklin, Nikola Tesla, and Robert Boyle. Gentleman scientists largely disappeared with the increase in government and private funding of science, mostly to universities, in the twentieth century.

[5] *On the Origin of Species by Means of Natural Selection, or The Preservation of Favoured Races in the Struggle for Life* was published on November 24, 1859. While controversial at the time of its publication and for many years afterward, it is now considered by scientists and historians to be one of the greatest achievements in the history of science.

of evolution had been proposed by others, but Darwin revolutionized evolutionary thinking.[6] In his writing, Darwin describes what happens when the characteristics of some members of a species predominate and, through his theory of natural selection, how this predominance comes about.

Robin Dunbar, the acclaimed evolutionary psychologist, described how Darwin's theory follows from a set of simple assumptions:

1. Individuals vary in the extent to which they possess a given trait.
2. Some of that variability is genetically inherited.
3. Some variants reproduce more successfully because they are better suited in some way to the environment.
4. The next generation will come to resemble the more successful variants.

The result is evolution. With enough new variants, a new species will emerge that is able to survive and flourish in its environment. Natural selection is all about survival and reproduction.[7]

Let's play this out. A population of mammals grows until it is faced with a dwindling supply of resources.[8] The mammals compete for those resources in what Darwin calls the "struggle for existence."

[6] A contemporary of Darwin, the British naturalist Alfred Russell Wallace is considered a codiscoverer of evolution. Other scientists and thinkers also described natural processes that transformed species over time, but Darwin was the first to build a detailed explanation for the process of evolution through the mechanism of natural selection. Gregor Mendel, an Austrian scientist and friar, published a paper in 1866 that laid out the principles of inheritance and genetics. His paper was written in German and was overlooked until the early twentieth century.

[7] Robin Dunbar, *Evolution: What Everyone Needs to Know* (Oxford University Press, 2020), 15.

[8] The geological record shows that multiple ice ages have occurred during the millions of years of mammalian evolution. These cooling periods followed by warming slowly but dramatically changed the environment.

Some individuals in the population have traits that increase their ability to survive and reproduce more successfully. These traits are thus passed on to the next generation. In our mammal population, over time, the traits that survive and reproduce predominate; the ones that don't eventually die out.

We will see later how bipedalism helped the earliest hominins to survive. Millions of years ago, the earth cooled, and rainforests, with their dense vegetation and lush fruits, shrank dramatically. The resulting woodlands were more seasonal in their production of fruit. Many of these earliest hominins were forced to leave their life of hanging in trees to travel farther to find food. Travel using bipedal locomotion conserves energy and is therefore significantly more efficient for long distances. Those individuals with biological traits favoring bipedal movement won out. Over tens of thousands of generations, a new primate emerged, one who walked standing up.

Let's Regroup

Before we transition to the next section, this is a good time to summarize some key points. Evolution happens through natural selection. Natural selection involves small, sometimes imperceptible changes to specific members of a population. At first these changes don't seem like a big deal. But over time—and this means over thousands of generations—these changes result in dramatic change at the level of the individual and the wider population. Looking back this may seem extraordinary, even unbelievable. But just take a trip to the Grand Canyon and see how a small stream, given sufficient time, can fashion dramatic new rockscapes.

Evolution is a process of building on what already exists. Species don't pop up out of nowhere. Over millions of years, natural selection does its work. Those first small mammals mentioned diverged into thousands of species that came to dominate all the lands of our planet. Most fantastically, from those first tree creatures emerged the first hominin ancestors.

I have mentioned how climate change intersects with natural selection to change life. One of the most significant changes was continental drift. About three hundred million years ago, all present-day continents were one land mass. Over time the continent broke apart. By the time the dinosaurs became extinct the land masses in the Southern Hemisphere were separated. The drift has been slow and steady through history and continues today.

The continental drift caused the evolution of thousands of creatures along distinct evolutionary paths (see African and Asian elephants, which have a common ancestor but have many distinctly different characteristics). It also led to further climate change. About six million years ago in what is now Africa, a unique set of environmental circumstances sparked natural selection to create a bipedal, large-brained hominin. In a real sense those earliest shrewlike mammals are our ancestors, and in these earliest human ancestors we can begin to see the beginning of us.

The classification of animals is a complex system for understanding how all organisms are related. In this system, humans are great apes. For a long time, scientists thought that our closest primate relative was the gorilla because of similar bone structures. With the sequencing of the genome of both humans and chimps, we now know that we share 98.6 percent of our DNA with chimpanzees (only 96 percent with gorillas). We didn't evolve from chimpanzees or any other species of monkey, but we do share a common ancestor. While there is much controversy on the date, and missing evidence in the fossil record, an estimated date of our last common ancestor is about five to seven million years ago.

We are primates. We are great apes. Our closest relative in the animal kingdom is the chimpanzee. Interesting, but why should anyone care about this distant evolutionary relationship? The main reason is that because we are apes, we inherited lots of ape adaptations. And understanding these adaptations gives us our first look into the main purpose of this book—understanding human behavior. As one quick example, primates are tropical animals. All primates are found in the Southern Hemisphere and are well adapted to warm tropical climates. Where do most people in the Northern Hemisphere take their vacations: Alaska or a sunny beach? Most of us prefer the beach or a green forest. This is the legacy of our evolution. Our bodies and brains love blues skies, greenery, and the glow and warmth of the sun.[9]

Our ancestors eventually ventured out of Africa, but only after we learned to cover our bodies, control fire, and build habitats. Compared with indigenous Northern Hemisphere mammals, we have a narrow range of temperatures we can survive without these adaptations. Clothes have become more ornamental, but they are necessary for survival in the cold. Polar bears, which evolved in the Northern Hemisphere, don't need clothing. Like

[9] Ecotherapy, or green therapy, is a mental health treatment that incorporates nature and outdoor activities (lots of green and blue) and seems to have a positive effect on mental well-being. Phototherapy, also known as light therapy, has been found effective in treating seasonal affective disorder (SAD), which mostly shows up in the fall and winter when there is less sunlight. If our ancestors had first evolved in Siberia, we may have been looking to vacation in subterranean resorts!

our great ape relatives, we are omnivores, but our teeth,[10] intestines, and even our eyes are well adapted to fruit eating. The latter are trichromatic, which allows us to distinguish between brightly colored fruit and young leaves from other vegetation, thus benefitting our survival.

We have nails rather than claws. On the opposite side of our nails is an area of skin called the tactile pad. This area has a high concentration of nerve endings that allows for the accurate manipulation of objects. Precision grip is an evolutionary advantage for several reasons. While claws are an obvious advantage for carnivores in the hunting, killing, and dissection of prey, our tactile pads aided our ancestors in gathering and eating fruit and later became helpful in making and using tools. We share our ape cousins' long-fingered hands, as opposed to the paws of most large animals. Opposable thumbs are unique in the animal kingdom. *Homo sapiens* and our primate cousins can bend and move our thumbs in a way that allows them to touch other fingers and grab on to objects. As our opposable thumbs evolved even further, they enhanced our ability to pinch, grasp, and manipulate objects, all critical in tool use.

Great apes are both arboreal and terrestrial. Ape bodies are designed[11] effectively for vertical climbing and movement in the trees, but apes can also walk on the ground. Standing upright and knuckle

[10] Humans and our ape cousins have the same number of teeth with the same combination of functional types including incisors, canines, premolars, and molars. Unlike carnivores, we do not have long, pointed teeth, which serve well in tearing and chewing meat, their primary source of nutrition. Our molars serve us well in chomping and grinding food such as fruit and tubers. These molars help our digestive system, which is less complex than that of large mammals that eat lots of high-fiber, plant-based foods. Those creatures have a digestive system with a fermentation chamber since high-fiber foods require more processing time to relinquish their nutrients.

[11] *Designed* does not imply the involvement of a conscious designer; it refers to the process of natural selection acting on heritable traits over time.

walking, the preferred ground locomotion for chimps and gorillas, is very inefficient and uses a significant amount of metabolic energy. Humans can climb trees, but not very easily or safely. But our bodies are designed well for standing and upright walking. The latter is highly efficient and allowed the first hominins to cover much larger territory compared to their ape cousins. In the next section we will cover how and why natural selection favored bipedalism.

Figure 2: Evolution of Bipedalism

Behavioral Adaptations

Most mammals live solitary lives, meeting only to mate and raise their young. But apes are highly social creatures. They live in social groups, within which individual members coordinate activities and communicate with one another in both friendly and unfriendly ways. Apes, as with most primates, spend significant time grooming one another. Grooming and play help build strong social bonds.[12] This phenomenon is unique in the animal kingdom. *Homo sapiens* have expanded this social nature in extraordinary ways. While our large brains and intelligence have played an important role in our expansion around

[12] Grooming was the source of a key insight into primate behavior by Dunbar. Apes spend significant time using their fingers to remove burs and parasites such as ticks, fleas, and lice from the fur of other group members. This grooming can be an act of simple bonding or one of reconciliation or conflict resolution.

the globe, it is our social nature, our ability to cooperate and develop culture, that has led us to dominate the planet.[13]

We generally eat three meals a day with plenty of snacking along the way. The three-meals-a-day routine is an invention of the Industrial Age with its standardization of working hours. We generally eat before work, at a midday break, and then after work. In some cultures, people eat smaller meals, more frequently. The ancient Greeks and Romans tended to eat one big meal in the middle of the day with lots of munching throughout the day. Whatever the customs in terms of what, when, or how, we spend lots of time eating.

The reason is simple: we need lots of energy to grow, maintain our bodies, and reproduce. At the root of understanding evolution is understanding how the search for sources of energy triggered natural selection to do its work on our bodies and our brains. As we have learned, we share a common ancestor with our chimpanzee cousins. In the rich tropical forests of central Africa, that chimplike creature survived largely from fruits and vegetation easily obtained from the environment. That small, tree-dwelling creature survived for millions of years until a significant climate event changed the trajectory of one line of descendants.

You may have heard the term "the missing link." This usually refers to a hypothetical extinct creature somewhere in the line between *Homo sapiens* and our earliest progenitor. Using a scientific technique called the molecular clock,[14] paleoanthropologists believe the last

....

[13] Joseph Henrich, *The Secret of Our Success: How Culture Is Driving Human Evolution, Domesticating Our Species, and Making Us Smarter* (Princeton University Press, 2016).

[14] The molecular clock is a concept in evolution that suggests a relatively constant rate of change in the molecular sequences of certain biomolecules over time. This concept is used to estimate the time of divergence between species. It can be used to determine the time since a common ancestor. Description obtained from ChatGPT 3.5.

common ancestor (LCA) existed about five to seven million years ago, although this timeline is still subject to much debate. Scientists have oodles of million-year-old bones to study, but the tropical forests of our earliest ancestors didn't fossilize bones very well. Once hominins moved beyond these forests, they left behind lots of bones and other evidence that tell the story of human evolution.

Climate change caused the forests to shrink, eliminating a major source of energy, the easily obtained fruits and leaves so important to those primarily arboreal ape ancestors. Forced to the ground to traverse long distances, natural selection favored more efficient travel. Bipedalism was the answer. It saves energy and also frees up the hands to search for and secure new sources of food. At some point you may have seen pictures of our chimpanzee cousins leisurely sitting on a branch munching away. Contrast that with upright apes traversing long distances while they dig up roots and tubers, their new sources of calories.

Now occurring on the ground more than in the trees, natural selection continued its work. About four million years ago the earliest hominins, the Australopiths,[15] began to spread throughout Africa. In addition to changes to their hips and feet that allowed them to walk upright, the Australopiths developed big, thick, flat cheek teeth so that they could chew food tougher than fruit. The ability to grind nuts, seeds, roots, and tubers was a favorable adaptation.

Australopiths are important in understanding our evolutionary history as they are a key intermediary between our chimplike ancestor and later hominin species. Our chimpanzee cousins' ancestors,

[15] *Australopith* is an abbreviated name for a genus of extinct hominins, or early human ancestors, that evolved in Africa approximately four to two million years ago. There were multiple species in the long transition from apelike to a more human form.

which remained in the tropical forests, were also shaped by natural selection. But ancient chimps were a lot closer anatomically and behaviorally to today's chimps. The upright, bipedal, but small-brained Australopith took us on a dramatically different evolutionary path, from the forest-dwelling last common ancestor to the apelike Australopith to modern humans. Bipedalism was a dramatically new trait that drove significant other adaptations.

I remember my grade school textbook depiction of human evolution, much like the one in Figure 2.

At that time, the evolution of humans was seen as a somewhat linear process. Evidence gathered over the last four decades shows that the story of human evolution is much more complicated and closer to Figure 3.

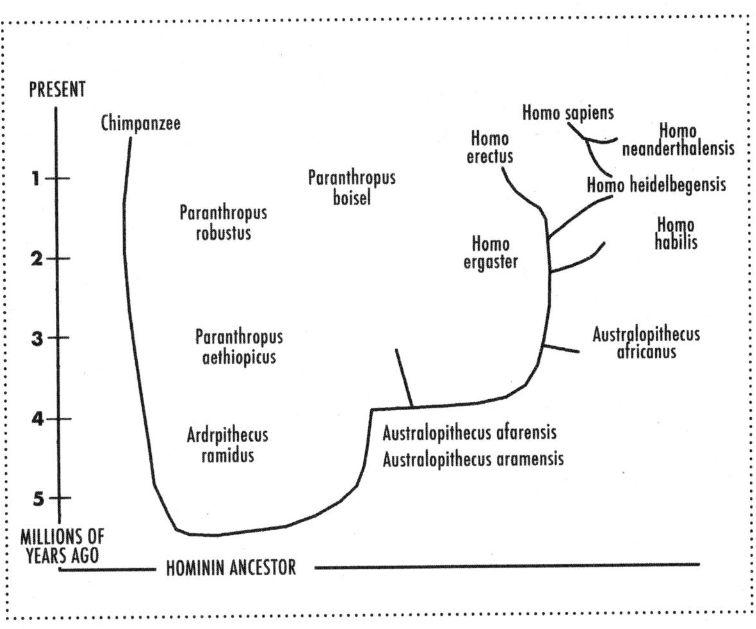

Figure 3: Hominin Evolution

A New Kind of Species

The Australopiths, which comprise at least ten separate species, proliferated in Africa for almost four million years. That's a lot of time, a lot of natural selection, and the formation of a lot of adaptive traits that created new successful species.

From one of those species, a new kind of hominin appeared in Africa. Unlike the Australopiths, early *Homo* species appear to have divided into only two consequential[16] (consequential in terms of their contribution to the development of later species including *Homo sapiens*, Neanderthals, and Denisova) species. They first appeared about two million years ago and were distinguished from the Australopiths by their emerging human characteristics—a significant increase in brain size, a remodeled skeleton that allowed even more efficient walking, and the loss of body fur and along with that an increased capacity to sweat.

These later features allowed them to dominate their home continent and eventually emigrate from Africa. Their large brains led to the increased use of more complex tools such as hand axes as the archeological record shows. While crude by modern standards, these new hand axes were far superior to sharp slices of rocks. Bigger brains also led to new problem-solving powers, and the early *Homo* species were extremely successful. The fossil record shows they moved from their home continent and colonized much of southern Europe and parts of Asia. There is evidence of fire use, meat eating, and—while still controversial as to the extent—the ability to communicate in

[16] Carl Linnaeus developed the classification system that organized the diversity of life on Earth. We are part of the genus *Homo*, which includes *Homo neanderthalensis*, *Homo erectus*, and other close extinct relatives. The step above in the hierarchy is family Hominidae, which includes our primate cousins such as chimpanzees, bonobos, orangutans, and gorillas.

crude, simple language. But most importantly, about five hundred thousand years ago they gave rise to another ancient ancestor, archaic humans.

This is where the story gets very interesting. These archaic humans had bodies and brains that led to a more advanced hunter-gatherer lifestyle, which would in turn further shape those bodies and brains in profound ways. The hunter-gatherer way of life led to increased species longevity. It is believed that *Homo erectus* was the most long-lived species of the *Homo* genus and a critical link in our ancestral chain. Archeological evidence shows that *Homo erectus* survived for a span of between one and a half to two million years. Again, climate change was a major factor in driving significant behavioral and biological changes.

About nine hundred thousand years ago, Earth began to experience a long period of dramatic climate fluctuations. These in turn altered habitats in favor of hominins with larger brains. These larger, more complex brains enabled early humans to interact with one another and solve more difficult problems presented by new and unpredictable environments. Cooking is believed to have played a role in the increase in brain size. Cooking significantly increased food efficiency as less food delivered more calories to energy-hungry brains. Humans were then able to spend less time foraging, chewing, and digesting food.

Let's play this out. Climate change alters habitats. Natural selection favors hominins with bigger brains that can adapt to new habitats. Cooking increases food efficiency, which allows brains to grow even larger. With less time spent looking for and processing food, hominins have more time to engage their brains, which placed further demands on energy needs. Natural selection favors continued brain growth, which allows for more complex problem-solving and higher levels of social interaction. The social brain emerges. Said another way: smarter, more socially adept humans survived, thrived, and had offspring. This allowed them to become our ancestors.

Multiple species of archaic humans emerged in both Africa and Eurasia, and it is clear that they bumped into one another and even interbred. One of these species is our most direct ancestor, although there is still much debate on how exactly this happened. Some scientists believe *Homo sapiens* are the result of a long period of evolution and inbreeding among other early *Homo* species. There seems to be a growing consensus that *Homo sapiens* evolved from *Homo heidelbergensis*. A small population in central Africa emerged about three hundred thousand years ago with adaptations that would allow the species to emigrate and eventually come to dominate the planet. More on that to come in later chapters.

One famous cousin of *Homo sapiens* is the Neanderthal. It is estimated that the Neanderthal and modern human lineages separated about five hundred thousand years ago. While this common ancestor lived in Africa, Neanderthals evolved in Eurasia around four hundred thousand years ago and became extinct around forty thousand years ago. That would put them in the same time and place with *Homo sapiens*. In fact, in addition to living alongside early modern humans, in some cases they were even more intimate. Through recent analysis of both human and Neanderthal DNA, we know that many of us with European or Asian roots have inherited around 2 percent of the latter's DNA. My 23andMe DNA report confirmed my Irish and German heritage, but it also surprised me by identifying 236 variants of the 7,462 tested that trace back to the Neanderthals.

Physically, Neanderthals were like modern humans in many

ways, but they were more muscular and stockier with significant differences in the face and head. While we have a flat face and somewhat round skull, Neanderthals had a "sloping forehead, elongated skull, heavy brow ridge, projecting midface and almost no chin." If you were to pass a Neanderthal male on the street, you might describe him as barrel-chested. "Their body proportions and muscular arms and legs allowed them to be well adapted to the colder weather of Europe and Eurasia."[17]

Neanderthals also shared many behavioral characteristics with humans. Their large brains indicate the capacity for significant intelligence and social sophistication. They made tools and were proficient hunters. The existence of a hyoid bone[18] and recent DNA evidence indicate that Neanderthals could talk, although not at the level of modern humans. They made and wore clothes, critical to their survival during the cold glacial periods of northern Europe. There is controversy over their extinction about forty thousand years ago. Were they wiped out by their smarter, more collaborative *Homo sapiens* cousins? Or did their small population slowly die out due to their inability to adapt? In any event, a part of them still resides in us in our DNA. And perhaps our *Homo sapiens* ancestors learned some important survival lessons as they moved from the tropical climates of Africa to the colder northern climes. This is *Homo sapiens*'s superpower, the ability to learn and pass on what they learned through culture.

Scientists believe that Neanderthals most likely emerged from an extinct species of archaic humans known as *Homo heidelbergensis.*

---

[17] "Neanderthal Facts," 23andMe.com, accessed June 2023.

[18] The hyoid is a u-shaped bone located in the neck just above the larynx. It plays a crucial role in the ability to speak.

This species is named for Heidelberg, Germany, the site of its first discovery in 1908. The fossil record indicates *Homo heidelbergensis* lived sometime between eight hundred to five hundred thousand years ago and was common in Africa and western Eurasia. It is thought to be the first human species to live in colder climates. There is evidence of controlled fire use, tool making, shelters, and hunting big game. The latter activity is significant in that it implies that these large-brained, highly mobile creatures were fully hunter-gatherers. This lifestyle would continue to dramatically shape their bodies and brains.

In Africa, *Homo heidelbergensis* evolved into Neanderthals. In Asia, it evolved into a more recently discovered subspecies called *Homo denisovan*. Denisovans exist not only in the fossil record but also in DNA found in several populations in Southeast Asia and Australia. In Africa, *Homo heidelbergensis* also spawned another lineage, the most significant species to ever occupy our planet, *Homo sapiens*. The fossil record and DNA evidence show archaic *Homo sapiens* in Africa about two hundred thousand years ago.

Human migrations out of Africa are believed to have begun as far back as two million years ago. The first wave was likely *Homo erectus*, followed by other archaic humans, including *Homo heidelbergensis*. *Homo heidelbergensis* gave rise to multiple species including Neanderthals in Eurasia, Denisovans in Asia, and *Homo sapiens* in Africa. A key point to make here is that for tens of thousands of years multiple human species in both Eurasia and Africa bumped into one another on a regular basis. Given that many people alive today have between 2 to 4 percent Neanderthal or Denisovan DNA, some of the bumping was quite intimate.

The fossil record and genealogy give us lots of information on human evolution. Scientists can make many inferences on human behavior, but we must use our imagination to speculate on the nature of the interactions among these multiple coexisting early humans. One attempt to do so was a novel published in 1980, *The Clan of the Cave Bear.*[19] Later made into a movie with the same title, the story centers on Ayla, an orphaned Cro-Magnon[20] who is found and raised by Neanderthals who call themselves "Clan." The story arc centers on tension between Ayla and her protector and other members of the group, who distrust a member of "the others" and fear the manifestations of their clearly superior intellect.

The Clan of the Cave Bear was preceded by another prehistoric fantasy adventure film, *Quest for Fire.*[21] While both movies contain many historical inaccuracies, they received positive reviews for their depiction of prehistoric life. I point them out here because they also highlight something that will be described in detail in the chapter on culture. Our success as a species is based on how we use our intellect to find solutions to problems and discover new ideas, then use culture to spread them.

Homo sapiens's emigration from Africa occurred between 80 to 150 thousand years ago. There may have been multiple groups that traveled first to the Levant[22] through northeast Africa but

....

[19] *Quest for Fire* was released in 1981 and received generally positive reviews. The movie *The Clan of the Cave Bear* was released in 1986 and starred Daryl Hannah. It was a critical and commercial failure. Both were criticized by academics for their significant historical inaccuracies.

[20] *Cro-Magnon* is a name used for early *Homo sapiens* who settled in Europe from about sixty thousand to forty thousand years ago.

[21] Readers will come away with a sense of the author's unusual taste in movies!

[22] *Levant* is a term used to describe the geographical region in the eastern Mediterranean. In the West it encompasses a territory called the Middle East. The region has a rich history and is significant in that it was at the crossroads of various ancient civilizations. It was probably the first step in most *Homo* emigration from Africa.

eventually died out. They may have been dominated by larger Neanderthal populations. But around sixty to seventy thousand years ago a wave of *Homo sapiens* landed in the Levant and then rapidly spread throughout the globe. They appeared in Asia about sixty thousand years ago, in Europe about forty thousand years ago, and eventually reached the "New World," most likely on a land bridge across the Bering Strait, sometime between fifteen thousand and thirty thousand years ago.

Eventually Neanderthals, Denisovans, and many other archaic human populations became extinct. Their extinction is still the subject of much controversy. Some scientists believe these species failed to adapt to their environments, which were altered by climate change. Others believe they were killed off or assimilated in Borglike[23] fashion by *Homo sapiens*. Most likely, crowding and competition for limited food resources were the causes.

Over a period of six million years, natural selection worked its magic to create modern humans. Environmental changes forced our chimplike ancestors onto the savanna and a new way of life, first as scavengers and ultimately as hunter-gatherers. The demands of the hunter-gatherer lifestyle shaped our bodies slowly but steadily. We became bipedal, powerful throwers, long-distance runners, and furless, sophisticated tool users. The latter is attributed to the most significant change, a larger and more complex brain capable of solving problems and managing a wide array of social relationships.

Critical to our understanding of human behavior, it is important to see how the hunter-gatherer lifestyle shaped human

[23] *Borg* refers to an antagonistic cybernetic species that wipes out other species through forced assimilation in the Star Trek fictional universe.

brain development and thinking. Our world has changed dramatically, starting with the Agricultural Revolution around ten to twelve thousand years ago. Civilizations emerged. Hunter-gatherer lifestyles began to change, and natural selection continued its work. But millions of years of programming will take millions more to overwrite. Said another way, as we approach our daily lives our brains are operating with the same software that allowed our ancestors to successfully thrive and pass on their genes. Our brains are mismatched in many ways to our modern environments.

Mismatch

We have seen that the human beings who join our workforces are the product of evolutionary forces that shaped our bodies and brains over millions of years. Over most of that time our ancestors lived as hunter-gatherers. For perspective, some scholars have compressed our evolutionary history into a single calendar year. With that frame in mind, our first ancestor arrived on January first and our transition from primarily hunter-gatherer didn't occur until the end of December. That is a long time for natural selection to do its work. The key point for this book, for understanding *us*, is to know that the neurocircuitry that creates our human nature is designed primarily for life as a hunter-gatherer.

In his enlightening book *The Story of the Human Body*, Daniel Lieberman describes how "millions of years of evolution favored ancestors who craved energy-rich foods, including simple carbohydrates like sugar, which used to be rare, and who efficiently stored excess calories as fat."[24] He goes on to describe many of the illnesses that plague modern humans (including heart disease, diabetes, hypertension, and others) as a result of cravings that were once adaptive but are now maladaptive to modern environments, which have a surplus of easily obtained simple carbohydrates and fats. This is what is known as the mismatch hypothesis, the idea that traits once advantageous are now unfit.

Steve Stuart-Williams tells a useful story about a hedgehog to explain evolutionary mismatch. Natural selection provided the hedgehog with a useful defense mechanism. When approached by a predator, it rolls up into a spiked ball. A predator is then dissuaded from making the hedgehog its next meal as the trouble seems much more than it's worth. Today, many a hedgehog can be found flattened like a pancake in the middle of the road. For most of its history the spiked ball thing worked well, but not so much against a two-ton metal vehicle. Natural selection takes a long time, and the hedgehog's defense mechanism is out of sync with its current environment.

Professor Stuart-Williams goes on to describe modern humans as being in the same boat as the hedgehog:

> We're not adapted to the strange new world we created for ourselves—this world of straight lines, right angles . . . and strict schedules; of cars, shaved faces, and designer jeans; of mirrors, cameras and cities as large as colonies . . . humans are adapted primarily for life as hunter-gatherers living in the savannah and woodlands

[24] Daniel Lieberman, *The Story of the Human Body* (Vintage Books, 2013), 16.

> of Pleistocene Africa. That's the world in which we spent most of our evolutionary history, and therefore that's the world we are designed to inhabit—the human equivalent to the hedgehog's road free forest.[25]

The pace of environmental and lifestyle changes has been much faster than the pace of evolutionary adaptation. Our brains and bodies are well equipped for our ancestral environment, but at times they are not a match for our modern world. This is evolutionary mismatch.

I found myself in another kind of mismatch as I walked into my first class at Harvard in 2022. I was sixty-seven years old and hadn't been enrolled in a college class since 1979. A retired banking executive, I was a member of the 2022 cohort of Harvard's Advanced Leadership Initiative (ALI). As an ALI fellow, I attended workshops and seminars on leading societal change. Participation in ALI served my post-retirement goal of making a positive impact on the world. It also met my need for learning and intellectual stimulation. As a member of ALI, I was able to enroll in any class offered by the university subject to professorial approval. My first choice was easy—I selected Human Evolution and Human Health taught by the paleoanthropologist I just quoted above, Dr. Dan Lieberman.

In the previous decade I had read deeply in the areas of human evolution, evolutionary psychology, and neuroscience. As the reader knows, I have had a long fascination with human behavior. Said another way, particularly as an HR executive, I was in a constant search for the answers to this book's opening questions: Why are

[25] Steve Stewart-Williams, *The Ape That Understood the Universe: How the Mind and Culture Evolve* (Cambridge University Press, 2018), 47.

people the way they are? Why do they think, feel, and act in often-peculiar ways? The biggest moments of insight came when I looked at human behavior through the lens of an evolutionary framework.

I was the first to arrive at the first session of Dr. Lieberman's class. Being on time was a discipline developed during my many years as a corporate executive, one not quite evident in many of my much younger fellow students. I sat down and pulled out my new bound notebook, a retirement gift from one of my favorite employees. Armed with my notebook and a fancy, ultra-sharp Pilot pen, I was ready to go. A few minutes before class was to start (and for a few minutes beyond the start of class) students poured in. Almost in unison, the students pulled out their laptops and popped open the lids. The slightly darkened room lit up from all the fluorescent screens. Classrooms set up for lectures in the computer age don't need the bright lights I was accustomed to in my undergraduate days. As Professor Lieberman lectured, I dutifully scribbled notes while hearing the clicking of keyboards all around me. It was then that I realized I had an analog-trained brain living in a now-digital world. This was a class on human evolution, and I had not quite evolved. Mismatch maybe?

One of Professor Lieberman's first slides contained a quote from pioneering geneticist Theodore Dobzhansky: "Nothing in biology makes sense except in the light of evolution."[26] The theory of evolution is fundamental to understanding the natural world. By studying natural selection and other related evolutionary processes, we can come to a better understanding of why all organisms are the way they are. At first, the study of natural selection was focused on

[26] Daniel Lieberman, *The Story of the Human Body* (Vintage Books, 2013), 16.

biology. Later, the principles of natural selection were used to explain human behaviors. It culminated in the creation of the field of study called sociobiology and later, evolutionary psychology. Dobzhansky's view applies not only to biology but to behavior.

Research and discourse in evolutionary psychology led to the discovery of important insights into the roots of human behavior. Natural selection shaped our larger, socially oriented brains to solve a particular set of problems. As we know from our reading to this point, our brains evolved over tens of thousands of years, during most of which we lived in small-scale hunting and foraging communities. Evolution is a gradual process that takes a long time. Our brains, well suited for a hunter-gatherer, haven't evolved at the same speed as the changes in our environment. The result is that the mechanisms that once served us well often suboptimize our thinking and behavior in the modern world.

chapter 3

The Ultimate, Survival Vehicle

Our species evolved to build, in the form of their societies, tribes, or cultures, a second body or vehicle. Like our physical bodies this cultural body wraps us in a protective layer, not of muscles and skin, but of knowledge and technologies, it gives us our language, cooperation and shared identity.

—Mark Pagel

Language, Information, Culture

As we have learned, *Homo sapiens* and our *Homo* cousins have been around for over two million years. Until about ten to twelve thousand years ago we lived as hunter-gatherers. The forces of evolution and natural selection shaped our biology and our brains to adapt successfully to that lifestyle. Our bodies are well designed for long-distance running, throwing, manipulating small objects, seeing color, and other skills that helped ensure our survival and the passing of our genes to the next generation. And our brains have a network of wiring that not only contributed to survival but became a force for further evolution through gene-culture coevolution. This term refers to the fact that cultural practices and behaviors, not just the environment, can impact genetic evolution.[1]

[1] Roy Baumeister, *The Cultural Animal: Human Nature, Meaning, and Social Life* (Oxford University Press, 2005), 12.

Early philosophers, most notably John Locke, believed that the human mind was a blank slate at birth, that it came with no inborn traits or processes. We now know that we are primed with many capacities, perhaps the most important being our innate drive to participate in a culture. One definition of culture is "an information-based system that allows people to live together and satisfy their needs." An important expansion of that definition comes from Joseph Henrich, who describes culture as "the large body of practices, techniques, heuristics, tools, motivations, values and beliefs that we all acquire while growing up mostly by learning from other people."[2]

The latter definition combines two distinct ideas. One is that culture is a vast system of knowledge, skills, expertise, and abilities gained through learning that is stored in the collective mind of its members. The other is that these processes and propensities—even "addiction"[3] to culture as Henrich believes—are embedded deep in our psyches. One example is language. The language we speak was obtained through our exposure to the speakers around us. If German-speaking parents have a child and give it up for adoption, the child will learn not German but the language of the adoptive parents. But the mechanism for learning language is innate.

As a cultural species, language is critical to sustaining culture. At the most basic level of analysis, language is the ability to extract meaning from sound waves through a complex set of rules that allows us to create words and sentences. Steven Pinker describes

---

[2] Henrich, *The Secret of Our Success*, 3.

[3] Henrich, *The Secret of Our Success*, 3.

language as an instinct[4] and says that the rules just mentioned were embedded in the brain by natural selection to enable communication among social hunter-gatherers. In support of this theory, scientists have identified unique parts of the brain that are key to language processing. For example, the Broca's area, located behind the left eye, is necessary for language formation. Damage to the Broca's area leads to the inability to form language even if one's motor ability to form sounds is working.

Language is foundational for culture. It is the conduit for connecting minds into one system, as in the first definition of culture mentioned. Individuals have many thoughts and ideas, but those ideas become most powerful when they are shared. Language starts with an electrical impulse inside the brain of an individual, but it only becomes language when it is shared with another person. Evolutionary biologist Mark Pagel describes language as "the most powerful, dangerous, and subversive trait that natural selection has ever devised,"[5] as it allows us to rewire other people's minds and allows others to rewire ours. This collective rewiring is culture.

Our species was named *Homo sapiens* by Carl Linnaeus,[6] known as the father of biological classification, and comes from the Latin words meaning "wise man." The name recognizes our large brains and significant cognitive capabilities. Originally, scientists focused on these intellectual strengths to explain our ability to move from Africa, develop tools and technologies, and eventually come

---

4 Steven Pinker, *The Language Instinct: How the Mind Creates Language* (Harper Collins, 1994).

5 Mark Pagel, *Wired for Culture: Origins of the Human Social Mind* (W. W. Norton & Company, 2012), 275.

6 Carl Linnaeus was an eighteenth-century Swedish botanist, zoologist, and physician who developed a hierarchical system for the classification of living organisms including plants, animals, and microorganisms.

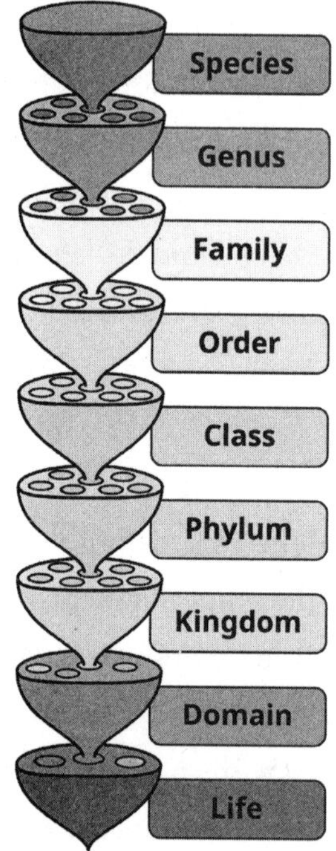

Figure 4: Linnaean Classification System

to occupy and dominate all corners of the planet. In recent decades, the focus has shifted to our ability to create and sustain culture as the more significant factor in our success. While our individual rationality is robust, it is our collective intelligence that explains our species's enormous success.

Culture is an adaptation in the same way as is the giraffe's long neck, the cheetah's speed, or the bonobo's long arms and legs. The giraffe's long neck enables it to eat vegetation high up in trees, the cheetah's speed is for capturing prey, and the bonobo's anatomy serves its energy needs and provides safety from potential predators. Human brains are equipped with dozens of mechanisms that enable them to collectively create culture. That culture in turn is beneficial for survival and, according to the law of natural selection, beneficial for passing genes to the next generation.

At this point, it is important to understand that these mechanisms were deeply imbedded into our psyche to allow us to participate in a culture. They manifest themselves as the cravings, desires, and drives that constitute human nature. As mentioned, we come into this world not with a blank slate but with a panoply of proclivities and emotions that push and pull us in directions that serve our long-term survival needs. Some examples come from evolutionary psychologist Steven Pinker.

> The emotions of sympathy, gratitude, guilt, and anger allow people to benefit from cooperation without being exploited by liars and cheats. A reputation for toughness and a thirst for revenge were the best defense against aggression in a world in which one could not call 911 to summon the police.[7]

Culture is common among other animals, particularly in our primate cousins. Franz de Waal, one of the world's leading primatologists, documented the importance of culture to chimpanzees. In a conversation with Professor Yascha Mounk, de Waal describes the criticality of culture.

> The most basic . . . is that they cannot survive without culture. Take for example captive chimpanzees. If you release them in the forest, they will die. They will die because they don't know what to eat. They don't know what dangers to avoid. They don't know how to orient themselves. They're just hopeless and helpless. Culture is absolutely essential for their survival; there are a lot of things that they eat that they learned from each other. Cracking nuts is a good example; there are chimpanzees who have nuts and stones in the forest and don't do anything with them and other chimpanzees where they have stones and nuts, and they crack the nuts with stones. They have a lot of extra food that way, because nuts are a very valuable food source.[8]

---

[7] Steven Pinker, *The Blank Slate: The Modern Denial of Human Nature* (Viking, 2002), 53.

[8] Franz de Waal interview with Yascha Mounk, *Persuasion* substack, March 2023.

Primatologists and other scientists have documented a great deal of behavioral variation across groups in many species. They used to think that much of animal behavior is instinctive, but we now know that a great deal of behavior is learned and transmitted through culture. For example, some primates use sticks to pry seeds out of fruit while other members of the same species living in another location have not mastered this skill. Scientists also see wide variation in foraging techniques and greeting and mating rituals. It appears that these variations are largely learned through imitation and subsequent trial and error. These collective differences between groups are culture.

Human culture shares an important characteristic with primate culture: observational learning. But human observational learning is vastly more complex and expands beyond imitation and emulation.[9] The most important feature of human culture is that "culturally transmitted adaptations accumulate over many generations, resulting in complex behaviors that no one individual could invent on his or her own."[10]

Michael Tomasello used the "ratchet effect" metaphor to elucidate how culture accumulations work. The ratchet effect is analogous to the mechanical ratchet, a tool with a set of teeth that engages and allows motion in one direction only. Humans continuously add on to existing knowledge through modifications and improvements. Through observational learning and trial and error, knowledge is generated and passed on so that it exists not only in the mind of the inventor or improver but in the collective mind of the group—its

[9] Robert Boyd and Joan Silk, *How Humans Evolved*, 9th ed. (W. W. Norton & Company, 2021), 430.

[10] Boyd and Silk, *How Humans Evolved*, 429.

culture. This is unique to humans. In fact, for many anthropologists, culture is the defining feature of what makes us human.

Let's imagine an example of how this might have happened. An ancient hunter-gatherer having moved from Africa to Eurasia lives in a cave with his clan for protection and warmth. One day he finds the remnants of burning logs from a lightning strike. Having experienced fire in the past, he recognizes the potential of controlled fire for warmth and protection. He takes one of the smaller smoldering logs back to the cave and creates and sustains a fire. Despite their best efforts, one day the fire burns out. The clan now understands the benefits of fire but doesn't know how to start a new one.

One day clan members are idly sitting around in the cave with one banging together two rocks, one with some shiny element filtered through it. In the darkness of the cave someone notices a spark fly and a small amount of smoke in a small stash of dry grass nearby. A eureka moment! The clan members gather more dry grass and start striking the two rocks together to repeat what had happened serendipitously just a few minutes before. The clan now knows how to initiate fire.[11]

Over time, innovations are added and the method is shared or traded with other groups. As the method spreads, more uses of fire are developed. Fire is eventually used for cooking, for lighting, and to scare away predators. Fire was also used to create advanced hunting tools. Fire enabled humans to travel farther and to adapt to colder environments. While cooking food was a key factor in our brain's development, perhaps the most important role fire played in human

[11] Evidence suggests that early humans began using fire about 1.5–2 million years ago. It is unclear when they first learned to control it, but it was probably *Homo erectus* around one million years ago. Cooking played a critical role in reducing pathogens and increasing nutritional value. The latter seeded the development of larger brains.

evolution was in allowing human activity to continue into the later hours of the day. Humans gathering around a blazing fire was foundational for shaping our highly social nature.

Gene-Culture Coevolution

This is a good place to explain gene-culture coevolution and how the ratchet effect makes our species so unique. We have learned how natural selection works: A variation occurs in an individual phenotype[12] that creates an adaptation that advantages the individual in its environment. That variation is then passed on and spreads through the population over time. We usually think of these adaptations as biological. For example, *Homo sapiens* moved to northern climates between twenty to fifty thousand years ago. They came with dark skin, which protected them from the harmful UV radiation of the equatorial regions of their birth. At some point one individual was born with a mutation: lighter skin that increased the absorption of vitamin D, which is crucial to absorbing calcium and keeping bones strong. With less sun and more clothing covering the body, lighter skin became highly advantageous. Over thousands of years this adaptation spread widely among the population.

The ratchet effect has led to tons of knowledge. Bigger brains that could store that knowledge were adaptive. Then those bigger brains retained even more knowledge. Brains that could learn, improve on, share, and even teach are even more adaptative. This is gene-culture coevolution at work. Joseph Henrich in *The Secret of Our Success* describes it best.

....

[12] A phenotype is an outward expression of genes. It is the trait that is expressed and observable. For example, eye color is a phenotype of a set of genes inherited from parents.

> [R]elatively early in our species' evolutionary history . . . we first crossed this evolutionary Rubicon,[13] at which point cultural evolution became the primary driver of our species's genetic evolution. This interaction between cultural and genetic evolution generated a process that can be described as *autocatalytic*, meaning it produces the fuel that propels it. Once cultural information began to accumulate and produce cultural adaptations, the main selection pressure on genes revolved around improving our psychological abilities to acquire, store, process and organize the array of fitness-enhancing skills and practices that became increasingly available in the minds of the others in one's group. As genetic evolution improved our brains and abilities for learning from others, cultural evolution spontaneously generated more and better cultural adaptations, which kept pressure on for brains that were better at acquiring and storing cultural information.[14]

One interesting sidenote that highlights the importance of culture and contrasts it with the power of human intelligence are the many stories of eighteenth-century European adventurers. Many tell of hardy and highly educated explorers who found themselves stranded in unfamiliar habitats. While some faced hostile enemies,

[13] The Rubicon is the river that marked the boundary between Gaul and Italy. According to Roman law, a general was forbidden from crossing the river with his army without authorization from the Senate. The law was established to prevent generals from seizing power. In 49 BCE, Caesar crossed the Rubicon. It is now used as a phrase to describe a significant event or decision that cannot be undone.

[14] Henrich, *The Secret of Our Success*, 57.

many perished because of their inability to adapt. One example is the Franklin Expedition of 1846.

> Sir John Franklin, a Fellow of the Royal Society and an experienced Arctic traveler, set out to find the Northwest Passage and spent two ice-bound winters in the Arctic. Everyone on his team eventually perished from starvation and scurvy. Their fate was tragic but also instructive. Members of the expedition spent their second winter on King William Island. The Central Inuit have lived on King William Island for at least 700 years, and this area is rich in animal resources. But the British explorers starved because they did not have the necessary local knowledge to make a living.[15]

While these explorers were smart by some standards, they didn't have the benefit of the accumulated knowledge of the Inuit who had built on innovation after innovation in making kayaks, dogsleds, and bows and had mastered the art and science of ice fishing. Culture wins.

[15] Boyd and Silk, *How Humans Evolved*, 428.

chapter 4

Your Brain Is Not For Thinking

To the extent that we can characterize evolution as designing our modern brains, this is what our brains are wired for: reaching out to and interacting with others. These are design features, not flaws. These social adaptations are central to making us the most successful species on the planet.

—Matthew Lieberman

I was anxious as I sat at my first formal dinner meeting with senior executives. I had recently been promoted to the prestigious management training program at the bank. Prior to that I had worked my way from my first job as a messenger to loan collector and then to consumer loan officer. A place in the training program was a big deal and a rarity for a working-class kid like me. Most of the trainees were college recruits from top business schools. Most were of middle- and upper-middle-class backgrounds. Most had been schooled in all the appropriate norms of business social engagements. As for me, not so much.

I was perplexed by the number of eating utensils and glasses. There was one big plate in front of me, plus one on the left and one on the right. All were jammed together on a too-small table. I sat frozen for a while. Which was my glass? Which small plate was mine—the one on the right or the one on the left? Which fork should I use first? I could feel my stress level rising. I wanted to make a good first impression. I wanted to fit in. I wanted to show I knew the appropriate rules of behavior for this important encounter with high status in the company.

Looking back years later, I know that this was my social brain at work. Our brain is a social brain because it is specialized to handle the complex social interactions that are critical to human survival and well-being.

We are a cultural species. Culture is the secret to our success, and that culture is an information-based system of social relationships. Our social brain was designed by natural selection to enable us to successfully participate in a culture by navigating this complex range of social relationships. This chapter will dig deeply into the mechanisms built into our brain over thousands of years of living in the small group lifestyle of hunter-gatherers.

As to the dinner and the many that followed, I learned to watch closely what everyone else did—particularly those higher on the food chain.

The Powerful, Confused Social Brain

Our understanding of the evolution of the human brain and social behavior comes from Robin Dunbar, a British anthropologist and evolutionary psychologist. Dunbar is most famous for his "social brain hypothesis," which suggests that the size of our brain is related to the complexity of our social relationships. Most of Dunbar's insights came from studying the grooming behaviors of primates, which spend over 20 percent of their day stroking and picking foreign elements from one another's fur. This mutual grooming has been shown to be the major way primates maintain their relationships with one another.[1]

According to Dunbar, the complexity of social relationships in primates increases as the size of the neocortex, the part of the brain associated with higher cognitive functions, increases. This relationship holds true across a wide range of primate species, including humans. Dunbar proposed that neocortex size in primate species, particularly the size of the prefrontal cortex, is a good predictor of the average size of their social groups. His hypothesis is based on the idea that social relationships are critical for primate survival and reproductive success. To maintain and navigate complex social networks, primates need advanced cognitive abilities, such as the ability to recognize individual faces, keep track of social hierarchies, and understand social norms and customs. These cognitive demands, in turn, require a larger and more complex brain.

Dunbar's research has shown that the average size of social groups in humans is around 150 individuals, a number now known as *Dunbar's number*. This suggests that the human neocortex is optimized for social relationships within a particular range, and that the size of our social networks is limited by the cognitive capacity of our brains. Dunbar's number also correlates to the approximate size of groups in our hunter-gatherer past.[2] Since we spent 95 percent of our time as a species living as

[1] Robin Dunbar, "The Social Brain Hypothesis," *Evolutionary Anthropology* 6 (1998): 178–90.

[2] "Hunter-gatherers typically live in camp groups or bands of fewer than fifty individuals, but these unlike most primate groups are embedded in higher level groupings—several camp groups make up a community, several communities a mega-band, several mega-bands a tribe." Robin Dunbar, *How Religion Evolved and Why It Endures* (Oxford University Press, 2022), 99.

hunter-gatherers, our brains evolved not to outsmart predators or to better understand the physical world, but primarily to enable us to maneuver successfully in a complex social environment.[3]

Our social brain is adept at interpreting and responding to social signals, such as facial expressions, tone of voice, and body language. We care deeply about what others think of us and we have a deep need for connection. We have a unique ability to understand and share the mental states of others (known as theory of mind). We also have a deep need to harmonize with others. As noted in my own story about the formal dinner at the opening of the chapter, we have a desire to learn and follow group norms and rules of behavior. And finally, we have a unique ability to step back and reflect on ourselves, to gain perspective and self-awareness, which in turn allow us to maintain healthy relationships.

For our ancestors, these abilities allowed them to be socially adept and, more importantly, kept them from getting kicked out of their social group. If one got kicked out of the hunter-gatherer tribe, they wouldn't be our ancestor. Now we can dig a little deeper into each of these tendencies, needs, and abilities and get a step closer to a better understanding of why people think and behave the way that they do.

We Have a Need to Connect

As social beings, humans have a fundamental need to connect with others. This need is deeply wired into our brains, is essential for

[3] In her book *Social Chemistry*, Marissa King documents that contemporary hunter-gatherer societies in Africa and Indonesia have an average group size of 148.4. Army companies from sixteenth-century Spain to the nineteenth-century US were comprised of 150 soldiers. The same pattern shows up in research on social media users, who seem to be able to maintain relationships with about the same number of other users. Marissa King, *Social Chemistry: Decoding the Patterns of Human Connection* (Dutton, 2021), 37.

our well-being, and can have a profound impact on our physical and mental health. In *Social: Why Our Brains Are Wired to Connect*, neuroscientist and social psychologist Matthew Lieberman explains not only the evolutionary rationale for human bonding but describes the connection of specific brain regions to human social behavior.[4] For example, Lieberman shows how a brain region known as the dorsal anterior cingulate cortex (dACC) is activated when individuals experience social rejection or exclusion. He calls this phenomenon social pain.

Lieberman describes the dACC as an alarm system. He compares it to the common smoke detector found in a home:

> The smoke alarm needs to let everyone in the vicinity know there might be a fire, to call 911, or to just flip the burgers so they stop burning. It has to be able to interrupt whatever else you are doing or focusing on. This is precisely what emotions do for each of us. The conscious distress of physical pain motivates us to take our hand off the stove; the pain of social exclusion motivates us to reconnect with others.[5]

"Social pain is real pain just as physical pain is real pain," writes Lieberman.[6] Physical pain forces us to change our behavior to protect our bodies. Since our ancestors depended on social bonds for safety and for successfully passing on their genes to the next generation, this

[4] Matthew Lieberman, *Social: Why Our Brains Are Wired to Connect* (Crown Publishers, 2013).

[5] Lieberman, *Social*, 62.

[6] Lieberman, *Social*, 46.

built-in alarm system is a critical element in our evolutionary design.

After I read Lieberman's book, I found myself fascinated with how our everyday language captures this connection between physical and social pain. After a breakup with a loved one, individuals often say they have a "broken heart."[7] Public criticisms in a meeting by one person to another are often described in terms such as "a punch in the gut," "he stabbed me in the back," or "she threw me under the bus." I once left a meeting during which there was no shouting or intense emotion, but some mild criticism was directed at a presenter. Afterward, the speaker described the scene to me as a "bloodbath." Our brains register rejection and criticism deeply.

The emotion of loneliness is another alarm system built into our psyches by natural selection. Loneliness is an adaptive emotion that signals we need to reach out for social connection to satisfy our fundamental need for social interaction. Just as thirst tells us to find water, loneliness is a warning that we are in a state of social isolation, and we need to do something. If we fail to drink, our body suffers consequences. In much the same way, social isolation can have significant consequences for both physical and mental health. Research has shown that "social isolation is on par with high blood pressure, obesity, lack of exercise, or smoking as a risk factor for illness and early death."[8] One study found that social isolation and loneliness have an impact on health comparable to smoking fifteen cigarettes a day.

Natural selection not only built in alarm systems to help us connect, it also built in reward systems. Oxytocin is a hormone

[7] Social pain is often physically felt in the heart. The phrase "broken heart" may have come from the Greeks, who thought the heart was the seat of the soul and emotions.

[8] John Cacioppo and William Patrick, *Loneliness: Human Nature and the Need for Social Connection* (W. W. Norton & Company, 2009), 93.

that plays a critical role in the birthing process and in mother-child bonding. It also plays a role in facilitating social bonding and attachment among individuals. It is often called the "love hormone" because it is released during positive social interactions, such as hugging, kissing, or intimate contact. It also promotes feelings of trust, empathy, and connection. When oxytocin is released, people report a feeling of warmth and closeness. Research shows that oxytocin also made people feel more charitable. Moreover, "oxytocin elicits prosocial behavior, and oxytocin is released when we experience prosocial behavior. . . . In other words, a warm and fuzzy feedback loop."[9]

On an interesting sidenote, storytelling has been shown to cause the release of oxytocin. Research has found that character-driven stories with emotional content not only result in better understanding of key points, but also lead listeners to connect with the storyteller. A leader who tells effective stories can build trust with and improve the motivation of followers. As a heart transplant recipient, I have been to many American Heart Association (AHA) fundraisers. The AHA has mastered the art of using the stories of survivors to loosen the purse strings of potential donors. Based on research, it works because the stories release oxytocin into their unsuspecting brains.[10]

Sometime around four hundred thousand years ago, humans learned to control fire. This breakthrough discovery allowed us to cook food. Cooking led to better diets, bigger brains, and more discretionary time. The light of the ancestral campfire allowed for a longer day and lots of time for storytelling. Research of more recent

9 Sapolsky, *Behave*, 113.

10 Paul Zak, "Why Your Brain Loves Good Storytelling," HBR Digital, October 28, 2014.

hunter-gatherer societies shows that nighttime conversations were filled with storytelling while daytime talk was more transactional. It is believed that campfire storytelling solidified social networks by "putting listeners on the same emotional wavelength and elicited understanding, trust and sympathy."[11] Here we have gene-culture coevolution at work. Through thousands of generations, our brains have experienced and then been shaped by storytelling. The shaping process involved building these alarm and reward systems into the brain.

Another reward system related to social connection is the mesolimbic dopamine system located in the ventral tegmental area (VTA) and the nucleus accumbens (NAcc) regions of the brain. I don't expect many readers are interested in learning a great deal about brain biology, but I include this information to show how what we experience as thoughts, feelings, and needs are the product of brain functions built in by natural selection in response to survival needs. We don't have agency over much of this. Research has shown that social connections activate the dopamine system, leading to feelings of pleasure and reward. Many positive social affirmations, such as a compliment, laughing at a story, or a hug, can all trigger a release of dopamine.

We Are All Kreskin[12]

My wife, Leslie, came home one day with an unusual frown. I could immediately tell something was wrong. When I asked if she was OK, she demurred. Later in the day she described an interaction with

[11] Michael Balter, "Ancient Campfires Led to the Rise of Storytelling," Science Online, September 22, 2014.

[12] George Joseph Kreskin, known as The Amazing Kreskin, became famous in the 1970s with hundreds of TV appearances during which he demonstrated fascinating intuitive abilities, including mind reading.

someone at the gym that had upset her. All of us have experiences like this. We notice a behavior or facial expression and infer an emotional state. Psychologists call this mindreading, the ability to attribute mental states (such as beliefs, desires, intentions, emotions, and so forth) to others and to use this information to understand and predict behavior.

The evolutionary roots of mindreading can be traced back to our primate ancestors. Primates, like humans, live in complex social groups and rely on social bonds for survival and reproduction. This means that they need to be able to understand the intentions, desires, and emotions of others to navigate social interactions effectively. This ability to read mental states expanded as human groups became larger and more complex. Mindreading enabled hunter-gatherers to cooperate more effectively, anticipate and avoid conflicts, form strategic alliances, and adapt to constantly changing social environments.

Matt Lieberman describes the specific brain regions that compose what he refers to as the mentalizing system. This system includes a range of cognitive processes related to social cognition, such as perspective taking, mental state inference, and empathy. Let's play out an example of this system at work. You are a presenter at a meeting, and you notice scowling and eye-rolling among participants. You infer from this real-time feedback that your talk isn't going well. You pause your remarks and comment on what you are observing. You open the floor for discussion and as a result can bring more clarity or make adjustments that win the group over. Your mentalizing system has saved the day.

Mindreading is ubiquitous and rarely conscious, but it is a critical feature of our social brain. As you go through the next few days, think about all the times you are activating this system. Perhaps you will see a friend for the first time in a while. What clues can you look for to determine their mood? You encounter someone at work who is crying. You don't know them well, but you feel an urge to comfort them, and you feel a little sadness yourself. You witness an argument between two colleagues. You don't have a stake in the outcome but find yourself trying to understand each person's perspective. These are examples of the mentalizing system at work.

Our mentalizing system ignites another important cognitive process known as empathy. Empathy enables us to understand and share the emotions, experiences, and perspectives of others. In the 1990s, researchers discovered the existence of neurons that fire when an individual performs an action and when they observe someone else performing the same action. Think about a time you saw someone yawn in a meeting, and you yawned almost immediately afterward, as did others around you. The existence of these unique "mirror neurons" gives more evidence of the social nature and structure of our brain.[13]

Mirror neurons are believed to play a key role in triggering empathy as they allow our brains to experience the emotions and experiences of others as if they were our own. Lieberman describes empathy as a "front-end process" that can lead to emotional or behavioral responses.[14] I once witnessed a baseball player get hit in the groin and fall to the ground holding his crotch and writhing in pain. I found myself wincing and grabbing my own crotch. My mirror neurons were lighting up. You have heard a common response to similar situations: "I feel your pain."

[13] Mirror neurons are neurons that fire when an individual performs an action and when the individual observes someone else performing the same action. These neurons were first discovered in monkeys. There is still some debate about their existence and role in humans.

[14] Lieberman, *Social*, 152.

In the baseball example the pain was physical, but in most situations the pain is social or emotional such as when we feel sadness for a friend who has suffered a setback, excitement for a friend who has just received news of a promotion, or anger when we see someone treated unjustly. These shared feelings connect us with others and solidify our social bonds. Looking through our evolutionary lens we can see how empathy played an important role in human success by enhancing cooperation and altruistic behavior.

Kumbaya Moments

Evolution has shaped our brain to create an urge to connect with others and the ability to understand what others are thinking and feeling. In addition to our need to connect and the ability to read others' minds, Lieberman describes a mental process that causes us to "adapt to the groups we are in and become the kind of people those people want to be around."[15] He calls this process harmonizing. According to Lieberman, harmonizing involves the synchronization of neural and physiological activity between individuals during social interaction.

I remember my first visit to Mississippi Boulevard Christian Church (MBCC). MBCC is a predominately African American congregation whose Sunday service shares all the great traditions of the Black church. During the sermon, church members responded in unison to the pastor's expressions that called for a customary response. Unlike many of my earlier church experiences, I felt myself almost immediately being pulled closer to the congregation. This sense of community was enhanced further by the gospel singing of

[15] Lieberman, *Social,* 178.

the large church choir. The rich vocal harmonies of the music had everyone standing, swaying, and singing along. I felt connected, part of something.

I felt this same sense of connection and synchronization during a visit to Cleveland one fall day in 1979. My friends and I decided to make the three-hour drive to the Ohio city to see a Steelers game. I have been a Steelers fan since I was a boy, so this was a much-anticipated trip. But as we approached the stadium, I became a bit anxious. The rivalry between the Browns and Steelers was, at the time, one of the most intense in sports, and we expected to be harassed by Browns fans. The Browns were having an off year, and the Steelers were the defending Super Bowl champs, so we expected the worst. But as we got closer to the stadium, we were relieved—the parking lots were filled with black and gold. When we entered the stadium, we were pleased to see thousands of Steelers fans waving their Terrible Towels. Our seats were in a section filled with Pittsburgh fans. We felt an immediate bond with all the people around us as we high-fived our way to our seats.

Other than it being a Steelers victory, I don't remember many details from the game. But I do remember the feelings I experienced. It was my first trip to another team's stadium, and it seemed that being in enemy territory enhanced the bond with the Steelers fans around us. We sang the Steelers fight song, waved our Terrible Towels, and cheered on our team to victory. Almost every fan recognizes how fandom contributes to our sense of social identity and a sense of belonging to a larger community. Being in a crowd enhances those feelings. The act of cheering and celebrating can trigger the release of neurotransmitters such as dopamine, which is associated with pleasure and reward. This neuro-mechanism is a product of our hunter-gatherer past. Evolution equipped us with the ability to form and maintain social bonds and alliances crucial for our ancestor's survival. In a sense, our experience at the big game is a recreation of the ancestral campfire that bonded our ancient forefathers.

Psychologist and neuroscientist Lisa Feldman Barrett describes how the people around us impact our emotional and physiological states. She calls this co-regulation.

> This co-regulation has measurable effects. Changes in one person's body often prompts changes in another person's body, whether the two are romantically involved, just friends, or strangers meeting for the first time. When you are with someone you care about, your breathing can synchronize, as can the beating of your hearts, whether you are in a casual conversation or a heated argument. . . . We often mirror each other's movements in a dance that neither of us is aware of and that is choreographed by our brains. One of us leads, the other follows, and sometimes we switch.[16]

Natural selection has wired our brains to create this physical and emotional synchronization. Have you ever had a profound sense of connection and understanding with another person? You might describe it as being on the same "wavelength." It feels profound because when both brains and bodies are in harmony, it is both physiological and cognitive.

[16] Lisa Feldman Barrett, *Seven and a Half Lessons about the Brain* (Houghton Mifflin Harcourt, 2020), 84. The title of this chapter is a quote from *Seven and a Half Lessons about the Brain.*

Synchronization is the alignment of neural activity among individuals that in turn can impact blood flow, heart rate, and other physiological processes. It creates the conditions for Lieberman's harmonizing. Going deeper, harmonizing involves aligning our thoughts, feelings, and behaviors with those of other people in order to connect with them and achieve shared goals. It is easy to see the evolutionary advantage of harmonizing. Early humans flourished against faster and stronger predators through high levels of cooperation and collaboration.

When we harmonize with others, we experience a sense of shared purpose and belonging, which triggers a dopamine release. As we have learned, dopamine is part of the brain's reward system and when it's released it gives us feelings of pleasure and motivation. I have worked on several executive teams that were highly aligned around a shared purpose and lofty goals. Those years were the best of my career. I have also worked on dysfunctional teams. Those were the worst. The former were times of joy, satisfaction, and growth; the latter were times of stress and feelings of being stuck in mud.

I was once asked to give a motivational talk to a group of employees at one of our neighboring companies in Memphis. AutoZone is a retailer of automotive parts and accessories with over six thousand stores in the United States, Mexico, and Brazil. Founded by a Memphian in 1979, it has grown rapidly because of its strong culture of customer service and employee satisfaction. Before I was introduced at the meeting, the leader called everyone to stand to recite the company pledge in unison. I had heard of this practice, but it was fascinating to experience it firsthand. The pledge is recited at every meeting as a reminder of the company's mission and purpose.

AutoZone
Pledge

- **AutoZoners always put customers first!**
- **We know our parts and products.**
- **Our stores look great!**
- **We've got the best merchandise at the right price.**

Figure 5: AutoZone Pledge

The AutoZone pledge, like the Japanese business custom of singing company songs, taps into the human need for connection. Harmonizing in this way makes the group bigger than the self. It reminds members of the group's shared vision and purpose. I noticed a few people in the meeting reciting the pledge in a rote manner. I assumed that those were employees less excited about the mission or about their jobs in general. But most employees were smiling and seemed all in on the practice. I have long thought that business leaders underutilize harmonizing as a business practice, while their peers in sports and the military use it frequently. Think of your favorite sports movie and the big motivational speeches, boisterous group exhortations, and team cheers.

In his fascinating book on the secrets of good timing, Daniel Pink cites research on the benefits of exercise, group singing, and dancing. Movement is great for the body but also for the brain. Studies show that "group singing calms heart rates and boosts endorphin levels. It improves lung function. It increases pain thresholds and reduces the need for pain medication."[17] More importantly, it synchronizes the group and creates a virtuous cycle. "Feeling good promotes social cohesion, which makes it easier to synchronize. Synchronizing with others feels good, which deepens attachment and improves synchronization further still."[18]

Think back to the ancestral campfire and the dancing and singing that created a sense of belongingness critical to both individual survival and group functioning. All good hunts started with proper planning and a bit of dancing and chanting to bind the hunters into a cohesive unit.

We humans are finely attuned to social norms, those unwritten rules that guide behavior and interaction within our groups. Norms lead to pressure for conformity to group beliefs and values. Our self is in constant tension between our need to express our beliefs, desires, and values and the goals and norms of the group. Henrich writes that humans have been endowed with a "norm psychology," meaning we "intuitively assume that the social world is rule governed." In Henrich's view this norm psychology has driven a process of "self-domestication."[19] At a young age we develop cognitive abilities that allow us to learn and adapt to norms but also to spot norm violations by others.

Following norms keeps us in good stead with our group, and for our ancestors, violating norms could lead to ostracization and an early trip to the grave. Thus, this norm psychology is deeply wired into our brains by natural selection. As to their purpose and benefit,

---

[17] Daniel Pink, *When: The Scientific Secrets of Perfect Timing* (Riverhead Books, 2018), 195.

[18] Pink, *When*, 195.

[19] Henrich, *The Secret of Our Success*, 189.

norms are highly beneficial to group functioning. They provide for predictability (we will learn more about this as a deep human need), structure, and order in social situations. Norms help group members avoid or navigate social conflict. Norms reflect and reinforce the values of the group, and they are passed on to new members and to the next generation, sometimes in formal ways but often through observational learning and modeling.

Social norms lead to conformity, which is perhaps the dark side of the harmonizing coin. As noted, there is a tension between the expression of self and following group norms. Social norms can limit individual freedom and creativity and can prevent individuals from exploring new ideas or expressing themselves in unique ways. Norms can also become so ingrained and automatic that group members are not aware of them. They can become outdated in new contexts—yet questioning them can be seen as traitorous to other group members.

Many readers may be familiar with the famous Solomon Asch conformity experiments. Asch asked research participants a question with an obvious answer. However, he presented the task to groups seeded with confederates who were working with him. Asch presented the subjects with a simple visual perception test involving the comparison of three lines to a separate standard line. The subjects were asked to state aloud which of the three lines matched the standard line. But the subjects were usually the last in the group to give their answer—after Asch's confederates, who were instructed to make a clearly wrong choice. In a significant number of cases, the subjects agreed with the confederates and chose an obviously incorrect answer. In other words, the subjects chose group conformity, a choice aligned with social brain theory.

Over the course of millions of years of evolution, our brains have been shaped by natural selection to have a primarily social orientation. We have a deep need to connect with others, we can read minds, and our reward systems are activated when we find ourselves in synchrony with the members of our group. When we try to understand the people we lead, the people we work with, and the people we love, we need to see their emotions, beliefs, values, and behaviors through the lens of the social brain. While we have amazing capabilities for reasoning, critical thinking, and problem-solving, we are much more *Homo socialis* (social man) than we are *Homo sapiens* (wise man). I hope this awareness of how our brain evolved and works provides insight that allows you to better understand others. Following I lay out thoughts on how to use the social brain perspective in everyday work and life.

Ideas and Applications

- Humans are social beings. We evolved to be social animals, and that has been the secret to our success as a species. We should remember to prioritize socializing and building relationships in almost all contexts.
- The degree of our need for socializing varies, but the need for healthy personal relationships is universal. Keep in mind that brains work better when social needs are met. Positive relationships are critical for brain functioning, and people are more creative and solve problems more effectively when they feel safe and secure in their relationships.

- Build relationships with the people you work with by sharing personal stories, particularly those that show vulnerability. The latter helps break down barriers and builds trust.

- Be aware of the software built deeply in our brains that has us constantly interested in what is going on in the minds of others. Think of the verbal and nonverbal signals we receive as an indicator light. Be careful not to jump to conclusions about what the other person is thinking or feeling. Use the indicator light as a signal to probe for more information.

- Find ways to bring people together to build group harmony. Organizational meetings should balance sharing information with group activities that promote bonding and a sense of shared purpose. Creatively add a little singing and movement. It may feel out of context at times, but it has been proven to promote group cohesion and cooperation.

chapter 5

Negativity Bias: The Boss Wants to See You

To survive, life has to win every day. Death has to win just once. A small error or miscalculation can wipe out all the successes. The negativity bias is adaptive, the term biologists use for a trait that improves the odds of survival for an individual or group.

—John Tierney and Roy Baumeister

Mystery Meeting

On Friday I received an email from Jill requesting a meeting with Bryan first thing Monday morning. Bryan was my boss and the CEO of our company; Jill was his executive assistant. Once I read the email, I had an immediate feeling of anxiety. My mind was filled with questions. Why did Bryan want to see me? Is something wrong? Bryan often stopped by my office to talk, and formal meetings like this were rare. I had a sense that I would be thinking about the meeting all weekend. I had a notion of calling Bryan, but I knew he had been out of town most of the week and I didn't want to disturb him.

I first met Bryan Jordan when we served on the executive management committee of another major regional banking company. We had come together as peers as the result of a merger. He was chief financial officer, and I was chief human resources officer. I gained immediate respect for him as a thoughtful and caring executive. A few years later we found ourselves involved in another merger. I left to become CHRO at First Horizon Bank and after a few months worked with the board to recruit Bryan to become CFO and potentially CEO.

The board was impressed by Bryan's business acumen and leadership abilities and promoted him to CEO about one year later. Over the course of our fifteen years of working closely together we shared a great deal of mutual respect. I admired him as a person and boss, particularly his calm in the face of storms. Our company faced many challenges because of the financial crisis of 2008. In that year, every day brought news of another bad loan or a big financial loss, yet I never saw him berate the bearer of bad news. And he always treated me with dignity and respect. I thought of him as a friend.

How do I explain that immediate sense of trepidation? Luckily, and as the reader can no doubt guess, I was familiar with the phenomenon social scientists call "negativity bias" (also known in the academic literature as negativity dominance or negativity effect). This bias refers to the universal tendency for us to give more weight and importance to negative information compared to positive information. It is a product of the way our brains were wired by natural selection to detect and respond to threats in the environment.

Remember the section on evolutionary mismatch and the story of the hedgehog whose physical response to threats in a modern world was no longer a match for the new challenge of two-ton, speeding automobiles. Despite my awareness of negativity bias and my strong history with Bryan, my amygdala reacted in a split second, sending signals to other parts of the brain to prepare for what it read as a threat. The hypothalamus activated the sympathetic nervous system, which led to the release of stress hormones. As with many social situations, this bodily response happened quickly and initially outside my consciousness. However, in this case the threat response was muted based on my experience and learning. I was able to talk myself into positively reframing the email and my expectations for the meeting. (As to the meeting request, Bryan just wanted to pass on some feedback from employees he had gathered during his visits to our out-of-town locations.)

When we face a potential threat—even a perceived one in our modern social world—sensory information is processed in the brainstem and sent to the thalamus, a kind of switching station in the brain. From there, the information can be sent to various areas of the brain for processing. However, in some situations sensory information about a potential threat can bypass the thalamus and be sent directly to the amygdala. As Jonathan Haidt describes it, "the amygdala has a direct connection to the part of the brainstem that activates the fight-or-flight response, and if the amygdala finds a pattern that was part of a previous fear episode (such as the sound of a hiss), it orders the body to red alert."[1]

We get lots of these red alerts during our daily lives. Recently, my wife, Leslie, grabbed me from behind to give me a hug. I thought she was out for the evening, so I jumped as soon as I felt her touch. My heart rate shot up and it took me a few seconds to calm myself. This physiological process evolved to ensure that we can respond quickly to potential threats without having to wait for information to be processed in other areas of the brain. It's easy to see how this quick reaction time had an adaptive advantage through most of

[1] Jonathan Haidt, *The Happiness Hypothesis: Finding Modern Truth in Ancient Wisdom* (Basic Books, 2006), 30.

human history. Threats often came in the form of stronger and faster predators. A slow response time would be fatal.

The same line of thinking can be applied to the negative bias. We have a strong tendency for negative events and emotions to affect us more strongly than positive ones. We remember bad events more vividly; we are stung by a word of criticism but quickly forget a paragraph of praise. Negative emotional experiences haunt us longer than positive emotions elevate us. Haidt calls it one of life's design principles: "bad is stronger than good." Natural selection again offers an explanation. Through our evolutionary history, our environment has presented us with many opportunities and threats. Haidt describes the process using fish. "The cost of missing a cue that signals food is low; odds are that there are other fish in the sea, and one mistake won't lead to starvation. The cost of missing the sign of a nearby predator, however, can be catastrophic. Game over, end of the line for those genes."[2]

On the ancestral savanna, the hunter-gatherers who survived were the ones who were more alert to danger. The brave, constantly reckless, and overly curious experimenter, the one who tried every berry and ran thoughtlessly after every tasty rabbit and welcomed every stranger, didn't contribute much to the gene pool. As Baumeister and Tierney wrote, "To survive, life has to win every day. Death has to win just once. A small error or miscalculation can wipe out all the successes."[3] Our brain's negativity bias is highly adaptive but "our fine-tuned sense of bad can be debilitating, and what worked for

---

2 Haidt, *The Happiness Hypothesis*, 29.

3 John Tierney and Roy Baumeister, *The Power of Bad: How the Negativity Effect Rules Us and How We Can Rule It* (Penguin Press, 2019), 11.

hunter-gatherers doesn't always work for us."[4] When trying to understand some of our opening questions, negativity bias explains a lot.

It is often said that people don't like change. That statement is too broad to be universally true. People often get very excited about changes, even very big ones such as marriage, a promotion, or a new home. While these events do bring some stress, we do look forward to them. But it is also fair to say that many people tend to exhibit resistance or discomfort when faced with significant change. Like many of the aspects of human behavior we have described thus far, responses to change vary widely in intensity based on individual traits and experience, but initial negative feelings about significant change are common.

While there are rational reasons to fear some change, much of the reaction can be linked to negativity bias. I made countless presentations to employee groups announcing organizational changes. At almost every meeting the first questions posed focus on the negative. Will people lose their jobs? Will there be cuts to compensation? Why do we have to do this now? Even the seemingly neutral questions show signs of concern or skepticism. The concept of loss aversion also helps explain this phenomenon. Loss aversion, a form of negativity bias, refers to our tendency to evaluate outcomes as gains and losses, and to feel that losses loom larger than gains.[5]

In my many conversations with employees during major change events, I have found that they take their current situation as a reference point. They have a bunch of stuff they like: the work they do, colleagues, boss, pay, workspace, and so forth. Change means

[4] Tierney and Baumeister, *The Power of Bad*, 11.

[5] Loss aversion is a concept developed by Daniel Kahneman and Amos Tversky. It refers to the tendency of individuals to prefer avoiding losses over acquiring gains.

they may have to give up some of this good stuff. A little evolutionary mechanism built into their brain says, *This may be bad.* And with loss aversion they are much more focused on possible losses than the fact that the change ahead may bring about gains. Of course, during these many change events, I have always come across some employees who are looking forward to the change. Most are positive people with a strong sense of security and a trusting relationship with leadership. A few just hate their jobs or their boss and are hopeful for a big severance payment!

Bad News and Biases

Loss aversion is one of the most well-known biases in behavioral economics because it defies the notion of rational economic decision-making. In hundreds of experiments, subjects become risk averse when making decisions that involve facing losses, even when one action is significantly more favorable mathematically than the alternative. Consider the case of a person who invests $1,000 in a stock. Over time the stock fluctuates in value but at one point decreases in value to $800. At any given time, the decision to sell or hold the stock should be based on estimates of its future value. But research shows that many people will hold on to the stock in hopes the value will rebound and thus avoid realizing a loss.

Negativity bias flows into many aspects of life. Psychologists studying people's reactions found that bad first impressions had a much greater impact than good first impressions.[6] I have seen this frequently in my time as a human resources executive. I remember

[6] Tierney and Baumeister, *The Power of Bad*, 65.

one example of an executive who joined our company from a major competitor. In her first meeting, Mary made the mistake of strongly touting some of the practices of her former employer. She turned off all her new peers almost immediately and in many meetings that followed her ideas were met with eye rolls and critical hallway conversations. But over time, and with a little self-awareness coaching from her friendly HR executive, Mary proved to be a thoughtful and effective leader. In Mary's case and many others, I have often thought about the waste of time and energy brought on by bad first impressions. I even added a little cultural indoctrination to my executive assimilation meetings to help new leaders avoid bad first impressions.

I found a great contrast to what happened with employees who made favorable first impressions. In the case of bad first impressions, it took a lot of time and contradictory information to change views. But in the case of those who made good first impressions, it was amazing how much grace was given even in the face of growing evidence that the new employee was either not competent or a bad fit for the role. (Also note the fact that hiring managers often compensate for weaknesses and give more time than they should because they don't want to admit they made a bad hire.)

Team performance is a rich area of study for social scientists. "Project Aristotle" was one recent and oft-quoted study conducted at Google. The primary focus of the study was to find out what makes some teams successful while others struggle. The findings pointed to psychological safety as a significant factor in determining team success. We will discuss the concept of psychological safety in detail in a future chapter. I bring it up now because our brain's negativity bias plays an important role in psychological safety.

In *The Power of Bad*, the authors document some of the "bad apple" research that shows how one team member (the bad apple) can ruin team performance. In one study of personality traits and team performance, researchers measured how well members communicated, avoided conflict, and liked one another and how fairly they shared the workload. "The scientists expected that performance would be best predicted by the average personality score of the team—after all, that would take into account everyone's strengths and weaknesses. But the strongest predictor of team functioning turned out to be the score of the worst person in the group. One lazy, disagreeable, emotionally unstable person was enough to sabotage the whole team, and it didn't matter if there was one particularly wonderful member of the group. The star couldn't compensate for the dud's damage."[7] It turns out one bad apple can spoil the whole barrel!

Natural selection shaped our brain with a powerful approach/avoid orientation. We move toward that which rewards us—food, sex, or a warm and smiling face. We move away from that which threatens us—a snarling sharped-tooth predator, the look and smell of disease, or the angry face of a stranger. The latter is prioritized by the brain. We are significantly more attentive to and influenced by negative than positive information. As we have seen with loss aversion, this asymmetry affects judgment and decision-making. It also impacts other aspects of our everyday lives.

I am confident you have been on the other end of a statement like, "I have some bad news for you." Or someone you know comes up to you with a facial expression that communicates you are about to receive bad news. You may remember your physical response as

---

[7] Tierney and Baumeister, *The Power of Bad*, 141.

your stress (avoidance) response kicked in. Your brain perceived a threat and in a split second released stress hormones such as cortisol and adrenaline. Your heart rate and blood pressure may have become elevated. You may have even experienced muscle tension and a change in your breathing. Your body was ready for action.

Your response was quite normal, but most likely a mismatch in the sense we have discussed previously. Our ancient ancestors faced many physical threats that could prove life ending. Our built-in fight-or-flight response[8] was a lifesaver. Most of our modern-day threats are not as dire. Bad news is never pleasing, but it is rarely life-threatening. Still, our biological system kicks into high gear. One significant side effect is that cognitive functioning—our ability to think, concentrate, and make decisions—deteriorates in real time. We are ready to react, but to think clearly . . . not so much.

We should remember this phenomenon when delivering bad news. When researchers tested the old line "I have some good news and bad news" by asking research participants what they wanted to hear first, more than three-quarters wanted the bad news first. Other researchers, looking at the best way to give feedback, found that giving praise first confused recipients and even made subsequent criticism more painful.[9]

As an HR executive, I have delivered bad news countless times. It was the part of the job I disliked most. From demotions to firings,

[8] The "fight-or-flight" system is scientifically known as the sympathetic nervous system (SNS), which is activated in response to stress, danger, or situations requiring a physical response. The SNS prepares the body for action by releasing adrenaline, which makes the heart beat faster and the lungs breathe more efficiently. This in turn increases alertness and sensitivity. Energy is mobilized for action. The SNS is balanced by the parasympathetic nervous system (PNS), which releases neurotransmitters and hormones to calm the body. Too much activation of the SNS takes a toll on the body.

[9] Tierney and Baumeister, *The Power of Bad*, 97.

layoffs, and poor performance reviews, I can sometimes still see the many faces of hurt and disappointment in my memory. The most important thing I learned is the phenomenon of cognitive disruption. Once you give the bad news, the recipient doesn't remember much of what you say afterward. What they do remember in part, they get wrong. I learned that for most bad news events, a follow-up meeting was necessary.

There is no simple formula for delivering bad news. Your objective and context are most important when deciding on an approach. With an employee I valued, one whom I considered important to the organization, I made sure I prepared lots of positive comments in advance of the meeting. More than just general praise, I made sure I commented on specific skills and successful projects. I also made sure that the feedback was also specific and actionable. These performance feedback conversations were designed to be highly engaging, with me asking and answering lots of questions. I always tried to have a follow-up session by the end of the next week. This gave time for the recipient to process the feedback and develop additional questions.

When firing people for performance or behavior issues, my meetings were highly choreographed: the purpose of the meeting came quickly and next steps followed in a caring but perfunctory manner. Early on in my career, I tried to go into detail to justify my decisions, but I learned that people in that situation can't really process information very well. Giving people detailed criticism right after you tell them you are firing them goes in one ear and out the other. In later years, I offered to have a follow-up conversation during which I could give more detailed feedback. Few took me up on the offer, but in the ones who did I could sense genuine appreciation for my time. In those who didn't, I could imagine my image on a doll with pins inserted in delicate places.

In *The Power of Bad*, the authors describe what sociologist Douglas Maynard calls the "perspective display sequence." When studying doctors, Maynard observed that those with effective bedside manner often started the process of delivering bad news by asking questions such as, "What have you learned so far?" or "What do you think is going on?" Experienced doctors learned that "asking questions allows the patient to be more than a passive audience."[10]

> The first impulse when gobsmacked with bad news is self-protection: the fight or flight response. Some patients try to shut out the bad news; others want to shoot the messenger, or at least argue with her. But if the patient is instead asked his perspective and is the first one to say something is wrong, then he's readier to face it and continue the conversation.[11]

This three-step process involves first seeking the patient's perspective, confirming it, and then following up with the details of the bad news.

I can confirm from my experience that delivering bad news is best as a dialogue. Again, if the goal is the maintenance of a long-term relationship, the deliverer of bad news should make sure the receiver knows why that relationship is important. Research has shown that overdone praise is usually more about the deliverer than

....

[10] Tierney and Baumeister, *The Power of Bad*, 100.

[11] Tierney and Baumeister, *The Power of Bad*, 100.

the recipient. People crave praise and recognition, the more specific the better. Evidence moves praise beyond flattery. I also ask a lot of check-in questions during a bad news conversation. Does what I said make sense? Am I being clear? I also try to leave space for quiet. People overcoming their initial negative arousal need time to process.

Our brains have a built-in rapid detection system that privileges threats above opportunities and rewards. This negativity bias is adaptive in an evolutionary sense and allowed our ancestors to survive and thrive. In simple terms what's left for us in our modern world is that bad is more powerful than good. There are "merchants of bad"[12] who prey upon this negativity bias. Some in the media, politics, and advertising grab our attention by focusing on bad events. They keep our aroused focus on their agenda; our eyeballs keep watching their network, reading their newspaper, or buying their useless products.

Ideas and Applications

- Stay aware that negativity bias is a powerful pull on our thinking. One technique that works is called labeling and reappraisal. When faced with an initial negative reaction to an event, name it and reappraise it. This is what I did with the opening message from my boss. My limbic system detected an immediate threat, but by naming it I brought it into conscious awareness and was able to reevaluate it as a nonthreat.

....

[12] Tierney and Baumeister, *The Power of Bad*, 214.

- Practice positive reframing. Every time you experience a negative event, step back and think about it from a broader perspective. What positive can come out of it? What did you learn? Consciously compare it to other events that turned out to have neutral or no long-term negative impact. Positive reframing not only helps counter negativity bias but also leads to personal resiliency.

- Challenge your thinking when feeling negative thoughts. Hold off on deciding about an idea or person based on a bad first impression. Initial negative thoughts are often based on cognitive distortions influenced by negativity dominance.

- Be mindful of your sources of information. Limit exposure to social media and sources that are constantly focused on bad news. Many in the media and politics understand negativity bias and are consciously attempting to keep your attention by activating your amygdala, the part of the brain that creates the fear response. Negativity bias served our ancestors well because it focused their attention, a psychological response that doesn't serve us well when we are drawn into a stream of media negativity.

- Balance your news input with sources such as goodnewsnetwork.org, positive.news, informationisbeautiful.net, and my good friend Bill Burke at theoptimisminstitute.com.

chapter 6

Us versus Them: Here We Go Steelers, Here We Go

As a lifelong Cleveland Browns fan, I grew up learning to hate the Pittsburgh Steelers. I hated their colors, their emblem, Three Rivers Stadium, and anything else that was Steeler related. I hated Franco Harris, Terry Bradshaw, and I especially hated Jack Lambert. Chuck Noll? Hated him! Art Rooney? Hated him too . . . as a Cleveland Browns fan, it was my sworn duty to be a devout hater of anything Pittsburgh born and bred.

—Mark Barnes, Cleveland Browns fan
(the Steelers are 46–7 vs. the Browns since 1970)

Terrible Towel

As you know from an earlier chapter, I am a Steelers fan. I have been one since I was eight years old. I proudly wear my Steelers T-shirts and hats (although I tend to wear them more after a win). My license plate is framed by the Steelers logo. All my friends and colleagues know I am a Steelers fan. Some of my most cherished memories are Steelers wins, particularly the six Super Bowl victories. I sometimes find myself tuned to the NFL Network watching replays of big games. I only stick with the ones I know we won. I am amazed at how I get a rush of excitement after a touchdown, or even a replay I have seen a dozen times. I love my team and often travel from my home in Memphis to watch them play.

In 2007, my wife, my son Jeff, and I traveled to Phoenix to watch a game against the Cardinals. Steelers fans have a reputation for large fan support at away games, so while we recognized we were entering enemy territory, we knew from previous trips we would not be alone. I remember the excitement of that day. This was the first big out-of-town Steelers trip for Jeff. Though he was very young when we moved from Pittsburgh, he'd adopted his dad's love for Pittsburgh teams. This was the trip where I would show him all the rituals of Steelers fandom.

As we arrived at the stadium, we were thrilled to see Steelers flags flying over tailgating parties and we could see a large contingent of Steelers fans heading to the gates. This would be an enjoyable day. But as we arrived in the stands, an uneasiness set about me. We settled into our seating section, and I could hear Spanish all around us. And the fans were different from the ones you would find at a Steelers home game: they were generally smaller in stature, their skin a little darker. My momentary unease was matched by a quiet embarrassment at what I was feeling.

But then the Steelers took the field. Everyone around us took to their feet. Off came their jackets and we found ourselves surrounded by a sea of Steelers game day shirts. Out came hundreds of Terrible Towels, the rally flag of my beloved Steelers. My unease quickly faded as I high-fived everyone I could. During the game, I learned that many of the fans were from Mexico, which has a large Steelers fan base. When Steelers tight end Heath Miller caught a pass early in the game, all the fans around me shouted "Heeeath," just as they do back in Pittsburgh. We all sang the Steelers fight song together: "Here We Go." My new friends knew all our rituals. I was with my peeps!

I have long reflected on that day, a classic example of how the us-them mechanism in our brains can momentarily flood us with primordial emotions. Evolution has shaped our brains to form this dichotomy beyond our conscious thought and with stunning speed. We are tribal. We love our groups. Our social brains have been wired to connect and coordinate with those around us. Our identities are forged by the groups we belong to. Our groups meet our need for belonging, safety, meaning, and purpose. Our "groupishness"[1] is the secret of our success. Yet our propensity for us-versus-them thinking runs deep.

Robert Sapolsky has studied the biology of us and them. His research shows how our brains and nervous systems have evolved to perceive and categorize others as part of an "in-group" or "out-group" based on ethnicity, skin color, and other observable traits. We also categorize others based on values, beliefs, and ideologies. The latter are identified by markers such as dress, hairstyle, or ornamentation. As Sapolsky describes, "our brains distinguish between in-group members and outsiders in a fraction of a second, and they encourage us to be kind to the former but hostile to the latter. These biases are automatic and unconscious and emerge at astonishingly young ages."[2]

Our prejudices and biases are learned and reinforced over time through social learning. "Yet the cognitive structures they require are

....

[1] A term attributed to the great evolutionary biologist Richard Dawkins in his influential book *The Selfish Gene*.

[2] Robert Sapolsky, "This is Your Brain on Nationalism: The Biology of Us and Them," *Foreign Affairs*, March/April 2019.

present from the outset."[3] As we saw in an earlier chapter, our brains come with a built-in apparatus to learn language, but the language we learn to speak depends on context. Likewise, we are wired to categorize. Learning who to trust and who to hate is just filling in the blanks. That process is facilitated by oxytocin, a compound known as the "cuddle hormone." As we discussed in chapter 4, oxytocin is central to mother-infant bonding, and it promotes emotional attachment between partners.

But oxytocin also has a dark side. It has been found to promote in-group favoritism and even hostility toward individuals perceived as being part of an out-group. This can contribute to tribalism and prejudice. If an individual is in an aroused state, oxytocin can amplify negative emotions leading to anger, aggressive behavior, and xenophobia. It is a double-edged sword. As Sapolsky explains, oxytocin "deepens the fault line in our brains between "us" and "them."[4] The momentary feeling I experienced as I sat in my seat at the Steelers game was likely a drip of oxytocin flowing through my system.

Scientists who first studied group formation were shocked at how little it took for groups to become tribes. In 1971, a research team led by Henri Tajfel was interested in learning about the causes of in-group favoritism. Their original goal was to form groups with meaningless connections and then add other variables to understand how in-group favoritism started. But their research plan "failed for a very revealing reason . . . the research team could never get to the starting point. They were unable to make a group that seemed so arbitrary and trivial that no group

[3] Sapolsky, "This is Your Brain on Nationalism."

[4] Sapolsky, "This is Your Brain on Nationalism."

favoritism was found. If the research team did nothing more than flip a coin to assign participants to a red team or a blue team,"[5] favoritism immediately followed.

This automatic attachment to and preference for a group is known as minimal group effect and has been robustly studied. Among the most fascinating results of Tajfel's studies was how in-group favoritism, even in arbitrarily assigned groups, influenced behavior. After these minimal groups were formed, participants were asked to distribute rewards between members of their own group (in-group) and members of the other group (out-group). Tajfel's team found that participants consistently showed a preference for distributing more rewards to members of their own group. Other researchers have found that in-group preference and out-group bias persist over time, even when group connections are trivial.

Being a Steelers fan is part of my identity. In many training sessions on diversity and inclusion, participants are asked to write a list of words that define them. My list always includes "Steelers fan." I am one because I grew up in Pittsburgh and it didn't hurt that during my early adult years the Steelers won a lot. It is unlikely that I would be a Steelers fan if I had grown up in Dallas. This example makes an important point about identity: we don't choose much of our identity; it is thrust on us. And most of who we are comes from our connection with the groups we belong to.

Professors Jay Van Bavel and Dominic Packer are psychologists who study identity, the importance of groups in identity formation, and its impact on behavior. Their research points out the important role that identity plays in creating our sense of self and our role in

---

[5] Roy Baumeister and Brad Bushman, *Social Psychology and Human Nature* (Cengage Learning, 2017), 461.

the world. Our identity is activated by the groups we belong to, and these groups in turn shape our beliefs and values. As a group member we conform to the norms of the group and actively align with group interests and support group goals. From an evolutionary perspective, our hunter-gatherer brains benefited from this connection of identity to our "groupishness."[6]

When we create and share social identities with others, good things happen. Our shared experience and close bonds create trust. We cooperate, we reciprocate, we share, and we treat other members of our group with compassion and generosity. Our social brains connect in synchrony. Our brains are flooded with neurochemicals such as dopamine and oxytocin. Every football fan who has lived through the moment of being in the stands when their beloved team scores the winning touchdown in a big game knows this feeling. It has brought in the harvest, built cathedrals, and even won battles.

But, as noted earlier, there is a dark side. As much as social identity can make people want to support members of their own group, it can also make them not support those belonging to other groups. Van Bavel and Packer describe how it can go to the level of harm and worse:

> When relations between groups harden and when we start to see "our" interests as fundamentally opposed to "their" interests, the natural positive and empathy we feel toward our own group can shift in a dangerous direction.

[6] Jay Van Bavel and Dominic Packer, *The Power of Us: Harnessing Our Shared Identities to Improve Performance, Increase Cooperation, and Promote Social Harmony* (Little, Brown Spark, 2021), 32.

> We start to think that we are not only good but that we're *inherently* good. And if that's true, then they must be intrinsically bad and should be opposed at all costs. Issues are moralized in ways that favor our point of view. We become less tolerant of dissent and vigilant against any deviance that threatens to dilute the all-important boundary between us and them.[7]

Any observer of today's political polarization can see this dynamic at play and accelerated by social and general media that create echo chambers and play to the worst parts of our us-them nature.

One of the great philosophical debates is about the nature of human beings. Often quoted are the contrasting perspectives of Thomas Hobbes and Jean-Jacques Rousseau. Hobbes was an Englishman who set out a doctrine about the role of the state. In his most famous work, *Leviathan*, he argued for a government with strong central authority. His thinking was founded on his pessimistic view of human nature, which he saw as being driven by individual desires and self-interests. Rousseau, on the other hand, believed that humans are born inherently good and compassionate, but are corrupted by society and its institutions. Both used their thoughts about human nature to support their arguments about governance. So, what is it? Are we fundamentally good or bad?

It seems that Hobbes and Rousseau did not have the benefit of modern insights into human nature. Our propensity for us-them explains a lot. We can be good when we are thinking

....

[7] Van Bavel and Packer, *The Power of Us*, 32.

about us and be bad when we are thinking about them. A bigger question is this: Why did natural selection build in this us-them orientation? First, it is important to remember that natural selection is not a conscious or intentional "designer" like a human architect or engineer. It does not have a goal or a preferred end state. Natural selection occurs when certain traits confer a reproductive advantage in a particular environment. These advantageous traits are then passed on to future generations, leading to their increased prevalence over time.

From this lens, the existence of "them" makes sense. In our hunter-gatherer days, as populations grew, we had to compete with others for scarce resources. Territorial behavior and intergroup aggression are common among our primate cousins, and evidence of violence and conflict exists in the fossil record of early humans. We know how intergroup competition can reinforce group cohesion, social cooperation, and cultural norms and traditions. Competition makes "us" stronger—clearly adaptive in an evolutionary sense. Think of sports teams. They are cohesive not simply because they wear uniforms of the same color, but because they must work together for the common good against an opponent. A team that merely practiced without ever facing an opponent would probably not be as successful as one that played strong competition.[8] Cohesive groups beat the less cohesive ones. Henrich adds to this, "Over time history suggests that all prosocial institutions age and eventually collapse at the hands of self-interest, unless they are renewed by the dynamics of intergroup competition."[9]

---

[8] Baumeister and Bushman, *Social Psychology and Human Nature*, 495.

[9] Henrich, *The Secret of Our Success*, 170.

The Perils of Us–Them Thinking

I have seen the us-versus-them dynamic play out countless times in my corporate life. The resulting conflicts were frustrating and often baffling to the executives who faced them. Once, I received a call from our bank president looking for help on a significant business problem. After a monthly financial update, the president learned that fee income was way off plan. He called a meeting with key leaders to investigate the matter. Instead of explanations of the fee decline and solutions to fix it, the executive heard a litany of complaints and recriminations between the product management and technology departments.

While he eventually learned that the fee decline was due to a flaw in the fee capture system, the bank president knew he had a deeper problem that a coding change wouldn't fix. That is when he called HR. After a series of interviews, we learned that there was significant animosity between the two teams, starting with the two department leaders, who were reported in the interviews to "hate" each other. While not completely true, that is what team members acted on. Us-them kicked in "in spades."

From the perspective of the product department, the technology team were "cowboys" who didn't listen and often went off creating systems and codes that didn't meet the necessary business requirements. As to the technologists, they viewed the product team as arrogant "prima donnas" who didn't communicate well and weren't good team players. Reputations were impugned, trust was nonexistant, and negative emotions were high. This state of affairs is what Amanda Ripley calls "high conflict . . . when conflict clarifies into a good-versus-evil kind of feud, the kind with an us and a them."[10]

I taught many conflict-management classes in my time as an HR leader. I usually start the session by asking a question: "What emotions come to mind when I say the word *conflict*?" I then list the responses on a flip chart. Here's a sample list:

- Upset
- Painful
- Frustrating
- Emotional
- Nervous
- Anger
- Exhausting
- Annoying
- Necessary
- Inevitable

I am sure you can see a pattern. Almost all the emotions are negative. Occasionally, a few people will add positive or neutral words, but I found the "going in" story on conflict to be "it is a bad thing to be avoided."

You might be able to guess the first point I make in the sessions: this is a framing problem. Our social brains don't like conflict, at least as most of us have experienced it. While some people enjoy engaging in some forms of conflict, like a robust political debate, most of us avoid it like the plague. When we think of conflict, it's Ripley's "high conflict." At a nonconscious level our brains are lighting up. We are

[10] Amanda Ripley, *High Conflict: Why We Get Trapped and How We Get Out* (Simon & Schuster, 2021), 4.

not wired to be like *Star Trek*'s Spock.[11] We want to be liked. We don't want to feel rejection. We don't want to be kicked out of our groups.

Reframing conflict allows us to assign new meaning to it and move beyond the initial orientation of our social brain. This first reaction emanates from the brain regions mentioned earlier in the book, such as the dorsal anterior cingulate cortex (dACC)—which acts as an alarm system and is the source of social pain—and the amygdala—the source of our emotional responses. Reframing taps the prefrontal cortex, particularly the dorsolateral prefrontal cortex (DLPFC), which is associated with executive functions such as cognitive control and decision-making. Daniel Kahneman would say we are engaging system two and overcoming system one.[12] Another way to think about it is that we are using conscious thoughts to offset the nonconscious tendencies of our hunter-gatherer brain.

Reframing can allow us to see healthy conflict as beneficial. Research shows that when different perspectives clash in a constructive manner, it often leads to innovative solutions and fresh insights. It can also improve decision-making by encouraging open discussion and constructive debate. Business consultant Howard Guttman describes these additional benefits:

- Stimulates healthy interaction and involvement in accomplishing a task

[11] For non–science fiction fans, Spock is the fictional character from the science fiction franchise *Star Trek*. Spock is Vulcan, a humanoid species known for valuing logic and rationality. Spock is also half human, and a major storyline involves his struggles with controlling his emotions.

[12] Kahneman introduced the concept of system one and system two in *Thinking, Fast and Slow*. He describes system one as fast and intuitive and system two as slow, analytical, and reflective. The system is metaphorical, as the brain is not functionally organized in this way, but it represents how decision-making is operationalized by the brain.

- Opens up issues of importance
- Strengthens team spirit and generates commitment to group goals
- Results in greater understanding
- Helps to build cohesiveness
- Helps individuals to grow
- Results in better solutions
- Improves the quality of the group's work[13]

Quoting from Takeo Fujisawa, cofounder of Honda Motor Co., Guttman describes the positive role conflict plays in keeping a company flourishing. He says managing conflict is like "orchestrating the discordant sounds inside the company into a kind of harmony."[14]

John Gottman is a renowned psychologist and researcher who has done extensive work on marital relationships. Gottman developed what he called the "magic ratio" of positive to negative interactions. He found that couples who have a ratio of at least five positives to every one negative interaction are more likely to have a stable and happy marriage. He also observed couples engaging in constructive conflict who ended the interaction with a closer and more harmonious partnership. Many couples report they experience their best lovemaking after an intense argument with each other. Yes, good conflict does have its benefits!

Our two bank teams were knee-deep in high conflict with all its dangerous attributes. Team members were trapped in binary us-them thinking, which had degenerated into "us good, them bad." At that

---

[13] Howard Guttman, *When Goliaths Clash: Managing Executive Conflict to Build a More Dynamic Organization* (Amacom Books, 2003).

[14] Guttman, *When Goliaths Clash*, 4.

point, it's not only them that's bad but their ideas and motives too. In the political arena this delves even deeper into dehumanization. This scenario is actually a composite of multiple high-conflict situations in which I have been asked to intervene. Fortunately, there is a time-worn and -tested strategy for unraveling team dysfunctions like this.

My first step was a meeting with the two leaders where I laid out the results of our interviews with team members. Like many meetings before this one, the initial reaction of the leaders passed through several of the steps in Kübler-Ross's five stages of grief: denial, anger, bargaining, depression, and finally acceptance. Yes, there is a problem. We are part of the problem. We need to do something. And then to me: What do we do? My answer was met with eye rolling and a great deal of skepticism. "Teambuilding, really. That's always HR's answer." But I was firm in my recommendation as I had experience and robust research on my side. There are no magic pills to resolve high conflict. Management decrees don't work and neither do sticks or carrots. Escaping high conflict is hard work.

The Contact Antidote

In the 1950s, psychologist Gordon Allport was interested in understanding the nature of prejudice. He started with two important questions: 1) Where does it come from? 2) How do you prevent it? After years of study, some in South Africa during apartheid, he came up with a simple yet elegant answer: contact. Now known as contact theory, it suggests that regular contact between members of two groups can reduce prejudice, improve intergroup relations, and promote social cohesion. The scientific community's first reaction to Allport's theory was largely negative. Its simplicity generated skepticism and even derision.

Yet after years of study and refinement, contact theory has proven to be an important first step in overcoming prejudice and breaking down us-them thinking. As Ripley writes, contact theory "is a way to help people recategorize one another by spending time together, under certain conditions. These encounters can interrupt the cascading assumptions we make about each other, essentially slowing down conflict and making space. Once people have met and liked each other, they have a harder time caricaturing one another." Once you have spent time with someone, learned about their life, struggles, and grandchildren, it's harder to think about them as "right wing nut jobs" or "left wing pinko extremists."[15]

The "certain conditions" is important; some experiments with contact theory have caused groups to end up hating one another even more. Fifty years of research solidified the following core principles of contact theory:

1. Positive conditions: The contact must be pleasant and positive and allow participants to open up and feel comfortable disclosing their beliefs and values.
2. Equal status: All participants must have equal status and see themselves on equal footing.
3. Common goals: Participants should share a common goal that they all care about.
4. Sustained contact: Participants should be in regular contact with meaningful interactions.
5. Aligned leadership: In situations involving levels of hierarchy, there must be alignment and support from leadership.[16]

[15] Ripley, *High Conflict*, 178.

[16] This summary was adapted from ChatGPT 3.5.

While easy to understand, contact theory is challenging in execution because of the complexities of human nature. We all enter social situations with our "going in story" about the other. Skilled, experienced facilitation and awareness of these five principles is the key to turning "Us" and "Them" into just "Us."

Our brains are constantly trying to save energy. The binary nature of us-them is one by-product of this evolutionarily designed process. Lisa Feldman Barrett provocatively declares that the brain is not primarily for thinking, it's for survival. Its most important task: passing on our genes to the next generation.[17] The brain runs myriad biological systems and is an energy hog. Scientists point out that the brain takes up only 2 percent of our body weight but burns between 20 to 25 percent of our calories. To conserve energy, it takes shortcuts. Binary thinking is a shortcut.

On the ancestral savanna, survival questions required split-second thinking—friend or foe, fight or flight. Binary thinking is useful: right/wrong, left/right, good/bad, true/false, black/white, always/never. It's easy to grasp and allows for quick action. It's system one thinking, engaged with little or no effort and often unconsciously. Shades of grey require system two thinking. Complexity and nuance burn lots of cognitive energy. If we are fatigued or facing uncertainty, even binary framing can overwhelm our thinking processes. Combining that with our brain's negative bias, the propensity for us-them thinking runs deep.

But Rutger Bregman is an optimist about human nature. In *Humankind: A Hopeful History*, he documents a counternarrative to historical events that portray humans as selfish, nasty, and inclined to

....

[17] Barrett, *Seven and a Half Lessons about the Brain*, 10.

conflict. He is also a big fan of contact theory and mentions the 515 studies that show that contact works.

> Contact engenders more trust, more solidarity and more mutual kindness. It helps you see the world through other people's eyes. Moreover, it changes you as a person, because individuals with a diverse group of friends are more tolerant towards strangers. And contact is contagious: when you see a neighbor getting along with others, it makes you rethink your own biases.[18]

When looking through the lens of the social brain hypothesis, contact theory makes sense. We are hardwired for kindness, altruism, and cooperation. Competition and conflict have been positive in developing our nature, but they linger on in our psyche to sometimes egregious effect.

Ideas and Applications

- Remember minimal group effect. It doesn't take much for us to form and/or embrace a group. And the next step is automatic—the tendency to contrast us with them and then label us "good" and the other "bad."
- Amanda Ripley recommends "complicating the narrative."[19] When faced with group conflict, think complexity, see shades of grey, and avoid binary thinking at all costs.

---

[18] Rutger Bregman, *Humankind: A Hopeful History* (Little, Brown and Company, 2019), 358.

[19] Ripley, *High Conflict*, 246.

Get curious, ask questions, take opposing perspectives, and look for nuance.

- Remember that there is often more variance within a group than among groups. Look for shared attributes and experiences. Use "us" language.
- Bring people together on equal terms. Remember the nature of our social brains—invest in building relationships even when the task is urgent. The investment will pay off down the road as the group process unfolds.
- Develop shared goals and redefine obstacles from "them" to the greater system you are working within.
- Become a systems thinker. Systems thinking is a conceptual framework for understanding, analyzing, and solving complex problems. Peter Senge describes all human endeavors as systems that are "bound by invisible fabrics of interrelated action . . . that take years to fully play out in their effects on each other."[20] Instead of focusing on "snapshots" (individuals or other pieces of the system), systems thinkers focus on the whole system. This runs counter to much of our learning, which teaches us to focus on finding who is accountable or to assign blame. But most complex problems are the result of breakdowns in a web of relationships and connections in the system. As an example, a failure at first viewed as being caused by a frontline customer service employee is likely caused by poor training,

[20] Peter Senge, *The Fifth Discipline: The Art & Practice of the Learning Organization* (Doubleday, 1990), 6.

misaligned incentives, inappropriate management pressure, poor product or process design, etc., as deeper analysis will bear out. Our brains go to blame "them" when we should kick in system two to analyze and understand.

chapter 7

Status: Do I Hear $5,000?

If I don't win, I just hope the winner isn't someone I know.

—Comment from a friend holding a Powerball ticket

The auctioneer looked over at me and in a rapid-fire voice shouted, "Do I hear five thousand dollars?" I looked around the table and saw the smiles and excitement of my colleagues. I raised my paddle again. I was the senior officer at a bank-sponsored table. The event was a fundraiser for a worthy cause, and the item being auctioned was an emerald ring. Emerald is my wife's birthstone. I had first raised my bidding paddle at one thousand dollars on a lark and to energize the table, but then a strange force took hold of me.

After the first few rounds, the bidders were down to two: myself and a man a few tables behind me whose face I could not see. I estimated the ring to be worth somewhere between two to four thousand dollars. As the bid moved past that high end, I could feel a deep tension inside my gut. My colleagues were cheering me on. The crowd was applauding every raised bid, and I could feel a hundred eyes on me. After every one hundred dollar increase by the auctioneer my competitor raised his paddle. Then I would raise mine in turn. I became determined to win. With the raising of that paddle to five thousand dollars, I heard, "Going once, going twice, sold!"

I immediately experienced an odd mixture of emotions. At first, I felt the satisfaction and confidence that comes with beating a competitor even though the context was a fundraiser and not an arm-wrestling competition. I also felt a sense of joy. In the final moment, Leslie, my wife, was beaming. My colleagues were high-fiving me. The crowd was applauding with approval. I could feel my chest raise up a bit. But then I felt an odd sense of embarrassment. Where was this sense of alpha male dominance coming from? And finally, a realization came over me: Did I just spend thousands more than the ring was worth? Oh well, it was all for a worthy cause!

Status Check

Winning the auction was a status-raising event for me. Our bodies and brains have a bunch of built-in mechanisms that make us pay attention to status and the interrelated concept of hierarchy. Think about my auction story. When males are in competition against another individual, testosterone is released. Testosterone is associated with an increased sense of confidence and dominance. The latter would have been clearly advantageous during our ancestors' time on the savanna. Studies have shown that testosterone levels tend to rise when a male wins a competition. That odd sense of feeling in my chest, the confidence rise after my big win, was testosterone doing its work.

But there's more. Winning a competition can also stimulate the release of dopamine and serotonin. You may remember from an earlier chapter that dopamine is associated with feelings of pleasure and reward. Serotonin is a neurotransmitter that promotes a sense of well-being and social dominance. Winning can also decrease levels of cortisol, which is often called the stress hormone. It rises during battle but then decreases—unless you lose, in which case it may hang around for a while.

That's enough for now on hormones and neurotransmitters. The bigger question is: Why is all this stuff wired into our bodies and brains in the first place? Let's start with some definitions. Social status (just *status* going forward) is the relative position of an individual in a society or culture. Hierarchy is a conceptual structure within a society or culture in which individuals are positioned in a vertical order, those with higher status (based on power, formal authority, knowledge, or some other factor) at the top and those with lower status at the bottom. While reading the definition may have taken a minute, scientists have shown that our brain recognizes status position in about forty milliseconds.[1]

A foundational premise is that all humans care deeply about status and their position in the social hierarchy. Donald Brown is an anthropologist who has developed a list of human universals, features that exist in all known societies. Brown has documented status hierarchies as a human universal. This evidence supports the notion that status awareness is a mental adaptation that served some evolutionary purpose. There are two types of status, one based on dominance and the other based on prestige. The former is most prominent among other species, including our primate cousins.

A study of the social behavior of chickens shows that they maintain a hierarchical structure in which an individual has rank or position relative to other chickens based on dominance. Those higher in dominance can peck those lower in rank and get access

---

[1] Sapolsky, *Behave*, 432.

to the best food and mates. Weak birds don't do well. This creates a functioning social system that allows the strongest birds to flourish. In other words, survival of the fittest. The term "pecking order" emerged from those studies and has been applied to understanding and explaining other animal and social dynamics.

In primate social structures, high status is based on dominance and power and also determines who gets access to the best food, mates, and other resources. Most of us have heard of the alpha male that rules over members of the troupe through brute strength. While dominance plays a large role, primate social structures have additional layers of complexity. Kinship and relationships are also important. As we have mentioned, most primates engage in a process of grooming, picking carefully through one another's hair, to promote comfort and health. Grooming builds bonds and allies. More allies mean higher status.

Human social structures are much more complex than our primate cousins'. In my section on the social brain, I wrote about Robin Dunbar and his theory that brain size is related to the size of the social group. Our human brains are larger, especially in the neocortex, because we need to be able to navigate complex social networks, particularly social hierarchies. Our brain is constantly scanning the social environment. Who is on top? Who has influence? Who can help me? One can easily see the adaptive advantage of this ability. For good reason, from the lens of evolution, we are exceptionally attuned to status.

Dominance plays a role in human social structures. Those with power and influence have higher status than those who don't. We follow and defer to those in positions of higher authority. Hierarchy helps create certainty and social order. There is a lot of complexity to this topic. Where does power and authority come from? Is it inherited? Allocated based on democratic or authoritarian processes? Earned based on knowledge or skill? That discussion is outside the scope of this book, but it is important to see why we are wired to pay attention to status. It is one of those predispositions that natural selection built into our psyche to enhance our ability to survive and pass on our genes to the next generation.

The second form of status is based on prestige. Prestige is a "freely deferred status granted to individuals because they help other individuals achieve their goals."[2] It's easy to understand how dominance status had an evolutionary advantage. The strong alpha male had access to the best food and mating opportunities, thus his genes were more likely to be passed on to future generations. Prestige-based status comes into play in the context of culture. Earlier in the book I wrote about gene-culture coevolution. Humans have a unique ability to transfer what they have learned through experience and innovation. Our brains also evolved to be good cultural learners. A transfer of useful knowledge led to the success of the group. Those with knowledge and skills were valued by group members and thus received attention, respect, and deference.

Joseph Henrich, in *The Secret of Our Success*, describes how prestige psychology evolved in our species:

> The key is recognizing that once humans became good cultural learners, they needed to locate and learn from the best models. The best models are those who seem to possess the information most likely to be valuable

[2] Mark van Vugt and Joshua Tybur, "The Evolutionary Foundations of Status Hierarchy," in *The Handbook of Evolutionary Psychology*, 2nd ed., ed. David M. Buss (Wiley, 2016), 790.

> to learners, now or later in their lives. To be effective, learners must hang around their chosen models for long periods and at crucial times. Learners also benefit if their models are willing to share nonobvious aspects of their practices, or at least not actively conceal the secrets of their success. As a consequence, humans reliably develop emotions and motivations to seek out particularly skilled, successful and knowledgeable models and then are willing to pay deference to those models.[3]

The hormones and neurotransmitters described earlier in the chapter are some of the biological mechanisms that drive our attention to status. Those with prestige experience psychological reward in the form of dopamine or serotonin that incentivize them to share their knowledge. The knowledge and skill gained by the received are rewards in themselves. But evolution also built in some negative incentives for those without status. More on that to follow.

When we meet someone for the first time, at a conscious but mostly nonconscious level we are trying to assess whether the person is friend or foe (us-them) and their rank in the pecking order (status). It is ubiquitous and fully human. We have membership in multiple hierarchies, and figuring out who has power and who is higher or lower in status can get quite complicated. As we have learned, our social brain evolved to be equipped to handle the task of navigating complex social systems. But modernity creates challenges that can cause errors in our behavioral calculations.

One humorous example (at least humorous for me) occurred

---

[3] Henrich, *The Secret of Our Success*, 119.

at work. I once played volleyball in a company league. The players came from all over the bank and occupied multiple levels in the organizational hierarchy. Now, I am not very athletic. In my youth, I was the guy often picked last for baseball and basketball games. The last words in many team drafts were, "OK, I'll take Daniel." This was particularly painful for me because in our working-class neighborhood, two abilities gave you status: sports and fighting. I was terrible at both. And to make matters worse, my younger brothers and sisters were fantastic athletes.[4] At the company volleyball matches, one talented player loved to spike the ball in my face and then taunt me with his prowess. I did not mind it too much. In that context, I was used to being in a low status role. The tide did turn a bit when I was invited to speak at a company meeting. My volleyball nemesis was sitting in the front row. When his manager introduced me to the group as Executive Vice President John Daniel and a member of the executive committee, I could see his face turn red. He came up to me after the meeting and apologized profusely for his taunting. While his testosterone levels may have been high during the game, that discolored face may have been a sign of the testosterone levels dropping in real time.

Envy and Scorn

Social encounters in our modern world are a constant stream of status assessments with profound implications for our health. In Michael Marmot's book *The Status Syndrome: How Social Standing Affects Our*

[4] I can proudly say that several of my siblings were great athletes. All three of my brothers were stars of their Little League and high school teams. Two of my younger sisters won awards at national track and field meets, and my sister Allison is in the Wichita State University Hall of Fame for basketball. I apparently did not inherit any of those genes!

Health and Longevity, the author makes a compelling case that status is the most important determinant of human longevity and health.[5] Princeton psychologist Susan Fiske, in *Envy Up, Scorn Down: How Status Divides Us*, describes how our focus on status leads to polarization and poor mental health. Fisk describes humans as comparison machines and shows the role of the amygdala, which becomes activated when we encounter people who matter to us; the anterior cingulate cortex (ACC), which is a discrepancy detector; and the insula, which triggers disgust. These brain regions play a role in the emotions of envy and scorn.

Envy and scorn are complex emotions that emerge out of our obsession with status. The purpose of emotions is to motivate our behavior. When facing fear, we focus on coping with a threat. Feeling guilty reminds us to make amends. Feeling jealous suggests that a relationship needs work.[6] Fiske describes the role of envy and scorn:

> Envy and scorn are no different than other emotions. Both envy and scorn identify a gap between what we have and what someone else has. . . . Scorn likewise compares self to other, with self coming out on top. Feeling envious signals inferiority; feeling scorn signals superiority. In envy, we might wish to attend to the gap, either bringing down the other, or bringing up the self.[7]

[5] Michael Marmot, *The Status Syndrome: How Social Standing Affects Our Health and Longevity* (Henry Holt & Company, 2005).

[6] Susan Fiske, *Envy Up, Scorn Down: How Status Divides Us* (Russell Sage Foundation, 2011), 36.

[7] Fiske, *Envy Up, Scorn Down*, 36.

Envy and scorn are useful emotions. For example, envy can motivate us to work harder, set goals, and strive for accomplishments similar to or higher than the person we envy. Scorn can serve as a mechanism for enforcing social norms. Used by a high-status individual, scorn can establish dominance and allow that person to maintain group order and cohesion.

But both emotions have a significant downside. Envy can lead to frustration, resentment, bitterness, and discontent. It can also strain relationships. When we are envious of someone, it may lead to feelings of jealousy and hostility. Scorn toward others can lead to isolation and alienation. Scorn can hinder empathy and understanding. Being intentionally closed off from those we scorn can lead to stereotyping, prejudice, and discrimination. Envy, when intense or persistent, can lead to increased levels of cortisol, which can have deleterious effects on health and well-being.

Jonathan Haidt, a psychologist we met earlier in the book, has been focusing recently on the negative effects of social media. Haidt shows that social media platforms encourage individuals to engage in constant social comparison. These comparisons are based on just a slice of others' lives and are often positively biased and unrealistic. The constant comparison can lead to deep feelings of envy, inadequacy, and diminished self-esteem. Haidt argues this is particularly damaging to teen brains and he has devoted considerable time to raising an alarm about the dangers of social media.[8]

Perhaps this is another example of evolutionary mismatch. Psychological mechanisms built into our brain to enhance survival

....

[8] See Greg Lukianoff and Jonathan Haidt, *The Coddling of the American Mind: How Good Intentions and Bad Ideas Are Setting Up a Generation for Failure* (Penguin Press, 2018); see also Haidt's *After Babel* substack.

can misfire. Our ancestors benefited from the ability to detect and pay close attention to status. Showing respect and deference to a knowledgeable, helpful other was often beneficial. Deferring to someone with more power made sense until there was a shift in the balance of power. Status and hierarchy also created certainty, a high human need. (More on that in chapter 10.) A clear pecking order saved mental energy, created coherence, and allowed everyone to find their place and individual identity.

Yet in today's complex world there are myriad representations that substitute for those basic elements of power and knowledge. Today, we assign status based on school, car, jewelry, neighborhood, clothes, and so forth. These are all markers for our ancestral brains. Status indicators surround us and flood us with thoughts and emotions. If left unmanaged, these can impact clear thinking. I am reminded of the famous celebrities who went to jail and damaged their reputations and pocketbooks when they cheated to get their children into prestigious schools. Most economists believe that there is little difference in the quality of education between a prestigious university and a marginally less prestigious one. Motivated students are just as likely to flourish at a good state school as they are at a higher-ranking private school. In fact, there is some evidence that good students suffer when attending highly competitive schools. For most of their academic careers, good students were top performers, and their status was recognized and psychologically rewarded. At top-tier schools, their ranking drops to the middle or bottom while their stress (and cortisol levels) increase.[9]

[9] Van Bavel and Packer, *The Power of Us*, 143.

SCARF

David Rock's insightful SCARF model[10] includes status as one of the five major domains of social experience that drives human behavior. The acronym of SCARF stands for:

> Status – our relative importance to others.
> Certainty – our ability to predict the future.
> Autonomy – our sense of control over events.
> Relatedness – how safe we feel with others.
> Fairness – how fair we perceive the exchanges between people to be.

Rock's model is built upon what psychologists call an approach-avoid framework. Approach is the motivation to experience positive outcomes. Avoidance is the motivation to avoid experiencing negative outcomes.[11] In simpler terms, we move toward that which rewards us and move away from that which threatens us. On the ancestral savanna, having a highly attuned approach-avoid response aided survival. Natural selection favored brains that could detect a threat automatically and quickly.

The amygdala can process a threat before it reaches conscious awareness. The resultant threat state allows for quick action such as the fight-or-flight response, which is universal among animals. The limbic system can also tag and record positive memories, which enhanced the survival of our ancestors. A fruit that was tasty and

---

[10] David Rock, "SCARF: A Brain-Based Model for Collaborating with and Influencing Others," *NeuroLeadership Journal* 1 (2008).

[11] Avoidance is part of the metaphorical system that results in our brain's negative bias.

caused no ill effects will be remembered. A hunter-gatherer coming upon that fruit in subsequent travel will feel the pull of an approach response. Enjoying the fruit created a reward state. Coming upon a growling, furry creature with big teeth created a threat state.

Neuroscientists have discovered that similar threat and reward states are experienced when we engage in the social world. Our social brain responds positively to words and actions that lead to acceptance and connection. This produces a reward state, which in turn positively impacts thinking. Through many clever experiments, psychologists have documented that people in reward states collaborate more effectively, are more creative, solve problems more quickly, and make better decisions. An insult, on the other hand, produces a threat state, which has a negative impact on thinking and collaboration.

In one of his early research papers on the SCARF model, Rock made a strong case for the importance of recognizing threat and reward states when trying to collaborate with and influence others. He showed the linkage of status to social connection. This is what he writes about status threats:

> It can be surprisingly easy to accidentally threaten someone's sense of status. A status threat can occur through giving advice or instructions, or simply suggesting someone is slightly ineffective at a task. Many everyday conversations devolve into arguments driven by status threats, a desire to not be perceived as less than another.[12]

[12] Rock, "SCARF," 4.

Rock goes on to report on studies that show how positive feedback, especially in public, showed activation in the brain's reward circuitry. People also feel a status increase when they are learning and growing. Promotions raise status but are limited in availability. Investments in personal and professional growth can be very powerful ways to increase status. I used coaching and mentoring to develop team members and was surprised at how it also boosted their self-esteem and status. It seems simply caring about and paying attention to an individual can increase status.

I once reported to a vice chairman who led our business unit. Keith was an effective leader who was open and trusting with his leadership team. He regularly shared confidential information with me about company plans and strategies. It was one of my first senior roles, and his trust and confidence had a positive impact on my confidence and self-esteem. I adopted that tactic when I became a chief human resources executive. I regularly shared confidential information about changes in company plans and strategies early to my team members. This positioned them to be mentally and emotionally ready to lead others. As it did for me, I could see that it had a positive impact on their status, and many of them confirmed that effect to me on multiple occasions.

Recently, I was honored to be asked to join an advisory board at my alma mater, the University of Pittsburgh. The athletic director, an outstanding leader, created the advisory board to promote the university's athletic program. Participation in the advisory board requires a significant donation to the athletics department. The athletic director invites board members to regular meetings, during which she seeks feedback and advice. She also shares unique insights, exclusive information, and early announcements on major events to advisory board members. This exclusivity enhances members' status; they feel they are getting insider scoops on their beloved teams.

Status enhancement is a longstanding fundraising strategy. Having one's name on a building or at the top of a list of donors is a proxy for demonstrating achievement and success to others. It is not socially acceptable to brag about money and success, but philanthropy is acceptable. It is also not socially acceptable to show scorn to someone of lower status or admit feelings of envy or schadenfreude.[13] Many people have these feelings and then feel embarrassed about them. Envy is one of Brown's human universals. Envy, scorn, and schadenfreude are one side of the same mental wiring that has us care deeply about status, comparison, and hierarchy.

Status and its antecedent social comparison precipitate a complex set of emotions. We have now seen status's evolutionary roots, as well as how low-status people experience high levels of stress and how social comparison leads to feelings of failure and inadequacy. But it is important to remember that status hierarchies have played an important role in the development of human societies and still contribute to human affairs in a number of ways:

1. Our status gives us our sense of identity, which largely comes from our membership in groups and knowing our place in formal and informal hierarchies.
2. People have a high need for predictability (a subject we will soon discuss in detail). Understanding our place in a system contributes to our sense of order and structure.

[13] *Schadenfreude* is a German word that refers to the experience of pleasure or joy derived from the misfortune, failure, or suffering of others, particularly a rival. The sense of satisfaction is recognized in most cultures, but this German word captures the emotion well.

3. Status helps with the division of labor, clarifies roles and responsibilities, and creates a framework for social interaction and relationships.
4. Individuals with higher status usually take on leadership and decision-making responsibilities, which can help the group achieve its mission and goals.
5. Status can fuel motivation. People lower in society can work hard and invest in their own development to improve their station.

Of course, not all human systems are just, and the values and benefits of status hierarchies vary widely. Status hierarchies have led to human plundering and suffering, but they have also contributed to democratic systems that do much to promote the common good.

Ideas and Applications

- Stay aware that nonconscious processes are constantly assessing our status and operating on our emotions. By understanding and then labeling these responses we can better control them. As an example, my wife occasionally gives me directions when we are driving, even when I have traveled the route many times before. As Rock pointed out, advice giving can often create a threat state. At first, I experienced a slight negative emotion (and a little voice in my head said, *She must think I have a bad memory*). Now I immediately acknowledge her behavior as "trying to be helpful" and remind myself of the times I missed a turn or went the wrong way. The initial threat state is normal in cases like this, but labeling almost immediately frees us from negative emotion.

- Remember that status enhancement is a powerful motivator. Research has shown that salespeople value membership in an achievement-oriented "President's Club" or "Diamond Circle" recognition. More money in the paycheck isn't public, and there are norms against posting your bonus on Facebook. But recognition events and membership in exclusive clubs are viewed by many people as highly desirable. In one study, salespeople sacrificed significant sales commissions by moving sales to another quarter to achieve "President's Club" recognition.[14]

- Remember the importance of praise and recognition. Given sincerity and specificity, it can be a significant status booster. In my decades of reviewing employee surveys, statements like "my manager gives me frequent feedback and praise" are rare. This contrasts with surveys from the managers themselves, which report above the ninetieth percentile in "giving frequent feedback and praise." This gap in perception is documented in national employee research studies as well.

- I once had a leader who regularly complimented his leadership team as a whole but rarely gave individual positive feedback. His leadership surveys consistently reported frustration by his direct reports on this lack of positive feedback. He was confused. In a conversation with me, he mentioned all the times he complimented the group. I pointed out to him that group feedback did not raise individual status—in the minds

[14] Lieberman, *Social*, 260. Some people are highly motivated by money but not by status. Based on my experience and some data, this appears to be a minority, but it is important to note. Know your team members' motivations.

of his reports, his positive comments were discounted. It is easy to praise a group. It takes significant emotional energy and preparation to give powerful, status-raising personal feedback.

chapter 8

Fairness: A Hershey's Kiss

The same brain regions that are associated with loving the taste of chocolate or any other physical pleasures respond to being treated fairly as well. In a sense, then, fairness tastes like chocolate.

—Matthew Lieberman

Alexis was a fantastic employee. She had been at the bank for over a decade, had received several promotions, and was flourishing in her role. Her manager gave her the highest performance rating and recommended her as a high potential during the talent assessment process. Alexis seemed to love her job and the people she worked with. She seemed to trust and respect her manager. Her manager reported she was happy with her pay and opportunities at the company. I had met with Alexis on multiple occasions as she participated in one of the company's employee resource groups. She always seemed happy and upbeat and, on several occasions, talked about how much she loved the company.

Then one day I received a call from her with an urgent request to see me. I could tell by the tone of her voice that something was wrong, so I invited her to visit my office at the end of the day. When she arrived for our meeting, she was visibly distraught. Before I could ask, she launched into her story while holding back tears. It seems earlier that day, she came upon a document at the copier that detailed the pay of all the members of her department. She apologized for looking at the document but said she couldn't help herself. One number that caught her immediate attention was an *8* in the salary of one of her peers. That single number flooded her with emotions and put her in an apoplectic state.

She laid out her story but started with a question: How could Matt, one of her peers in the same job, be earning $78,000 per year when her salary was only $76,000? Alexis pointed out that she had been at the company longer, had been in the role longer, and had received excellent reviews and feedback from her boss. The latter detail was evidence to her that the pay difference was not because Matt was a better performer. In fact, she pointed out that on many occasions she had provided coaching and assistance to Matt as he was learning his job. Her voice quivered as she talked, and I could tell she was holding back tears. At last, she summed it all up. "This is just not fair!"

Reciprocal Altruism

Alexis's story is one I have seen multiple times. A happy, productive employee suddenly becomes unhappy and less productive. And the change is usually not incremental. This contrasts with other events in the workplace that can have an impact on an employee. A poor performance review, a high volume of work, and conflicts with colleagues all generate some level of emotion, though usually with much less fervor. But when an issue comes up related to an employee's sense of fairness, the level of emotional intensity can be extremely high. Our human sense of fairness is deeply embedded in our psychological machinery and has evolutionary roots.

Our hunter-gatherer ancestors thrived on cooperation. The propensity and capacity to cooperate has clear adaptive advantages. Five wolves working together can bring down big prey. One large elk for all to share is better than one rabbit captured by a lone hunter. In fact, species from lions to army ants cooperate, and cooperators do better than noncooperators. With most species, cooperation is mutually beneficial, but transactional and short-term in nature. With humans, cooperation is a more complex and long-term phenomenon. It involves giving something of value to someone today with the belief that you will receive something of similar value in the future. This behavior is called reciprocal altruism.

Reciprocal altruism was a fascinating puzzle to the first evolutionary biologists. Evolutionary theory explains why members of a species help family members: family members share genes, so if you help family members thrive you are indirectly passing on your shared genes to the next generation. But human cooperation evolved so that individuals engaged in exchanges that involved a cost to the giver in the short term in return for benefit in the long term. Natural selection favored reciprocal altruism and built its behavioral dispositions into our brains.

The theory was first proposed by evolutionary biologist Robert Trivers[1] and is considered one of the most significant insights in evolutionary theory. Trivers and others that followed proposed that several conditions occurring together led to the development of reciprocal altruism. "Individuals must 1) have an opportunity to interact often,

....

1 Boyd and Silk, *How Humans Evolved*, 187.

2) be able to keep track of support given, and 3) provide support to only those that help them." Our ancestors' hunter-gatherer lifestyle created the perfect setting for reciprocal altruism. Generosity today meant costs in the short term but benefits later. Trivers described it as cooperation smeared across time.[2]

But there is a fly in the ointment when it comes to reciprocal altruism in practice—the free rider problem. In cooperative exchange, both parties negotiate and come to agreement about the fair value of what is exchanged. Cheating is limited. Unless some kind of force or deception is used, the parties come to some mutually beneficial exchange in real time. With reciprocal altruism, the beneficiary of generosity can fail to live up to his responsibly to share down the road. Free riders unchecked will do better than reciprocators. Too many free riders and groups don't thrive. Natural selection had a solution for that problem, a repertoire of preferences and emotions like the one experienced by Alexis in our opening story.

On the positive side, humans love giving and receiving. "When someone does something good for us, we feel gratitude. This motivates us to return the favor later, thereby continuing the mutually beneficial cycle of reciprocal exchange."[3] The positive emotions of gratitude and appreciation build trust and thus enhance group bonding. Free riders, on the other hand, will experience anger from other group members. Individuals will refuse to help cheaters the next time. Gossip is an often-used way to turn other group members against the cheater. We have a robust set of words to describe those who don't pull their weight: parasite, leech, scumbag, slacker, slug,

[2] Stewart-Williams, *The Ape That Understood the Universe*, 192.

[3] Stewart-Williams, *The Ape That Understood the Universe*, 196.

malingerer, scrounger, sponger, bloodsucker, moocher. Ostracism is also a significant punishment for consistent free riders. And as we have learned about our ancient hunter-gatherer days, getting kicked out of the group didn't help with the passing of genes to the next generation.

The primary purpose of emotions is to motivate us to do things. Guilt and shame are two emotions wired into our psyche to help support reciprocal altruism. If we feel guilt or shame because we cheated or failed to carry our fair share of the load, those emotions motivate us to change our ways. Gratitude motivates us to give. Sympathy motivates us to help someone in need. This set of emotions is part of what is called having a conscience. H. L. Mencken said, "Conscience is the inner voice that tells us someone might be looking."[4] That inner voice is natural selection's programming to support reciprocal altruism, which in turn contributes to our human capacity for hyper-cooperation.

Psychologist Jonathan Haidt names fairness/cheating as one of his six moral foundations, an innate human basis for moral reasoning. On innateness, Haidt writes that "the brain is like a book, the first draft of which is written by the genes during fetal development, no chapters are complete at birth." Haidt goes on to agree with Pinker that the brain is not a blank slate at birth either. He quotes neuroscientist Gary Marcus.

"Nature provides the first draft, which experience then revises . . . 'Built in' does not mean unmalleable; it means 'organized in advance of experience.'"[5]

....

[4] Stewart-Williams, *The Ape That Understood the Universe*, 196.

[5] Jonathan Haidt, *The Righteous Mind: Why Good People Are Divided by Politics and Religion* (Vintage, 2013), 153.

Haidt points out that culture begins revising the first draft at childhood, which explains the wide variability of moral reasoning. For example, one person may see fairness as everyone being rewarded in proportion to what they contribute, while others see it as some proportional level of sharing for everyone. All are finely tuned to pay attention to fairness.

Haidt writes about the beginnings of fairness as a moral foundation.

> Human life is a series of opportunities for mutually beneficial cooperation. If we play our cards right, we can work with others to enlarge the pie that we ultimately share. Hunters work together to bring down large prey that nobody could catch alone. Neighbors watch each other's houses and loan each other tools. Coworkers cover each other's shifts. For millions of years, our ancestors faced the adaptive challenge of reaping these benefits without getting suckered.[6]

Our human history has allowed us to move beyond seeing life as a zero-sum contest. We cooperate with those who cooperate with us and punish those who try to take advantage of us. Our brains have a fairness/cheating module that protects us individually but also leads to group success.

Games for Understanding

Unlike in many sciences, the hypotheses of evolutionary psychology

[6] Haidt, *The Righteous Mind*, 159.

are difficult or impossible to test. While evolutionary biologists have a fossil record, there is no record of human behavior beyond a few thousand years ago. So how do scientists provide evidence to support their theories? One place to look is the lives of modern hunter-gatherer societies. And the good news is that there is a robust record of the lives of hunter-gatherer societies as documented by the first anthropologists, who studied those societies in the early part of the twentieth century. There are even a few such cultures alive today and, while touched by modernity, their lifestyles provide evidence and insights into the field.

Another tool used by evolutionary theorists is game theory. Game theory is a branch of mathematics that deals with decisions people are predicted to make depending on the strategies of others. One of the most famous examples of the use of game theory was a series of computer simulations and tournaments conducted by the political scientist Robert Axelrod. The results of his studies were groundbreaking and widely praised for their insights on engaging in everyday negotiations as well as their demonstration of the underlying logic of reciprocal altruism and its origins.

Axelrod used a classic game called the prisoner's dilemma. In the game, two individuals, each accused of a crime, are given the option to cooperate with each other or betray each other. The outcome of their decision affects their respective prison sentences. The dilemma arises because each player can choose to cooperate (remain silent) or defect (betray the other person). The payoff structure is such that both players receive a higher individual reward if they defect while the other cooperates. However, if both players defect, they both receive a lower payoff than they would have had they both cooperated.

The players tested several strategies (always cooperate, always defect, other more predictive strategies) but what emerged from the research was a winning one: "tit for tat." TFT is a simple strategy that begins with cooperation and then replicates the opponent's previous move in subsequent rounds. If the opponent cooperates, TFT continues to cooperate. If the opponent defects, TFT retaliates by defecting as well. The strategy is forgiving, as it is always willing to revert to cooperation if the opponent cooperates again. This retaliatory but forgiving approach creates a balance between cooperation and defection.[7]

Tit for tat proved effective not only because it was easy to understand and execute but because it had three strengths. First, it is nice. It never defects first, which means it encourages cooperation. Second, retaliatory defection occurs only and immediately after the opponent has defected. And third, it is forgiving. If a previously defecting opponent cooperates, TFT will immediately also cooperate.[8] TFT showed how reciprocal altruism could have emerged in hunter-gatherer societies. The strategy is based on the principle of "you scratch my back, I'll scratch yours." The norm of reciprocity exists because the tendency has been wired into our psyche by thousands of generations of successful cooperation. We scratch one another's backs, but we remain attuned to cheaters and freeloaders. Along with the tendency to reciprocity comes the set of attendant emotions I've mentioned—gratitude, guilt, sympathy, anger—to enforce the reciprocity norm.

Matt Lieberman also used games in his research on fairness.

---

[7] The summary for TFT was adapted from ChatGPT 3.5.

[8] Lance Workman and Will Reader, *Evolutionary Psychology: An Introduction*, 4th ed. (Cambridge University Press, 2021), 203.

As you may remember, Lieberman is a foremost authority in social neuroscience. He is interested in how the brain responds to social experience and uses brain scans to detect neural activity. In one experiment, he recruited individuals to play a variant of the Ultimatum Game while lying in an MRI scanner. Two players were asked to come to an agreement on how to split some amount of money, say ten dollars. Lieberman describes what happened.

> One player, called the proposer, makes a recommendation about how much each of them should get, and the other player, called the responder, then decides whether to accept the offer. If the responder accepts, then both individuals get the amount suggested by the proposer. But if the responder rejects the offer, both players get nothing. A proposer might suggest that he gets $9, and the responder get $1. And if you guessed that the responder might be insulted by this kind of offer, you would be right. Responders commonly reject highly unfair offers, preferring to get nothing at all rather than let this insult go unpunished.[9]

The responders' behaviors will seem unsurprising to most readers, as Lieberman points out this is contrary to the notion that people act in line with their rational self-interest. Perhaps a more interesting outcome of Lieberman's and others' studies was the location of brain activity during fair exchanges. The ventromedial prefrontal cortex (VMPFC) and the ventral striatum (VS)

[9] Lieberman, *Social*, 73. This chapter borrows its title from *Social*, chapter 4, "Fairness Tastes like Chocolate." The epigraph is from page 75.

were activated. These regions make up the brain's reward circuitry. "Being treated fairly turned on the brain's reward machinery regardless of whether it led to a little money or a lot."[10] We learned in our chapter on the social brain how physical pain and social pain share the same neurocognitive processes. The same is true for physical and social rewards. Fairness is a vital element in social exchange and in fostering trust and cooperation. Our brains light up in a positive way when we experience fair exchange and in a negative way when we are cheated. It is wiring deeply embedded in our nature.

Unfairness Is a Threat

Using the language of David Rock as we discussed in chapter 7 on status, the perception of being treated unfairly triggers a "threat response." The amygdala becomes more active, and our brains and bodies experience a cascade of neurochemical and physiological changes. Our bodies are now ready for a fight-or-flight response, though in most of our modern exchanges these responses are a mismatch.

A threat response also reduces activity in the prefrontal cortex, which is responsible for higher order thinking and problem-solving. Back to Alexis, she was clearly in a threat state when I met with her. It took several meetings during which I explained salary compression as the cause of her pay gap and assured her she was a valued employee. I also worked with her manager to adjust her pay.

N. Gregory Mankiw, a Harvard economist, once wrote that "Fairness, like beauty, is in the eye of the beholder."[11] While we have seen

[10] Lieberman, *Social*, 74.

[11] Arthur Dobrin, "Fairness Is Innate to Human Nature," Psychology Today Online, January 12, 2013.

evidence that fairness is a critical human value rooted in our basic nature, determining what is fair can be complex and subjective. Most people have a good sense of when someone is cheating or not carrying their load. But there is no formula or algorithm for determining fairness. As an HR executive I was constantly faced with questions of fairness, and I often found myself struggling to make decisions that most would see as fair. And when the decisions were around questions of pay, benefits, and career opportunities, the stakes were typically very high.

One example of the dilemma I often faced was job postings. Most companies have some sort of job posting system. When a job is open, the company policy generally states that the job will be posted so that all employees have a shot at applying for the job. The rationale for such a system is that it creates a culture of opportunity and upward mobility. I believed in job posting and touted it as a benefit to our employees. Our policy stated that all jobs would be posted. But in many cases, managers developed employees through the company's talent management program and slotted them as successors to certain jobs, usually higher-level roles. In these cases, managers pushed back hard when we asked them to post their open position.

Here's where the debate about fairness comes in. For my HR team, the policy states that all jobs will be posted—there should be no exception to the rule. Not to post the job would be unfair. The managers' view was that the job should not be posted because the decision about who would fill the role had already been made. For them, to post a job and raise the hope of candidates was more unfair. In this example, like many I faced in HR, there is no easy answer. Comments about our unfair job posting system were aways among the top of employee complaints.

Most of those complaints were not about the postings but

about the hiring decisions of managers. Research shows that hiring decisions are one area steeped in human bias. Many managers make their hiring decisions based on a job interview, yet traditional interviews have a poor record of predicting subsequent job performance. In *Noise: A Flaw in Human Judgment*, Daniel Kahneman, Olivier Sibony, and Cass Sunstein report that interviews as a decision-making tool are "somewhat better than flipping a coin."[12] Hiring managers are regularly impacted by the halo effect,[13] similarity bias, and confirmation bias just to name a few potential pitfalls.

Candidates also often suffer from their own biases. Research shows that most people rate themselves as higher performers than they are. Some have what is called the Dunning-Kruger effect, the tendency of individuals with lower skills or competence to overestimate their ability. The latter were often the most difficult to settle after a complaint. They complained that they were treated unfairly but did not have the ability to comprehend the gap in their skill set. As we end this chapter on fairness and recognize Professor Mankiw's comment on the relative perception of fairness, here are some thoughts about creating a culture of fairness and reducing the threat states of people we are trying to lead or influence.

---

[12] Daniel Kahneman, Oliver Sibony, and Cass Sunstein, *Noise: A Flaw in Human Judgment* (Little, Brown Spark, 2021), 302.

[13] The halo effect occurs when an interviewer forms an impression based on a single characteristic such as if the candidate is well dressed or went to an Ivy League school. Similarity bias occurs when the candidate shares a similar background, experience, or appearance. (I once had a manager tell me she hired a candidate because she had great taste in shoes—a proxy for good decision-making!) Confirmation bias occurs when the interviewer looks for information to confirm a preexisting belief or initial observation.

Ideas and Applications

- Develop and espouse a set of values around fairness. The interpretation of a value can be subjective, but declaring it sets the foundation for a culture of fair dealing.

- Develop, communicate, and follow a clear set of policies and procedures. One place people see unfairness is when a policy is not followed. There are cases when policy exceptions are warranted; no policy or procedure can anticipate and cover every possible scenario. When this is the case, be transparent about the reasons for an exception. (In the example on job posting, one solution to posting a job that is already targeted to be filled through succession planning is to note that on the posting. That will alert candidates to the reality of their chances—and who knows, the process may find an even more qualified candidate. This will also aid candidates who want to promote their abilities and experiences to hiring managers.)

- Be transparent about decision-making processes when making changes that affect people. Make decision-making rubrics, formulas, and steps taken available. For example, layoff decisions are often made based on performance reviews. But research shows that performance ratings suffer from idiosyncratic bias[14] and other missteps. Many companies use competency models instead. With these models, a job analysis identifies the four or five most

[14] Idiosyncratic bias occurs when a rater evaluates or scores something in a way that is consistent with their own personal preferences, tendencies, or biases. The bias is specific and may not be representative of the general population. As an example, a manager who has meticulous standards of dress may rate an employee who has lower dress standards more harshly despite that fact that the employee's job performance is excellent. In my experience, ratings usually say as much or more about the rater than they do about the ratee.

important competencies needed to perform the job successfully. Candidates are then assessed by multiple raters and the results reviewed by HR. The competency model and the ratings can be shared with all the individuals involved in the process. With a process like this, I saw a significant drop in complaints about fairness, and there was less intensity of emotion around layoff decisions. Employees did sometimes debate the ratings, but most perceived the process as more open and fairer.

- In the absence of policy, follow precedent. When facing a decision not covered by policy, look at similar decisions made in the past. Treating an employee one way and another employee less or more favorably will usually trigger a perception of unfairness. While the factors used in some decisions may not be widely known, assume every decision you make that affects people may become public knowledge. As Supreme Court Justice William Douglas once said about transparency, "Sunlight is the best disinfectant."

- Use structured processes and objective criteria when making decisions that impact the lives of people. The book *Noise* documents the biases that negatively impact human decision-making.

- Involve impartial others to review decisions that impact people. Outside input can bring alternative perspectives and help expose unconscious bias and favoritism.

- Finally, ask yourself: Does it pass a basic smell test? Does the decision feel morally right and ethically sound? How would you feel if it impacted you?

chapter 9

Autonomy: Control Freak

Control leads to compliance; autonomy leads to engagement.

—Daniel Pink

In my early days as a recruiter, I interviewed hundreds of candidates. I learned interviewing techniques by observing my recruiting manager since I had received no interview training at that point. Paul had a set of questions he asked every candidate. He said these questions were important to help assess a candidate's cultural fit to the company and role. One of his favorite questions was, "What kind of manager do you like to work for?" It seemed like a good question, so I started asking that question to everyone I interviewed. Stop for a minute and think about how you would answer it.

It did not take long for me to see a pattern. I imagine that the answers I heard were like those of many readers. Here are some examples of the responses:

- "I don't want to work for someone who hovers over me."
- "I prefer a manager who gives me goals and leaves me alone."
- "I like someone who gives me freedom to decide the best way to do my work."
- "I hate working for a micromanager or control freak!"

The latter often stirred a bit of emotion, as if the interviewees were reliving a moment with a former manager. It didn't take long for me to realize there was some kind of universal principle at work, particularly since I had strong feelings about the matter myself. I once worked for a micromanager and hated it. I stopped asking the question because I kept getting the same answer. Years later I learned about self-determination theory (SDT).

My House, My Rules

In the opening chapter, I wrote about the carrot or the stick, the oft-used metaphor for extrinsic motivation, and its flaws. In the 1970s, social psychologist Edward Deci was one of the leading researchers who claimed that money and other externally administered rewards destroyed intrinsic motivation. As you may remember, intrinsic motivation refers to the internal drive or desire to engage in an activity for its own sake, without external rewards or pressure. Deci argued that extrinsic rewards are perceived as controlling and thus ineffective except in certain situations.[1] The finding that even positive forms of control led to negative impacts stimulated more research, which led to self-determination theory. In brief, SDT states that humans have three basic psychological needs: competence, relatedness, and autonomy. Giving people freedom to make personal choices not only leads to higher levels of self-motivation but also improves well-being.

Psychologists have long known about the human desire for autonomy and personal control and see it as part of a set of innate

[1] Latham, *Work Motivation*, 105.

tendencies most likely shaped by natural selection. "The quest for control is very deeply rooted in the human psyche, and it deserves a prominent place in any account of human motivation. People want to have control; they like to gain it; they resist losing it; and they are better off if they have it. . . . Power, mastery, money, skill, possessiveness, territoriality, self-efficacy, liberty—all these common human motives are fundamentally about control."[2]

Control over their environments would have been very advantageous and adaptive to our hunter-gatherer ancestors. Control over territory, food sources, and other groups supported survival and reproduction. Recent research on the need for autonomy in a wide range of cultures supports the idea that the need is a human universal. But more importantly, the more people receive support for this basic psychological need, "the better is their well-being and the better their functioning will be."[3]

In a fascinating rethinking of human history, professors David Graeber and David Wengrow studied early Native American cultures, modern hunter-gatherer societies, and archeological evidence to make the case that human social history did not evolve in the linear fashion[4] described by many historians. In making their case, Graeber and Wengrow describe early human societies as experimenting with

....

[2] Baumeister, *The Cultural Animal*, 91.

[3] Valery Chirkov, "Culture, Personal Autonomy and Individualism: Their Relationships and Implications for Personal Growth and Well-Being," eds. G. Zheng, K. Leung, and J. G. Adair, *Perspectives and Progress in Contemporary Cross-Cultural Psychology: Proceedings from the 17th International Congress of the International Association for Cross-Cultural Psychology*, 2008, 256.

[4] Some philosophers and historians view the historical development of society as a macrocosm of individual human development. Humans begin as helpless infants and move through levels of maturity to adulthood. But there is not a constant line of development to a higher level of society.

a wide variety of social and political organizations. At the core was a wide respect for individual freedom and autonomy, even for women, who were able to "live their lives and make their own decisions without male interference," individually and collectively. Autonomy, it seems, is not just a modern value but a basic human need. "Humans . . . appear to have begun (their history) with a self-conscious aversion to being told what to do."[5]

Without romanticizing the lives of our hunter-gatherer ancestors, there is a growing body of evidence that their lives were not, as philosopher Thomas Hobbes famously described, "nasty, brutish, and short." Anthropologist Richard Lee spent one year living with the Ju/'hoansi people in western Africa in the early 1960s. He chose the Ju/'hoansi because he believed their lives more likely mirrored those of our early ancestors. Lee found that these modern-day foragers devoted only twelve to nineteen hours per week to hunting, gathering, and other work to support their basic needs. Much more of their time was spent socializing, dancing, and engaging in other ritualistic practices.[6]

Another anthropologist, Marshall Sahlins, was well known for his famous essay "The Original Affluent Society." Sahlins's views were developed after extensive reading of "anthropological texts, colonial reports, and other documents that described encounters between Europeans and hunter-gatherers."[7] Considerable archeological evidence of cave paintings, jewelry, ornaments, and ritualistic

[5] David Graeber and David Wengrow, *The Dawn of Everything: A New History of Humanity* (Farrar, Straus and Giroux, 2021), 133.

[6] James Suzman, *Work: A Deep History, from the Stone Age to the Age of Robots* (Penguin Press, 2021), 136–142.

[7] Suzman, *Work*, 143.

practices supports the notion that early life was not just a constant struggle for survival. In Sahlins's telling, hunter-gatherer affluence came from "desiring little" in contrast to our modern view of affluence. Other researchers believe the quality of life was enhanced by high levels of egalitarianism and personal freedom. It seems the human need for autonomy was nurtured and supported over thousands of years of human history.

The Agricultural Revolution

Homo sapiens lived as hunter-gatherers for over two hundred thousand years. About twelve thousand years ago, in different parts of the world, societies began a significant shift by settling into farming communities. As these societies grew, complex social structures emerged. Two (of huge significance) were the establishment of standing armies and the beginning of large-scale slavery. While soldiers can be aligned around a common mission, their control, structure, and obedience were critical to high functioning. Slaves were often enemies who were captured and put into bondage. Work was extracted from slaves through domination, small rewards, and lots of punishment. An organizational paradigm built around hierarchy, power, and submission emerged and influenced thinking about the way to achieve group goals. Freedom of choice and personal autonomy were not part of the equation.

Some accounts of hunter-gatherer lifestyles, as documented by European travelers in the sixteenth and through the nineteenth centuries, often describe them as idyllic. The concept of the "noble savage" emerged and was popularized by French philosopher Montaigne. "It captures the belief that humans in their natural state are selfless, peaceable, and untroubled, and that the blights such as greed, anxiety, and violence are the products of civilization."[8] The notion of the "noble savage" was the strawman in a long-lasting debate about the nature of man and thus the best form of governance to ensure a stable and flourishing society. Hobbes's view was that humans are brutes who need to surrender their autonomy to a strong state to avoid a "hellish" existence.

Genevan philosopher Jean-Jacques Rousseau was a critic of Hobbes. He saw an innate goodness in human nature that aligned with the concept of the "noble savage." Rousseau and other enlightenment philosophers were engaged in a great philosophical debate in reaction to the emergence of political and social structures that ruled over men and created vast inequalities. The Agricultural Revolution had led to the creation of huge cities, vast empires, and large monuments and buildings (think pyramids). Society moved from a demand economy to one that created a surplus of food and domesticated animals. New social innovations were needed. We have already noted slavery and the military. Others were the expansion of the division of labor—which in hunter-gatherer societies was largely gender based so that women could focus on child-rearing—and the creation of bureaucracies to better run empires.

Over thousands of years, these innovations created waves of rising and falling societies. Change and history marched on. Feudalism emerged and created a huge peasant class. Incremental improvements in technology such as the wheeled plow, crop rotation, and the horseshoe improved agricultural productivity. A ruling class emerged that extracted a disproportionate share of the surplus.

8 Pinker, *The Blank Slate*, 6.

The result was a vast increase in inequality, a significant reduction in the quality of life, and the ongoing erosion of human freedom and autonomy. For most people, the misery index (had there been such a thing) would have been high. As Harari writes in *Sapiens*:

> The agricultural revolution certainly enlarged the sum total of food at the disposal of humankind, but the extra food did not translate into a better diet or more leisure. Rather, it translated into population explosions and pampered elites. The average farmer worked harder than the average forager and got a worse diet in return. The Agricultural Revolution was history's biggest fraud.[9]

Harari goes on to describe a trap. As farming led to surplus and then population growth, there came a point when people couldn't return to their hunter-gatherer past. The freedom and autonomy humans had experienced for thousands of generations was lost for most people.

The lives of hunter-gatherers were neither idyllic nor hellish. They faced periods of hardship, shortages, and violence, but their lives were marked with high degrees of personal autonomy. The Agricultural Revolution and the political and social structures that emerged from it dramatically changed the lives of millions of people. A small number of emperors, landowners, and kings ruled, and the ability of the rest to make choices about their own lives was lost. Freedom thus became an important topic for philosophers as they debated human nature, morality, and governance.

[9] Yuval Noah Harari, *Sapiens: A Brief History of Humankind* (Harper Collins Publishers, 2015).

The Enlightenment, the cultural and intellectual movement that emerged primarily in Western Europe in the eighteenth century, challenged what the Agricultural Revolution had wrought. The movement promoted reason and new methods of scientific inquiry. It also inspired new thinking about individualism, human rights, and governance. Its ideas laid the groundwork for the American and French Revolutions. Freedom did expand for many, but during this exciting intellectual period a new revolution was unfolding that would submerge the human desire and need for personal autonomy for many.

The Industrial Revolution

It is difficult to identify the precise point at which the Industrial Revolution began, but most historians point to the second half of the eighteenth century. Enlightenment nourished reason and scientific thinking, which in turn encouraged innovation. New technologies such as the invention of the steam engine, the mechanization of textile production, and advancements in the production and use of iron and coal produced new industries. Large factories emerged, and people who had once worked the land now found themselves employed in factories. The Industrial Revolution brought about profound changes in society and the economy. Significant increases in productivity created vast new wealth, remarkable new inventions, and a subsequent improvement in the quality of life for many.

But in the early stages, workers faced harsh working conditions, long hours, and low wages. The Industrial Revolution also exacerbated inequalities; wealth and power were concentrated in the hands of a small number of industrialists and their political sponsors.

By the middle of the twentieth century, social and political movements such as labor unions and the progressive movement in the US created a healthier balance of power and economic rewards.

But this section is not intended to cover all the complexity and impacts of the Industrial Revolution. What is important for our purposes are the norms, practices, and organizational structures that emerged and the impacts they had on personal freedom.

Large manufacturing businesses needed a framework to operate. In the beginning, the only models for overseeing the work of large numbers of people were the two we mentioned earlier: the military and the plantation. Neither was ideal for nurturing freedom and autonomy. Managerial role models were military officers who operated in highly defined hierarchies with power concentrated at the top. Foremen barked orders to ensure the workers followed the pace and rhythm of the factory instead of their own. While there may have been a few kind souls at the top, leadership as we know it today was not even considered. Foremen used more sticks than carrots—and in some cases, sticks were literally in use. Low pay and extrinsic motivation ruled the day.

The division of labor expanded dramatically into the twentieth century. Tasks were broken down into finer and finer activities.[10] This culminated with the introduction of the assembly line by Henry Ford in the production of his new automobile. Ford has been quoted as saying, "The problem with workers is they bring their brains to work along with their hands."[11] Unlike the artisanal system that produced

[10] The English economist Adam Smith famously described and praised an example of a detailed division of labor and specialization in his seminal book *The Wealth of Nations*.

[11] I could not assign this Ford quote to a definitive source. Another version is, "How come when I want a pair of hands, they come with a brain attached?" The sentiment does seem to capture the known views of Ford's time on industrial production and labor relations.

most products before the Industrial Revolution, workers performed one repetitive step again and again. Artisans made shoes, clothes, or baked goods from beginning to end. While artisans were only a small percentage of the population, they had the freedom to contribute their own ideas to a product, had control over their time, and could feel a sense pride in their finished work.

The factory worker, on the other hand, worked long hours doing the same task and had no sense of connection to the final product. The brain's only use was to manipulate hands and body to align with production.

> One man draws out the wire; another straightens it; a third cuts it; a fourth points it; a fifth grinds it at the top for receiving the head; to make the head requires two or three distinct operations; to put it on is a peculiar business; to whiten the pin is another; it is even a trade by itself to put them into the paper; and the important business of making the pin in this manner divided into 18 distinct operations, which in some manufacturers are all performed by distinct hands, though in others the same men will sometimes perform two or three of them. . . . Ten persons, therefore, could make upwards of 48,000 pins a day.[12]

In the opening chapter, I wrote about Frederick Winslow Taylor, who rose to fame during the early part of the twentieth century as industrialization matured and science began to shape

[12] Randy Hodson and Teresa Sullivan, *The Social Organization of Work*, 5th ed. (Wadsworth Cengage Learning, 2012), 23.

management practices. The social and political movements that we mentioned also led to change in factory life, largely for the better. But even as work transitioned from the factory to service and knowledge work, bureaucracy, hierarchy, control efficiency, and extrinsic motivation dominated management thinking late into the twentieth century. Daniel Pink, in his discussion on the importance of autonomy, summarizes the legacy:

> We sometimes forget that "management" does not emanate from nature. It is not like a tree or river . . . It's something humans invented. As strategy guru Gary Hamel has observed, management is a technology. And . . . it's a technology that has grown creaky. While some companies have oiled the gears a bit, and plenty more have paid lip service to the same, at its core management hasn't changed much in a hundred years. Its central ethic remains control; its chief tools remain extrinsic motivators. That leaves it largely out of sync with the nonroutine, right brain abilities on which many of the world's economies now depend.[13]

Pink continues his indictment of most modern management thinking by declaring that it is based on a flawed set of assumptions about human nature. More specifically, it is based on the belief that humans need to be prodded, pushed, directed, or rewarded to get moving.

[13] Pink, *Drive*, 88.

Back to Self-Determination

At the beginning of this chapter, I mentioned self-determination theory, and then I took a wide sweep through history, philosophy, and the evolution of work. My purpose was to show that the need for autonomy is a universal and foundational trait, that our ancestors lived with significant autonomy, and that since the Agricultural Revolution powerful forces, acting in their own interests, defaulted to create conditions that squelch human freedom, particularly in the workplace. Political and social movements in the early to mid-twentieth century led to significant improvements in physical working conditions, pay, and benefits, but did little to change the culture of most organizations or the mental models used to run them.

Starting with Taylor and his contemporaries, scientists began research to better understand human behavior to improve productivity and worker satisfaction. After overcoming the strong and stifling impact of behaviorism, a steady flow of new ideas emerged that positively influenced management thinking. Goal setting, reward, and other motivational theories were in wide use. In much of the research something fundamental to human behavior seemed to rise to the top. Workers seemed happier and more productive when they set their own goals, when they had control of task execution, and when they had a say in how rewards were structured. In the 1970s, influenced by successful tactics used by Japanese manufactures, participative decision-making came in vogue. Management journals and consultants spread the gospel.

I had my first exposure to participative management in the late 1970s while working at Mellon Bank. At the time there was significant worry that Japanese companies—which began dominating the

US market with innovative electronics and fuel-efficient, reliable, and affordable cars—would surpass American manufacturing capabilities. The "Japanese economic miracle" captivated US business leaders, who tried to emulate Japanese management and production methods. One of these was the use of quality circles. Quality circles are small groups of employees who voluntarily come together to identify, analyze, and solve production and quality problems. As a "high potential," I was enlisted to attend QC training and then use the tools and principles to improve work processes in the operations group.

Quality circles turned out to be a fad that was soon abandoned by most companies, including Mellon Bank. I remember the first few meetings our QC teams had with bank managers. The group's ideas were contrarily questioned and criticized, and few were ever implemented. I don't have fond memories of management from those days. Many of the men (and they all were men then) were ex-military and had a command-and-control mindset and set of practices. While there were many good leaders, too many barked orders, did not take kindly to feedback, and certainly didn't encourage new ideas. As many companies of that era found out, participative management and command-and-control inherently don't mix well. While QCs were a key part of Japanese manufacturing success, other factors such as just-in-time inventory systems, continuous improvement, waste reduction, and closer attention to customer satisfaction were even more important and would soon find their way to the US.

Eventually, concepts like participative management would find their place in American business culture. Behavioral scientists focusing on motivation began to recognize a hierarchy of factors that impacted worker motivation. Values, personality traits, culture, person-job fit, and job design were all important, but what seemed to come first in importance was the need for physical and psychological well-being. This brings us back to self-determination theory and two researchers, Edward Deci and Richard Ryan. Their earlier work had surprised many when they noted the distinction between extrinsic and intrinsic motivation. They also demonstrated how extrinsic motivation, the primary tool of many managers, often had a negative effect because individuals felt controlled.

In one fascinating study, Deci conducted an experiment in which college students were asked to solve puzzles. Some participants were offered monetary rewards, while others were not. The results showed that those who were not offered monetary rewards displayed higher levels of creativity and interest in solving the puzzles as compared to the reward group. In another study, children were given markers and asked to draw pictures. Some of the children were promised rewards for drawing, while others were not. The results showed that the children promised rewards became less interested in drawing compared to those who were not promised awards. A similar result occurred when Pizza Hut offered a reward for reading program. Children did read more at first, but they tended to pick books that were short and less challenging. The rewards also diminished their interest in reading. As one psychologist remarked when asked about the Pizza Hut reading incentive, it would probably produce "a lot of fat kids who don't like to read."[14] Alfie Kohn summed it up well in his book *Punished by Rewards*: "Rewards are usually experienced as controlling, and we tend to recoil from situations where our

[14] Alfie Kohn, *Punished by Rewards: The Trouble with Gold Stars, Incentive Plans, A's, Praise, and Other Bribes* (Houghton Mifflin Company, 1993), 73.

autonomy has been diminished."[15]

Deci and Ryan's research on motivation happened during a time when psychologists were focusing on universal human needs. Their research, and the influences of others who studied innate needs, led to the development of self-determination theory (SDT), which, as mentioned earlier, made the case for three primary inborn needs: relatedness, competence, and autonomy. We covered the first of these in detail in chapter 4 on the social brain. SDT "states that giving people the freedom to make personal choices leads to personal empowerment, a higher sense of autonomy, and a higher interest in the task."[16] Their research showed that giving autonomy led to higher levels of persistence, creativity, and problem-solving. Even more surprising, in the same way that healthy social relationships do, self-determination was beneficial to happiness and a sense of personal well-being.

David Rock includes autonomy as one of his five major domains of human social experience as described in his SCARF model. Looking from the lens of neuroscience, he describes how the freedom to make choices activates the brain's reward systems. On the other hand, people who don't have control over their decisions experience higher levels of stress. Some people believe that executive jobs must have elevated levels of stress, and I can say for sure that they do. But many studies have shown that low-level employees report higher levels of stress and more stress-related health problems (including cardiovascular diseases, mental health issues, and even

....

[15] Kohn, *Punished by Rewards*, 78.

[16] Latham, *Work Motivation*, 155.

higher mortality rates) than those in executive positions.[17] Other research shows that having a sense of autonomy is a better predictor of psychological well-being than economic prosperity.[18]

As I moved through my career in HR, I took a particular interest in watching successful leaders and comparing them to less competent ones. The view of a human resources executive is unique. You get to see lots of data on who is perceived as a good leader by their employees (employee survey data, upward and 360-degree reviews, exit interviews, turnover data, focus group reports, and so forth). A chief human resources officer also has access to business performance data (profits, performance to goal, revenue growth, efficiency and quality data, customer service results, and so on). Combine the two and you can determine the great ones and the not-so-great ones. For over thirty years I observed the great ones and looked to understand what made them successful. I discovered three things that made them stand out. First, and perhaps not surprising, they were good with people. They were respectful, listened well, and showed genuine concern for others. Not a screamer in the bunch. And they ran the gamut when it came to personality types: some were extroverts, some more introverted. Some were charismatic and good storytellers; some were quieter but still good communicators. Second, all had a strategic mindset. They were common sense smart, usually good readers, able to integrate global and national trends into their daily thinking, and they paid attention to the world. They were good at translating the what

---

17 David Rock, *Your Brain at Work: Strategies for Overcoming Distractions, Regaining Focus, and Working Smarter All Day Long* (Harper Collins, 2009), 124.

18 David Rock and Christine Cox, "SCARF in 2012: Updating the Social Neuroscience of Collaboration with Others," *NeuroLeadership Journal* 4 (2012), 134.

and why of events for the team members. And finally, they seemed to have an intuitive sense of the power of autonomy.

The Popwell Method

David Popwell's office was next door to mine for over fifteen years. David served in several executive roles at my last company, First Horizon, but for most of the time I worked closely with him he was the president of banking. David is an exceptional leader and true to the model I described. There were many things I admired about David, but his willingness and ability to empower his people was his competitive advantage. One crucial leadership moment exemplified his strength. In 2017, First Horizon completed the largest merger in its history, with Capital Bank of North Carolina. Those of us in management were excited about the merger, our new status as one of the largest banks in the growing Southeast, and the prospects for long-term growth. Our excitement seemed to catch on with our employees, our customers, and the board. The future looked bright.

While the merger eventually became a success story, not long into the integration period our financials came in lower than expected and cost trends didn't look good. Our CFO presented the management team with a challenge—we needed to cut costs quickly if we were going to hit our financial targets. Cost cutting during a merger is normal and expected. But those initial cuts were behind us; more cost cutting would cut deep. In banking, the highest noninterest expense is personnel, so reducing costs meant layoffs. Firing people is never easy, but doing so when employees think layoffs are behind them and the business seems to be doing well is extremely challenging. David managed the largest division in the bank, making his cost targets very painful to achieve.

As he had during the financial crisis, David relied on his leadership skills and intuition about people. At the executive team meeting when he first shared the news about the coming cuts, David laid out the case for why the cuts were necessary and then he just listened. As described by one of the participants, the tension and anger in the room was palpable. The bank leaders in attendance quickly realized that to achieve the bank's goals, they would have to displace good people, their long-term colleagues and friends. Cost cutting is a painful process, and these leaders needed to blow off steam. Some leaders shut down these kinds of emotional conversations. They might just say, "Suck it up, that's just the way it is, so let's move on." Good leaders recognize that allowing people to process through their emotions allows them to get to problem-solving. It is a multistep process. Shutting people down leaves them resentful and angry.

But the next step in David's leadership was the key to his success. Many executives take the easy route when they get a cost-cutting goal from their CFO. They take the target and divide it through some kind of mathematical formula, assign a sub target to each leader, and ask for a plan to achieve the goal. David took a harder path but one that usually results in better decision-making. After laying out the case for action and allowing his leaders to pour out their emotions, he facilitated a series of conversations that aligned all his team members to hit the target. He then stayed engaged as he empowered his team to come up with the best plan for the bank as a whole. The team identified a list of activities that were deemed low value and could be cut from the budget, while areas critical to customer service and profitability were retained. Working as a team can feel like a reduction in autonomy, but David's empowerment gave the team a sense of agency and control.

On three separate occasions, I was hired by a CEO to take over an HR department that was underperforming. I love the challenge of a turnaround. Who wants to take a leadership role in an organization that is running like a fine-tuned machine? With a turnaround there's usually no place to go but up! In all three cases I followed the same process for leading the change process. First, I spent a few months doing research. I interviewed the CEO and company leaders about their views of HR. I also conducted interviews with HR employees and sent out surveys. I did a little management by walking around, observing processes, and checking in with people just to get the lay of the land. Then I decided upon my leadership team. Using interviews with leaders and key clients, I decided who to retain and who to let go. In all cases, I brought in a few experienced HR leaders from outside the company who shared my vision for a business-oriented HR function.

Next was the most critical step: the creation of a vision, strategy, and action plan for the department. Using my decades of experience in HR, my reading, research, and talking with other successful HR executives, I had a pretty good idea what made a great HR department. But I also knew that edicts from the boss were disempowering. I had also learned from experience that the best ideas often come from the group, not from me. While I had deep experience and knowledge of best practices, I didn't understand the company as well as members of my team. Context often matters as much or more than the brilliance of an idea. Using an offsite meeting to start, I engaged all the members of my extended leadership team (my direct reports and their direct reports) in a series of conversations about the company, the business environment, the HR department, and the future. I was thrilled with the results of my first offsite strategy/visioning meeting, so I used the same process the next two times.

After laying out my thoughts about HR and the future, I assigned subgroups to design the organizational structure, write a vision statement, and set strategies and a detailed action plan for the first eighteen months. After reports from the subgroups, we all worked together to develop the first draft of a plan. There were times when I disagreed with the group's direction, but rather than just overrule them, I made my case about what I thought was a better way. If my objection was based on a foundational principle of mine, I was usually successful in bringing the team around to my way of thinking. But most of the time their decisions were different but still workable. I knew the key to team members buying into the plan was that they felt ownership of it.

David Rock describes autonomy as the "perception of exerting control over one's environment; a sensation of having choices."[19] I trust you can see that even with teams, leaders can foster a sense of individual autonomy by empowering people and getting them involved in the decisions that impact their lives. As noted earlier, a lack of control—an absence of autonomy—can create a threat state, and threat states decrease the quality of decision-making, creativity, and the ability to resolve conflict. A long-term lack of autonomy can lead to increased stress and anxiety and a reduction in psychological well-being. In *Drive*, Pink closes his chapter by quoting Professor Ryan.

....

[19] Rock, "SCARF," 5.

> The course of human history has always moved in the direction of greater freedom. And there is a reason for that—because it is in our nature to push for it . . . somebody stands in front of a tank in China. Women, who've been denied autonomy, keep advocating for rights. This is the course of history. This is why ultimately human nature, if it ever realizes itself, will do so by becoming more autonomous.[20]

If you are a leader, you will find ways to grant autonomy as often as you can. In a world of chaos, control only comes when we surrender it to others.

Ideas and Applications

- Recognize the deep need people have for autonomy and find creative ways to empower people. Delegate decision-making and encourage people to take ownership of their areas of responsibility as if they were entrepreneurs.
- Grant maximum flexibility on time and place when the nature of the work allows it. The pandemic's one gift has been showing how flexible arrangements can work in many more situations than originally imagined.
- Recognize even the perception of autonomy by facilitating conversations that allow people to express their views and provide input into decision-making in a group format. This

[20] Pink, *Drive*, 108.

can lead to better ideas, higher buy-in, and a mental reward state due to an increased sense of autonomy.

- Allow people to set their own goals within the context of overall group goals. When possible, allow them to have input into the latter.
- Establish the appropriate boundaries and policies within which people can make their own decisions about how to proceed with their work.
- Allow people the freedom to make choices about their hairstyle, clothing, personal space, and work tools within the parameters of an established culture. Sometimes clear rules and policies are needed, but culture is broad enough to manage behavior while allowing freedom for people to make choices.

chapter 10

Certainty: Our Brain Is a Prediction Machine

Prediction is very difficult,
especially if it is about the future.

—Niels Bohr

A Scare

When I pointed out the small lump in her breast, she discounted it. "In my family, we have dense breast tissue," she said. But I was a wreck. Les and I had only been married for a few years. She had been a rock during my long journey through two open-heart surgeries, the latter one a heart transplant. Friends and family told me later she had struggled emotionally during the whole ordeal, but I never saw it. She was always positive and supportive. Now it was my turn, so I tried to keep cool. My anxiety was magnified by the fact that I had lost my first wife, my partner of thirty-eight years, to a long battle with cancer. *Not again, not fair, keep calm, stay positive . . .* My mind was a jumble of thoughts and emotions.

I insisted Les set up an appointment to get the lump checked out. She agreed, but my emotional state fed hers. She began to worry. A few weeks later, we found ourselves in a doctor's office, a few days after the initial tests. When the doctor walked in, we could see the concern on her face. The tests results showed a mass that was concerning. The only way to know for sure was a biopsy, which we scheduled immediately. The next ten days were torture for both of us. It took time to set up the biopsy and then to get the results. Our imaginations were fed by anxiety. She prayed. We talked. But mostly we were quiet. The old worry principle had worked for me many times in business: determine what is the worst that can possibly happen, prepare to accept the worst, then try to improve on the worst.[1] It didn't help in this situation. The scenarios were daunting—surgery, mastectomy, radiation, body mutilation, long recovery, no recovery. The uncertainty was killing us.

And then came the news. It was cancer. Remarkably, our mood changed almost immediately. Questions were asked and answered. Expert surgeons and oncologists were consulted. An action plan was determined. Les once again was a trooper. There was no feeling sorry for herself, no complaining. "We got this" was our constant refrain. As the process moved along, we got lots of good news: mastectomy on only one breast, no chemotherapy, and in this type of cancer the reoccurrence rate in ten years was very low. The next few months were no picnic for Les, but together we attacked the treatment and recovery plan like it was another one of life's projects. The worry, the dark moods of those first few weeks, were long gone. Les even joked to her close friends, "I got a free boob lift out of it." As I write this Les is still doing great.

....

[1] I learned about the fundamental principles for overcoming worry in a Dale Carnegie Course in Effective Speaking and Human Relations in 1979. The class was recommended to me by my manager at the bank, who thought I needed to become more assertive. I enjoyed the class, and after a few years of training became a certified instructor, which ignited my career development—particularly because of the improvement in my ability to deliver effective presentations. Managing stress and speaking effectively are critical abilities for everyone, but they are extra critical for someone in an executive role.

Leslie

Certainty Is Bliss

It is a story recorded countless times: a diagnosis of cancer or other serious illness results in a more positive emotional response than the period of not knowing. This seems a bit irrational. According to researchers, imaging tests that indicate possible cancer find cancerous cells less than 50 percent of the time, and for many cancers the results show malignancy only 10 to 20 percent of the time. Of course, my readers know by now that our brains have a bunch of stuff wired in that don't fall into the bucket of rationality. We are not Spock, consciously calculating probabilities and risks. We hate the unknown. We crave certainty.

Scientists demonstrated this point in several human studies using electrodes that delivered a harmless but slightly painful shock. While delivering the electric shock to the skin, the scientists measured physiological responses that tend to correlate with stress. "In study after study, the researchers found that any element of unpredictability significantly increases people's discomfort, despite there being no objective difference in the intensity of the shock, for example, compared to situations in which there is a 100% certainty that they would be shocked."[2]

Lisa Feldman Barrett has spent her life studying the brain. One of her main conclusions is that our brains are not primarily for thinking but evolved to keep us alive and pass our genes on to the next generation. She points out that the brain uses about 20 percent of our caloric energy. Hunter-gatherers faced constant pressure to find calories, so the brain evolved to conserve energy where it could. One of the best ways to do that was to avoid surprises.

> When it came to body budgeting, prediction beat reaction. A creature that prepared its movement before the predator struck was more likely to be around tomorrow than a creature that awaited a predator's pounce. Creatures that predicted correctly most of the time, or made nonfatal mistakes and learned from them, did well. Those that frequently predicted poorly, missed threats, or false alarmed about threats that never materialized didn't do so well. They explored their environment less, foraged less, and were less likely to reproduce.[3]

---

[2] David Robson, "Why We're so Terrified of the Unknown," *BBC Worklife*, October 26, 2021, 3.

[3] Barrett, *Seven and a Half Lessons about the Brain*, 6.

Natural selection thus shaped brains that are very good at prediction. Successful prediction creates a reward state. Memories are formed to allow for repetition in the future. Predictability good, uncertainty . . . not so much.

Professor Barrett claims that our brains predict almost everything we do. It is so fundamental to how the brain is organized that neuroscientists have described the brain as a prediction machine. This metaphor is somewhat controversial given the organic nature of the brain, but it seems to bring clarity to what the brain is doing in almost every situation. Neuroscientist Lars Muckli describes it this way: "The main purpose of the brain . . . is it is a prediction machine that is optimizing its own predictions of the environment it is navigating through."[4] The brain starts with an expectation of what's around the corner. Once you turn the corner, the brain takes inputs to confirm the prediction or adjust and make new predictions. The brain does this quickly and initially outside conscious awareness.

Building Reality, Preparing for the Worst

How does the brain work as a prediction machine? First, let's nix the idea that the brain is like a recording machine that retains an accurate picture of reality. The brain can process and store vast amounts of information, but it is highly selective on what it retains based on attention, perception, and prior knowledge and experience. The brain actively constructs reality. Here's Professor Barrett again:

[4] Kevin Casey, "Theory of Predictive Brain as Important as Evolution," *EV Magazine*, May 29, 2018.

> From the moment you are born to the moment you draw your last breath, your brain is stuck in a dark silent box called your skull. Day in and day out, it continually receives sense data from the outside world via your eyes, ears, nose and other sensory organs. This data does not arrive in the form of meaningful sights, smells and sounds, and other sensations that most of us experience. It's just a barrage of light waves, chemicals and changes in air pressure with no inherent significance.[5]

Drawing on the memory of a lifetime of experience, the brain makes sense of the data and chooses a path of action, again mostly outside conscious awareness. Neuroscientist Jeff Hawkins describes prediction as a "ubiquitous function of the neocortex." He describes learning as the continuous flow of verified predictions with an error response mechanism when a prediction is incorrect. "A mis-prediction causes you to attend to the error and update the model."[6]

Let's play this out for one of our hunter-gatherer ancestors. Amoukar (a character from *Quest for Fire*) is out on a hunt with his fellow tribesman Naoh. They are traveling along a familiar path usually occupied by small game animals. Suddenly, Amoukar hears a low growl. This is unexpected. He freezes and slowly turns to his left. His brain is in an elevated threat state. As his head turns his eyes lock on to the eyes of a large creature with big sharp teeth. His brain has stored a category. If it growls, has thick fur, and bares sharp teeth, that's a "not good" category. Amoukar's brain has already sent

---

[5] Barrett, *Seven and a Half Lessons about the Brain*, 66.

[6] Jeff Hawkins, *A Thousand Brains: A New Theory of Intelligence* (Basic Books, 2021), 31.

hormones flowing through his body—his heart rate and blood pressure have increased. His sympathetic nervous system is fully engaged. He is ready to fight or run like hell.

Just like the brain stored a furry, big teethy, growly category, Amoukar has another memory: how it feels when faced with furry, big teethy, growly. Remember our chapter on negative bias? Amoukar's brain will remember his first moment facing big, teethy, growly for a long time. Most of what happened right before and after that first time he probably won't remember. Because he survived, he learned something. That's called experience.

Amoukar may have other memories and learning. Maybe he once saw an older, experienced hunter slowly move backward while closely watching the creature but not staring straight into its eyes. In his own encounter, Amoukar's brain was rapidly combining incoming sensory information with experience and learning. His brain was also making multiple simultaneous predictions, first to interpret and then to act. This response contrasts with instinctive behavior, which is innate and characteristic of many nonhuman behavioral responses.

Amoukar's encounter involved a moment of uncertainty with the first growl. The uncertainty produced a threat state. His brain then started running several scenarios and predictions, mostly outside his conscious awareness. Let's imagine that when he turned his head, he found himself staring into the eyes of a snickering fellow tribesman. He had been punked. Amoukar responds with laughter after an immediate release of some of the tension, but his heart rate and blood pressure remain high. His heavy breathing and dilated pupils slowly return to normal. His brain made a prediction, and his body was ready for a response before he could consciously process the moment. It would take a few minutes for his body to return to a normal state.

Our brain is constantly trying to predict what will happen next, allowing it to prepare the body and mind for the most-effective response. When faced with uncertainty, predictions are a lot more difficult. For our ancestors, the lack of prior learning or experience could generate the wrong response, which could be deadly. As a result, natural selection favored brains that erred on the side of caution, "either by avoiding the uncertainty altogether or by putting the brain and body in an aroused state that is ready to respond to a changing situation."[7] Uncertainty creates a threat state. Threat states can be helpful when faced with physical threats such as those faced by our ancestors. Threat states prepare the body and mind for action. But in our modern world these threat states are another evolutionary mismatch.

Amoukar and other members of his tribe spent most of their lives hunting and foraging in familiar terrain. While nomadic, moving from location to location in search of food and resources, their lives had a somewhat predictable pattern. Deviations from that pattern—the growl of a large predator, a sudden storm, a flash flood, the sight of a bitter enemy—could be life threatening. These threats of physical harm generated an immediate and automatic biological response shaped over millions of years of human evolution. This response was crucial for survival, but it is a mismatch in today's world. The threats we encounter today are not short-term physical dangers, but mostly psychological stressors such as work demands, social anxieties, or financial setbacks. These challenges require calmness and clear thinking, which is difficult when our brains and bodies are flooded with hormones and neurotransmitters that are preparing us for fight or flight.

....

[7] Robson, "Why We're So Terrified of the Unknown," 4.

Fear of the unknown and discomfort with uncertainty are legacies of our ancestral past. Even a small amount of uncertainty can generate a modest threat state. But the biological responses we experience with uncertainty are not always negative. Recently, I was driving a rental car in Boston, which has been ranked as the worst-driving major city in America. The road systems are convoluted, but the local commuters are familiar with the patterns and drive very aggressively. When driving in my hometown of Memphis, I can get to my destination without thinking; I am even able to concentrate on the news or listen to music. I turned the radio off while driving in Boston. I was in a moderately stressed and uncomfortable state, but the chemicals flowing through my body put me in an alert state. I was able to concentrate and focus on getting to my destination, albeit with a little help from the voice of Christina Aguilera on the direction-finding app called Waze.

Much of the resistance to change that leaders see from employees in the workplace is triggered by our natural discomfort with uncertainty and fear of the unknown. The announcement of a major organizational change, a new boss, or a merger can initiate a stress response and a state called allostasis.[8] This process prepares the body and brain to respond to short-term challenges in the environment. While helpful to Amoukar when he faced off against a saber-toothed tiger, the flood of cortisol and adrenaline isn't usually helpful in today's world. The resultant increase in heart rate and blood pressure clouds thinking, and if employees stay in a state of allostasis, health and well-being are impacted. Leaders who ignore or discount employee concerns only heighten anxiety. Conversely, the

....

[8] David Eagleman and Jonathan Downar, *Brain and Behavior: A Cognitive Neuroscience Perspective* (Oxford University Press, 2016), 446.

act of creating some sense of certainty can lead to big payoffs.

Stressed in Uncertainty

In 2003, I was leading human resources at Union Planters, a regional bank headquartered in Memphis. At that point, I had been the head of HR for a few years. I had built a strong team of HR professionals from both inside and outside the company, and I had worked hard to shape a strong culture of professionalism and service. The morale and engagement of the team was high. Our CEO sold me on joining the bank with his excitement about the potential and his vision of building a major banking franchise in that fast-growing part of the country. I shared that vision and excitement with my team, and for the first few years of my tenure our growth plan worked. Then came the big news. In January of the following year, Union Planters and Regions Bank of Birmingham announced a merger of equals. Jack Moore, my boss and the CEO, was closer to achieving his vision.

But the news was unsettling to my staff. Many of my team members had been through acquisitions on the buying side. In an acquisition, the impact on staff of the buying company is usually minimal. But in a merger of equals, significant changes affect employees in both companies. Merger cost savings targets for support groups can be as high as 30–40 percent of personnel-related expenses. That translates into layoffs, job content changes, the possibility of job relocation, and more. It also means many work processes are replaced or reengineered. When I met with my team on an all-employee conference call right after the announcement, I tried to balance my enthusiasm for the deal with the hard truth about the many coming changes.

After the conference call, feedback from my leadership team was immediate. While some employees were excited about the merger and optimistic they would land a spot with the new company, many were struggling with the uncertainty of the situation. In acquisitions, the buying bank often converts the systems and processes of the acquired bank into their own. Conversion planning is simply mapping one set of systems and processes to the other. In a merger, organizational design and conversion planning take longer as both companies want to retain the best system and processes and people. This can lead to a long period before employees learn how their jobs are impacted or whether they have a spot in the new company.

As the surviving HR executive, I was the decision-maker on systems, processes, and people, so I immediately put together teams to start the planning process. But I also initiated a weekly call with all HR employees in both companies. In the first call, I advised the combined team that the organizational structure and work processes would be designed by representatives from both companies and then laid out a timeline of when decisions would be made. That reduced uncertainty a bit. Then I promised that I would lead a call every Friday morning for all HR employees who could attend. On that call I would update the team on our progress, tell them everything I knew that was not confidential, and answer any questions they might have. At a time of great uncertainty, I introduced one certainty—that Friday call. I knew at the time it wasn't a panacea, but after the merger integration was complete, many of my team members told me that those weekly calls made a big difference reducing their level of anxiety. I continued the practice in many subsequent mergers and during other times of dramatic change.

There is a strong link between uncertainty and stress. As noted, the brain operates as a prediction machine using "sophisticated statistical methods" and "probabilities."[9] When those predictions are incorrect, uncertainty arises, and the brain requires more cerebral energy. This need kicks in a stress response, which elevates heart rate and blood pressure. Multiple hormones are released into the body, and it is ready for fight or flight. This response is lifesaving when facing an acute physical crisis. But if the stress response system is activated for psychological reasons, bad thinking and poor health results. Robert Sapolsky has written extensively on the stress response. Here he summarizes the impact:

> Sustained stress has numerous adverse effects. The amygdala becomes overactive and more coupled to pathways of habitual behavior; it is easier to learn fear and harder to unlearn it. We process emotionally salient information more rapidly and automatically but with less accuracy. Frontal function—working memory, impulse control, executive decision-making, risk assessment, and task shifting—is impaired, and the frontal cortex has less control over the amygdala. And we become less empathetic and prosocial.[10]

In brief, uncertain employees are unhappy and unproductive in almost every domain of human engagement. Long-term uncertainty and the corresponding stress response lead to significantly

....

[9] Achim Peters, Bruce S. McEwen, and Karl Friston, "Uncertainty and Stress: Why It Causes Diseases and How It Is Mastered by the Brain," *Progress in Neurobiology* 156 (September 1, 2017), 164–88.

[10] Sapolsky, *Behave*, 136.

reduced health and well-being.

Our response to uncertainty is another example of evolutionary mismatch. Our brains have mechanisms that served us well as hunter-gatherers, but most of the uncertainty in our modern lives is psychological in nature. Our brain's response to those situations should be different. The good news is that our brains are also wired to learn and change. It is important to point out here that many people have different responses to uncertainty based on their personality, upbringing, past experiences, and coping skills. Some individuals even thrive in uncertainty and find it energizing. I know this was true for me in the latter years of my career. I flourished in times of ambiguity and uncertainty when many around me struggled to cope. It became a differentiator for me, and it led to higher levels of happiness and enjoyment in my work.

In my later years as an executive, I was often asked to give talks to young professionals and interns. The title of my talks was usually something like "What I Wish I Knew Then." In other words, a talk on key life and career lessons. I included tips about the importance of self-awareness and resilience, and I always included points about the importance of thriving in times of ambiguity and uncertainty. As it was for me, I saw tolerance for ambiguity as a career differentiator. I shared my three main strategies:

1. Reframe uncertainty as an opportunity for both learning and personal growth.
2. Use an old Dale Carnegie worry principle: "Live in day-tight compartments." In other words, focus on the task at hand and don't allow too much time to speculate and worry about the future.
3. Maintain perspective—keep in mind it's not about you.

What happens in life is the result of complex forces and people with competing interests focusing on their goals. A singular focus on how change impacts us as individuals may have been lifesaving in our ancestral past, but it distorts reality in unhealthy and unproductive ways. Be curious and try to understand the bigger picture.

One way for leaders to reduce uncertainty is to maintain emotional stability. My father struggled with alcoholism and low self-esteem during my formative years. He was a good storyteller and, at times, could be warm and engaging. At other times his mood was volatile, and he could be mean and belittling. If we sensed the latter, my brothers and I would take off and avoid contact. One brother, who was very sensitive, once confided in me that he wished Dad was just mean all the time. He couldn't deal with the Dr. Jekyll and Mr. Hyde uncertainty of his moods. In *Primal Leadership*,[11] the authors describe resonant leadership, a style that emphasizes the importance of emotional intelligence. Emotional intelligence is largely being aware of our own moods and their impact on others and controlling those moods to create a positive emotional environment. Resonant leadership works because it allows people to be "in sync." When people are on the "same wavelength emotionally," uncertainty is reduced.

Ideas and Applications

- Create organizational processes, such as group meetings, one-to-one check-ins, staff meetings, and so forth, that follow regular and consistent patterns. Keep in mind

[11] Daniel Goleman, Richard Boyatzis, and Annie McKee, *Primal Leadership: Unleashing the Power of Emotional Intelligence* (Harvard Business School Press, 2002), 19.

people's need for autonomy; these should not be project management updates (although those are necessary at times) but opportunities for company or business unit updates, conversations, and questions. The engagement should be two-way—not long speeches from the leader. People want to know what's going on and where they fit in, but dialogue is the best method of delivery.

- With team involvement, create a business strategy and a plan of action for the unit you lead. Also, document your organizational structure that shows the role each team member plays and their accountabilities. I have never had a plan that played out the way we expected. We were constantly changing and adapting, but the documentation and discussion of the unit's direction seemed to give team members a greater sense of control and certainty.

- Break down complex projects into smaller steps with clear goals. With this and the previous point, it is important that you don't overdo it. Keep it simple and easy to read and follow. Almost nobody reads complex strategy and business plan documents. A few pages will suffice.

- Recognize the wide variability in people's tolerance for change and ambiguity. Some people will experience higher levels of stress and will need some personal attention. Advising them not to worry or discounting their fears and concerns only makes matters worse; people need to label and verbalize their emotions. Through questioning and support, emotionally resonant leaders will help team members process their concerns. The payoff in alignment and productivity is usually worth the effort.

- Acknowledge uncertainty and give updates and reassurance. I have experienced many flight delays while traveling. The uncertainty of not knowing whether I will get to my appointment in time or make my connection can be very stressful. It is worse when I get no information from the airline staff. On a recent flight delayed due to a mechanical issue, I noticed my mood was much better because the airline employee gave us updates every ten minutes with details on what was happening and possible scenarios if the flight didn't take off.

chapter 11

Irrationality: Ice Cream Thinking

When teaching my cognitive psychology course,
I use the example of broccoli and ice cream.
Some cognitive processes are demanding but necessary.
They are the broccoli. Other thinking tendencies
come naturally to us and they are not cognitively
demanding processes. They are the ice cream . . .
[we have] a natural tendency to resort
to ice cream thinking.

—Keith Stanovich

A Cautionary Tale

In October 2006, I arrived at a place with a lot of ice cream thinking. A merger involving my previous bank had caused the elimination of my job. That was the month I started my new job as the executive in charge of human resources at First Horizon. The company's headquarters has been in Memphis since 1864. It's been my hometown since early 2000. My two older sons were in high school, and my wife was battling cancer. The opportunity to stay in Memphis and provide stability for my family was too hard to pass up. But with over three decades of HR and banking experience under my belt, the opening at First Horizon was serendipitous and I was excited to get started.

My previous employer had been a major competitor so I knew a great deal about First Horizon. The bank was founded in 1864 and over its long history it had developed a reputation as a well-run, community-oriented enterprise. It was also recognized as a great place to work. In 2005, First Horizon became one of only twenty-two companies in *Fortune* magazine's Hall of Fame, having made the list of the best one hundred companies to work for since the list's inception in 1998. The bank also had a reputation for great customer service. I had many friends and neighbors who would share stories about the people and their experiences at the bank. It contrasted starkly with my previous company. When I mentioned I worked at Union Planters, I would often get a long list of complaints or would be enlisted to help solve someone's personal banking problem.

While excited, I also entered my new role with a bunch of questions. I had worked at three major banking companies up to that point. They were all significant consumer and commercial banking companies, and they all shared a similar strategy: don't let your mortgage business get too big. Housing demand and valuations are highly cyclical, so earnings in the mortgage business are volatile. Bank investors generally don't like volatility, so a large mortgage portfolio could impact investor expectations of steady earnings-per-share growth. There were also credit concerns. My first bank, Mellon Bank, nearly went bankrupt in 1987, due in part to huge losses in real estate lending. Mellon was swept up in the financial crisis of the mid-1980s, which ultimately led to the failure or sale of over two thousand banks and savings and loans. I loved my first job at Mellon; it, too, was a proud hundred-year-old institution with a strong culture. But its struggles caused thousands of layoffs, deep cost cutting, and the loss of its pristine reputation. I felt that loss personally. I learned early in my career that mortgage lending was a tough business and here I was starting at a company that was one of the largest mortgage originators in the country.

I used the same game plan when I started all of my new executive roles: do research and a lot of listening before planning any changes or launching any new ideas. In my first three months at First Horizon, I set up interviews with over sixty executives and senior leaders and sat in on several focus groups of frontline employees. My questions were basic ones: What's your view of the company? What's going well in the company? What needs improvement? What's your view of the leadership and direction of the company? I also asked questions about human resources, but my main goal was to get a feel for the company and its culture. I got an earful, and the overall picture wasn't pretty. While all the employees I spoke to loved[1] the company, most disliked and did not trust the CEO. Worse, many of the veteran leaders I spoke to on the bank side hated the mortgage business and were worried about the future of the company.

I was surprised by the bifurcated views of my interviewees. They loved the culture, the people, and the history of the company but had negative feelings about the CEO and his business strategy. An us-them dynamic had also settled over the company. First Tennessee Bank employees described First Horizon Mortgage[2] as gung-ho,

....

[1] Social belonging is a fundamental human need. Group cohesion was the key to our survival for millions of years. The need for attachment is hardwired into our DNA. When an employee feels a sense of belonging and connection to their employer and place of work, it meets that basic human need, and the word *love* flows freely to describe the emotion they are feeling.

[2] First National Bank of Memphis began acquiring banks in the rest of the state and thus changed its name to First Tennessee in 1971. Twenty years later, the brand was one of the strongest in the state. In the early 1990s, the bank began acquiring mortgage companies throughout the country. In 2004, the company adopted the name First Horizon for its holding company and its mortgage operations but kept First Tennessee as its bank name in its home state. First Horizon eventually operated in forty-six states before the collapse. The names contributed to the us-them dynamic in the company because it enabled easy labeling of the other.

greedy, materialistic, and only concerned with themselves. They contrasted that with their view of bank employees as loyal, dedicated, and focused on customer needs instead of their own pocketbooks. Mortgage employees saw the bankers as stodgy, overly conservative, and risk adverse. I had seen culture clashes during mergers before, but the emotions I experienced during those interviews were unlike anything I had ever seen. As the executive responsible for partnering with the CEO to shape culture, I could see I had my work cut out for me.

It didn't take long for me to understand the widespread dislike for the CEO who had hired me. During the interview process and in response to my questions, he assured me that he wanted executives who spoke their mind and weren't afraid to challenge him. I learned that this was not how most of his leaders viewed him. My first significant meeting with him was to communicate the results of my interviews. When I shared the concerns I had gathered about the culture and the business strategy, he became immediately dismissive and defensive. Then he peppered me with questions. How many people did you interview? Who were they? Are you sure you heard right? I attempted to balance the negative feedback with positives about the culture and the quality of the people I met, but he couldn't get his mind off the negative comments. Any brief summation of his response would be inadequate, but it went something like this: these people don't know what they're talking about, and I will set the record straight.

Before I go on, here's some background. The housing market in the US expanded rapidly in the early 2000s due to a prolonged period of low interest rates. In 2003, long-term mortgage rates were the lowest they had been in a generation. Low rates fueled demand, which led to double-digit home price acceleration. Investors, looking for high-quality, high-yield assets, entered the market in droves. *Flipping* became the word du jour to describe the process of buying, rehabbing, and selling properties for a profit—except during this growth spurt there was not much rehabbing, just reselling after a short holding period. With cheap credit, people also took advantage of high home valuations by taking out home equity loans. In *The Big Short*, Michael Lewis's book about the financial crisis, he tells an anecdote about a stripper he met at a subprime mortgage conference in Las Vegas who reported she had five separate home equity loans.[3] The country was now in a full-scale boom.

This is where "ice cream thinking" comes into play. Remember Daniel Kahneman's system one thinking? System one refers to the intuitive, automatic, fast mode of thinking. It allows us to make snap judgments and to respond to gut feelings. It serves us well when quick decisions are necessary. This kind of thinking doesn't use much cognitive energy; it comes to us effortlessly and quickly. It feels like eating ice cream (that is, of course, unless you're lactose intolerant). By contrast, system two refers to a deliberate, analytical, and slow mode of thinking. System two thinking is hard and burns a lot of cognitive energy. This mode of thinking is required when dealing with complex problems and when critical thinking is necessary. It feels like eating broccoli (that is, unless you eat your broccoli with lots of cheese and salt, which sort of defeats the purpose, but I trust you get the point).

Boom periods bring lots of ice cream thinking with all its biases and errors. At the peak of the housing boom, many,

[3] Michael Lewis, *The Big Short: Inside the Doomsday Machine* (W. W. Norton & Company, 2010), 152.

including the CEO and many of the mortgage bankers at First Horizon, thought the world had changed. One of their rationales was securitization, a financial device that packaged individual mortgages into securities and then sold them to investors. Investors thought they were buying a safe, high-yield asset (at least high-yield relative to the historically low short-term interest rates). Bankers thought they were moving risk off their balance sheets. Securitization had been around for decades, but the housing and lending boom led to the creation of more innovative and higher risk forms of securitization. Boom thinking brings with it unbridled optimism, speculative behavior, and irrational risk-taking. As it turned out, economic fundamentals hadn't changed at all; there was just a lot more complexity. Figuring it out required system two thinking, but participants throughout the economic system wanted in on the action. Quick decision-making replaced thoughtful, rigorous decision-making. Fear of missing out replaced fear of bandwagon jumping.

The US financial crisis of 2008, otherwise known as the Great Recession, was caused by the bust of the housing market. While I have explained some of what happened, the causes of the crisis were many and complex. Yet like many economic crises, the boom period before the bust was characterized by a mass psychology of risk-taking that seems clearly irrational in hindsight. I would like to tell the reader that I saw the crisis coming at both the bank and the national levels, but that would be hindsight bias.[4] But I was troubled by what I heard when I spoke with the mortgage bank leadership. One was petitioning the bank's credit function to loosen lending standards

[4] Hindsight bias is also known as the "I knew it all along" phenomenon. It captures the tendency of people to perceive events as having been predictable, at least for them.

in late 2006. There were already signs of a housing slowdown, but First Horizon mortgage bankers wanted to keep their growth engine revved up—their big bonuses relied on it. And I was shocked when I saw the company announce the acquisition of a mortgage banking origination company in Las Vegas in May 2007.[5] At the time, it reminded me of Mellon's expansion into the Houston mortgage banking market in the 1980s, right before the oil bust and a huge increase in mortgage defaults that cost the company millions in losses. My intuition was right; a few years later Nevada led the nation in the rate of home foreclosures. But then again, maybe it was my own hindsight bias!

The mortgage company's regular requests to loosen credit standards weren't completely irrational. The sales staff were competing in a market that offered mortgage products with never-before-seen lending criteria including lower credit scores, lower down payments, and teaser rates. I was once a consumer credit lending officer; I understand the basics of good lending. The consumer should have a low debt-to-income ratio, a verified source of income, and an appropriate loan-to-value ratio with real estate. During the boom, mortgage banks offered products with unreasonably high debt-to-income ratios and financing with little or no down payment. (At the time, I had a wonderful young woman helping us clean our home while my wife was going through her cancer treatments. I knew she was living on the edge because she often asked, and I granted, small loans to help her through car breakdowns or unexpected health care bills. During one of her visits, she proudly announced she had bought

[5] In 2007, the Las Vegas housing market was experiencing a speculative boom characterized by high demand and rapid price appreciation. To experienced bankers, the market mania seemed like a classic economic bubble set up for a crash.

a new home. When I inquired as to the details, she let me know she had received a mortgage loan with no down payment and a low teaser rate. I was happy for her but concerned. One year later her house was repossessed. She was one of tens of thousands of victims of the crisis.)

One of the products that best exemplified the excesses of the time was something called a "no-doc" or "stated income" loan. Basically, it allowed borrowers to state their income without providing detailed documentation to verify it. These loans became known as "liar loans."

First Horizon resisted the worst behaviors of some financial companies, but the damage to the company was severe. Securitization wasn't as safe as most people had thought, economic cycles were still a reality, and the basics of good lending hadn't really changed. The federal government took over the GSEs[6] that securitized mortgages and forced the banks that originated the mortgages to put them back on their balance sheets. As foreclosures increased, banks were forced to cover huge losses. As one of the largest originators in the country, First Horizon took an economic beating, made worse by the disproportionate share the mortgage business had of the company's earning streams. The recession also took its toll. Over the five-year period from 2007 until 2011, the bank took losses of over a billion dollars. The company shrank from $40 billion in assets with ten thousand employees to $25 billion in assets and fewer than five thousand employees.

[6] Government sponsored enterprises (GSEs) are financial corporations created by Congress to enhance the flow of credit to the housing market. They include the Federal National Mortgage Association, better known as Fannie Mae, and the Federal Home Loan Mortgage Corporation, better known as Freddie Mac.

Placing Irrational Bets

Classical economic theory is based on the assumption of rational choice theory: individuals make choices that give them the best result. *Homo economicus* is the term used to describe man as an economic actor who weighs costs and benefits, seeks information, and recognizes both the short- and long-term consequences of decisions. Behavioral economics is a field of study developed in the latter part of the twentieth century that challenges the assumption of pure rationality. Daniel Kahneman and Amos Tversky—two psychologists, as you will recall—were among the first and certainly the most famous to show that human decision-making, particularly in situations of risk and uncertainty, defies classic economic models. In fact, Daniel Ariely, a psychologist and behavioral economist, describes human decision-making as predictably irrational, a victim of systemic flaws in human thinking. Ariely describes humans as "pawns in a game whose forces we fail to comprehend."[7]

Ice cream thinking is a metaphor for one of those flaws, a tendency to act on intuition without taking the time and energy to engage Kahneman's system two. The Great Recession is a fascinating case study in human irrationality. How was it that so many smart, experienced people with much on the line made so many bad decisions? The Federal Reserve, with all its brilliant PhDs and experienced financial veterans who fed the boom with too much easy money. Regulators who missed the changing risk dynamics in the markets. Experienced bankers who filled their balance sheets with what turned out to be high-risk assets. Homeowners

[7] Daniel Ariely, *Predictably Irrational: The Hidden Forces That Shape Our Decisions* (Harper Collins, 2008), 243.

who bought homes and took out mortgage loans too big for their budgets. And investors who were swept up in the euphoria of the moment. Economic cycles come and go. During the boom, some people thought that market innovations had cured us of cycles—not so much. This one was made worse by the flagrant violation of basic lending principles such as documented steady income, good credit ratings, debt-to-income ratios that supported the debt services, and houses borrowers could afford.

Michael Burry was not one to fall victim to ice cream thinking and he made a fortune because of it. Burry, a self-described obsessive who may have Asperger's syndrome, noticed something amiss with the fast-growing mortgage bond market during the boom. Burry was a part-time investor who abandoned a career as a doctor to become an investor and hedge fund manager. Maybe because of his syndrome, he was comfortable spending time alone digging deeply into financial documents. In 2004, Burry conducted extensive research and analysis of mortgage-backed securities and collateralized debt obligations.[8] His research led him to believe that most of these securities were overvalued and likely to default when the housing market collapsed. Burry raised money on his theory and shorted the mortgage bond market using an innovative financial product called a credit default swap.[9] After a brief period of uncertainty and anxiety, his theory proved correct. The mortgage bond market collapsed in late 2007. It is estimated that Burry and his investors made over $700 million on his bet.

....

[8] Lewis, *The Big Short*, 27–60.

[9] A credit default swap (CDS) is a financial derivative contract that allows an investor as creditor to hedge against the risk of default on a debt instrument, such as a loan or a bond. A CDS is a useful financial tool for managing risk, but before the financial crisis the contracts were used for speculative purposes without adequate collateral.

There are many theories as to the causes of the Great Recession. Populists argued that greed caused the crisis and called for market participants to go to jail for their misdeeds. Despite multiple investigations, only a few people were found guilty, and only one person served time in prison (a former Credit Suisse executive who misrepresented the value of mortgage-backed securities to clients). Some researchers made the case that the federal government caused the crisis by aggressively pushing the expansion of home ownership. Brookings published a paper in November 2008 that describes the innovation and complexity of the financial system that masked risk. In their summary they note that escalating housing prices and the corresponding dramatic increase in borrowed money was "bound for catastrophe," yet they make the following point:

> What is especially shocking, though, is how institutions along each link of the securitization chain failed so grossly to perform adequate risk assessments on the mortgage-related assets they held and traded. From the mortgage originator to the loan servicer, to the mortgage-backed security issuer, to the CDO issuer, to the CDS protection seller, to the credit rating agencies, and to the holders of all those securities, at no point did any institution stop the party or question the little-understood computer risk model, or the blatantly unsustainable deterioration of the loan terms of the underlying mortgages.[10]

[10] "Crisis and Response: An FDIC History 2008–2013," FDIC.gov, accessed June 21, 2024.

Biases, Biases, Biases

Borrowers, lenders, investors, and regulators all fell victim to cognitive biases and irrational behaviors that led to the financial collapse. Greed, complexity, and misaligned incentives played a significant role in the crisis, but bandwagon bias, overconfidence bias, anchoring bias, optimism bias, endowment effect, and the availability heuristic all contributed to the environment that made the crisis possible.

WELL-KNOWN COGNITIVE BIASES

- **Bandwagon bias:** *the tendency to believe something because other people believe it.*
- **Overconfidence bias:** *the tendency to overestimate one's own abilities.*
- **Anchoring bias:** *the tendency to rely too heavily on the first piece of information encountered when making decisions.*
- **Optimism bias:** *the tendency to believe that one is less likely than others to experience a negative event.*
- **Endowment effect:** *the tendency to believe something one owns is more valuable than it is.*
- **Availability heuristic:** *the tendency to rely on information that is readily available when making decisions.*

Psychologists and behavioral economists have documented over two hundred cognitive biases. These are flaws in human rationality, flaws that contributed to the financial crisis and that continue to bedevil us individually and as a society. As I write this, 30 percent of Americans, according to a poll by Monmouth, believe President Biden's victory in the 2020 election was due to voter fraud. This belief persists despite multiple investigations that found no evidence that widespread fraud "substantially affected the outcome of the 2020 election, and virtually all of the dozens of legal cases filed by former President Donald Trump and allies were dismissed or withdrawn."[11] This belief is largely promulgated by the former president himself. Trump allegedly made over thirty thousand false or misleading claims during his term as president.[12] He also tended to make outrageous predictions that defied science and common sense. In February 2020, while COVID-19 was raging around the world, he predicted that the virus would disappear "like a miracle." He also endorsed multiple quack cures. Yet Trump still has the support of millions of Americans. Is this another example of the failure of rationality?

In his latest book, *Rationality*, Steven Pinker addresses this question, but first runs through a litany of "weird beliefs."[13]

....

[11] Ben Kamisar, "Almost a Third of Americans Believe the 2020 Election was Fraudulent," NBC News, June 20, 2023.

[12] Glenn Kessler, Salvador Rizzo, and Meg Kelly, "Trump's False and Misleading Claims Total 30,573 over 4 Years," *Washington Post*, January 24, 2021.

[13] Steven Pinker, *Rationality: What It Is, Why It Seems Scarce, Why It Matters* (Viking, 2021), 286. "Weird beliefs" is attributed to Michael Shermer.

> Many people endorse conspiracy theories like Holocaust denial, Kennedy assassination plots, and the 9/11 "Truther" theory that the twin towers were felled by controlled demolition to justify the American invasion of Iraq. Various seers, cults, and ideologies have convinced their followers that the end of the world is nigh; they disagree on when but are quick to postdate their predictions when they are unpleasantly surprised to find themselves living another day. And a quarter to a third of Americans believe we have been visited by extraterrestrials, either the contemporary ones that mutilate cattle and impregnate women to breed alien-human hybrids, or the ancient ones who built the pyramids and the Easter Island statues.[14]

Pinker describes Trump's support as well as the explosion of conspiracy theories, science denialism, and quack medical remedies as raising widespread doubts about our human "collective capacity for reason."[15] He then discounts current explanations for the seeming increase in irrationality. For example, social media has spread falsehoods and conspiracy theories wider and more quickly than at any time in our past, but both have been a part of human social experience for all recorded history. Human irrationality isn't new.

In his opening chapter, "How Rational an Animal?" Pinker briefly chronicles the vast successes of human rationality. Our species has "dated the origins of the universe, plumbed the nature of matter

14 Pinker, *Rationality*, 286.

15 Pinker, *Rationality*, 284.

and energy, decoded the secrets to life, and unraveled the circuitry of consciousness."[16] We have put a man on the moon, dramatically reduced poverty, and extended our lifespans by over forty years in the last century alone. More recently, we sequenced the genome of the virus that causes COVID-19 and produced a vaccine that saved millions of lives within a year. (A vaccine that millions refuse to take because it may include a Bill Gates chip!) Clearly, *Homo sapiens* has a great capacity for reason. This cognitive gift is the result of natural selection. Our hunter-gather ancestors relied on rationality for its primary life-giving activity, persistence hunting.[17] Our ancient ancestors weren't faster or stronger than most of their prey, but our two-legged, hairless bodies allowed us to wear down our prey over long distances. Our big brains gave us the capacity to coordinate with others as well as to track fleeing animals and recognize hoofprints, effluvia, and spoor. Our ability to reason allowed us to recognize weather patterns, understand geography and distance, and fabricate tools to make the whole process easier.

Pinker points out that even the holders of "weird beliefs" can be very rational in many contexts. They "hold down jobs, bring up kids, and keep a roof over their heads and food in the fridge."[18] Daniel Ariely has conducted most of his studies of irrationality at Duke and MIT, two of the most selective colleges in the world. Yet in almost every

....

[16] Pinker, *Rationality*, 1.

[17] Persistence hunting is a method of hunting that involves pursuing large prey over long distances until the animal is exhausted and more easily killed. Humans are not very fast compared to most mammals, but we are very good long-distance runners. It is believed that the persistence hunting of our hunter-gatherer ancestors contributed significantly to our bodies and brains. Our bodies shed fur and evolved to sweat while running. Our two-leggedness and upward stance gave us the ability to run efficiently. Our brains became wired to foster cohesion and cooperation for successful hunting.

[18] Pinker, *Rationality*, 288.

experiment, his brilliant students and study subjects fell victim to flaws in thinking. In one fascinating study, students were asked to put the last two digits of their Social Security numbers at the top of their answer sheet. They were then asked to bid on several products. His subsequent analysis of the data showed an anchoring effect. "The students with the highest-ending social security digits (from 80–99) bid highest, while those with the lowest ending numbers (1–20) bid lowest."[19]

Reason as Adaptation

So how do we explain this paradox? *Homo sapiens*, "wise man," is capable of extraordinary feats of reason yet vulnerable to fallacies and flaws like ice cream thinking. Cognitive psychologists Hugo Mercier and Dan Sperber tackle this "double enigma" of reason. Reason has been described by philosophers as the differentiator between us and other beasts. It is the "superpower" that natural selection has bestowed upon us—yet, as we have noted, it can be deeply flawed. In *The Enigma of Reason*, Mercier and Sperber use the framework of evolutionary psychology to make the case that reason can be understood only in the context of our evolutionary path. They argue for a new scientific explanation of reason that solves the double enigma.

> Reason . . . far from being a strange cognitive add-on, a superpower gifted to humans by some improbable evolutionary quirk, fits quite naturally among other human

[19] Ariely, *Predictably Irrational*, 28.

> cognitive capabilities and, despite apparent evidence to the contrary, is well adapted to its true function.[20]

Their theory suggests that human reasoning evolved primarily to serve the function of argumentation and persuasion, not as a mechanism for achieving accurate beliefs. The so-called "flaw" in human reasoning is "not a bug but a feature."[21]

In Mercier and Sperber's telling, our hunter-gatherer ancestors relied on cooperation and collaboration to survive, thrive, and pass on their genes. Reason is an adaptation, like many other cognitive capabilities, that "helps solve the problems of coordination, reputation management and communication."[22] The primary function of reason is persuasion through argumentation. We have been programmed by natural selection to try and convince others, take sides, and defend our positions. Reason's original purpose was not to ferret out the truth or get things right but to generate arguments. Today we use reason to understand the natural world. In that context, it has served us well. But the so-called flaws in reasoning show up most often and can only be understood in the context of its roots in the social world.

We are all biased in the sense that we easily produce arguments to support our point of view. This is called "myside bias." Reasons often flow effortlessly as we try to persuade or justify our actions. I remember one incident early in my HR career when I missed a deadline on a project that was important to my boss.

....

[20] Hugo Mercier and Dan Sperber, *The Enigma of Reason* (Harvard University Press, 2017), 5.

[21] Mercier and Sperber, *The Enigma of Reason*, 219.

[22] Mercier and Sperber, *The Enigma of Reason*, 278.

When she called me out in a meeting about the late project, I immediately produced multiple reasons for the failure to hit the due date. I effortlessly ticked off a dozen other projects I was working on, the long list of phone calls and requests that sat on my desk, the unrelenting demands of the role. On and on I went with a little emotion added in as icing on the cake. While frustrated, she agreed to extend the due date and sent me on my way. As I reflected later, I knew that the missed due date was due to my view that her project was not that important, and I was embarrassed to admit to myself that I had just procrastinated. But even today I remember the incident because of how easily I was able to generate arguments without preparation.

I also remember a similar situation with my first wife. I had promised to complete and submit a FAFSA[23] application for our oldest son to receive a Tennessee Lottery scholarship. The application interface was terrible, the amount of the scholarship was small compared to the total cost of tuition, and I hated filling out government forms, so I procrastinated. But I didn't respond to her question with the truth. My myside bias quickly produced a half dozen reasons why I hadn't done it. Only after I completed the process the next day did I admit to myself and to her that it was just plain old procrastination. These two examples show the lawyerlike quality of reasoning. But Mercier and Sperber note that the lawyer analogy "shouldn't be pushed too far."[24] Reason's best work is done not to deceive or manipulate but to use argumentation to produce a better solution. While reason serves us well in a zero-sum game

---

[23] The Free Application for Federal Student Aid (FAFSA) is used to determine eligibility for student aid. At the time, the application process was dated and cumbersome.

[24] Mercier and Sperber, *The Enigma of Reason*, 219.

such as a court trial, strong arguments can help win the day. But in a positive-sum contest, reason can be a powerful ally.

As I have noted, I used my leadership team to help me make most major long-term decisions such as organizational structure design, program and policy changes, and key leadership hires. My approach was to share my goals and must-haves and then let the group develop the final solution. During one of our major organizational restructurings, I laid out a nonnegotiable that said the recruiting function must report directly to me. I saw talent acquisition as critical and wanted to have direct input and access to the team. My leadership team disagreed. When they met with me, I could see they had spent a lot of time gathering arguments to overcome my nonnegotiable. (I am sure they spent a lot of time together deciding on what reasons to use to convince me and who would make the case. They chose wisely; the key presenter was someone I had worked with for a long time and held in high esteem.) After a long give and take, I eventually could see the logic in their arguments. At one point I had an aha moment. The team's arguments were sound, and my upfront stipulation was not so nonnegotiable after all. Time proved them right, the new structure worked, and myside bias in the context of positive-sum argumentation produced a better result.

In addition to producing arguments, reason has a second purpose: argument evaluation. "Reasoning is not only a tool for producing arguments to convince others; it is also, and no less importantly, a tool for evaluating the arguments others produce to convince us. The capacity to produce arguments could evolve only in tandem with the capacity to evaluate them."[25] There is significant evidence

[25] Mercier and Sperber, *The Enigma of Reason*, 332.

that humans are vigilant in evaluating arguments. It seems we are not good at seeing the flaws in our own arguments—that's myside bias at work—but we are very good at seeing the flaws in others' arguments.

False Beliefs Will Punish You

But it seems our evaluative abilities have limits. "In everyday life, when interacting with people we know, cues telling us to change our minds abound: we have time to ascertain goodwill, recognize expertise, and exchange arguments."[26] But in the larger realm of life we sometimes fall victim to irrationality.

Steven Pinker explains a strange paradox we see every day with human reason: How can it be that humans are so good at evaluating arguments yet so many of us fall victim to false beliefs, fake news, and wild conspiracy theories?

> People divide the world into two zones. One consists of the physical objects around them, the people they deal with face to face, the memory of their interactions, and the rules and norms that regulate their lives. People have mostly accurate beliefs about this zone, and they reason rationally within it. Within this zone, they believe there's a real world and that beliefs about it are true or false. They have no choice: that's the way to keep gas in the car, money in the bank, and the kids clothed and fed. Call it the reality mindset.[27]

---

[26] Hugo Mercier, *Not Born Yesterday: The Science of Who We Trust and What We Believe* (Princeton University Press, 2020), 259.

[27] Pinker, *Rationality*, 299–300.

In this zone, beliefs are testable.[28] You can hold a belief that hot coals won't harm you or that gravity doesn't exist until you walk on the coals barefoot or jump off a roof. False beliefs will punish you.

"The other zone is the world beyond immediate experience: the distant past, the unknowable future, faraway peoples and places, remote corridors of power, the microscopic, the cosmic, the counterfactual, the metaphysical."[29] In this zone, beliefs are distal, there is no way, through personal experience, to find out if the beliefs are true or false. Millions of people believe that extraterrestrials have visited us, that 9/11 was an inside job, that the Democrats were running a child sex ring, and that the COVID-19 vaccine contained a microchip to track people. Pinker calls this zone the "mythology mindset."[30] It is likely an offshoot of the same mental mechanism that supports religious beliefs. Religion reduces uncertainty and gives us comfort and an explanation for events. For some people, conspiracy theories may serve the same purpose. Beliefs originate and are supported by the people in our social circle. Holding seemingly irrational beliefs may be the result of rational behavior if espousing those beliefs binds us to our social circle. Shared beliefs make an individual one of "us" and not one of "them." Given our highly social nature, that is rational.

Keith Stanovich develops this argument by differentiating myside bias from the other two hundred or so cognitive biases. Daniel Kahneman argued that cognitive biases are basically shortcuts (heuristics) in our thinking to allow rapid decision-making. Our ancestors often faced life-threatening situations that required

---

[28] Pinker credits social psychologist Robert Abelson, who first distinguished between distal and testable beliefs in "Beliefs Are Like Possessions."

[29] Pinker, *Rationality*, 300.

[30] Pinker, *Rationality*, 301.

a quick response. In today's complex world, these same cognitive processes can lead to errors. (This is another example of evolutionary mismatch.) Stanovich argues that myside bias, in addition to enabling an individual to generate and evaluate arguments, also fosters group cohesion.

> Being a good group member almost by definition requires that the members display considerable myside bias when encountering ideas that contradict group beliefs. It is almost always the case, however, that the costs of the inaccuracies introduced into a particular member's belief network by the myside bias are outweighed by the considerable benefits provided by group membership.[31]

As an example, consider the case of election denial. Trump supporters have no way to directly check whether the election was stolen. By espousing the belief that it was, they are bound to other MAGA believers. It fits a worldview that a cabal of elites are the winners, and they are collectively being screwed by the system. Trump's rhetoric rationalizes and reinforces this worldview.

Research shows that we all have a bias blind spot. "Bias turns out to be relatively easy to recognize in the thinking of others, but often difficult to detect on our own."[32] There is some good news in the research—more intelligent people are less likely to fall victim to most cognitive bias. People who score high in open-mindedness can sometimes override cognitive bias. This does not hold true for

[31] Keith Stanovich, *The Bias That Divides Us: The Science and Politics of Myside Thinking* (MIT Press, 2021), 47.

[32] Stanovich, *The Bias That Divides Us*, 95.

myside bias. In multiple studies, high intelligence and elite education may lead to an even more intense "bias blind spot."

> If you are a person of high intelligence, if you are highly educated, and if you are strongly committed to an ideological viewpoint, you will be highly likely to think you have thought your way to your viewpoint. And you will be even less likely than the average person to realize that you have derived your beliefs from the social group you belong to and because they fit with your temperament and your innate psychological propensities.[33]

This bias blind spot may be the cause of some of the perceived arrogance of Democratic Party leaders who use belittling terms to describe Republican voters. For example, Hillary Clinton described Trump supporters as a "basket of deplorables." Obama was more nuanced, but he was patronizing in describing small towners as "bitter" and clinging "to their guns or religion or antipathy toward people who are not like them."

Convince Me

We have seen that reason and myside bias can be an evolutionary mismatch in our modern world, but not all our inherited hunter-gatherer behaviors are. Reason evolved in our hypersocial environment. Cooperation led to survival and genetic longevity. Today, in our postindustrial, digital workplace, cooperation in the form of

....

[33] Stanovich, *The Bias That Divides Us*, 96.

group problem-solving and innovation is highly prevalent. Myside bias, in a positive-sum scenario, can lead to superior results. In meetings, individual group members' reasons and beliefs are discussed, evaluated, and debated. "In problem solving, the performance of a group tends to be much better than the average individual performance of the group's members."[34] Reasoning, in many contexts—such as when reasoning alone or reasoning in homogenous groups about the group's beliefs—is prone to bias. But argumentative reasoning, its primary evolutionary purpose, serves us very well. In business I have heard many leaders discredit group problem-solving meetings. But the research is clear: groups usually outperform individuals in problem-solving and innovation. As Mercier and Sperber point out, a camel is a marvel of nature.[35]

I opened the chapter with a business case, my firsthand account of First Horizon at the beginning of the financial crisis. At the time, the company was led by smart and previously successful business executives. Despite their experience and intellectual abilities, they fell victim to multiple cognitive biases and flaws in reasoning. These biases and flaws seemed obvious to people from outside the company and to those looking back through a rearview mirror, as is often true. In the last few years of my career, I found some satisfaction is spotting errors in others' reasoning and my own. Awareness of specific cognitive biases is a big help in spotting them and subsequently improving problem-solving and decision-making. Yet as I embark on a new business venture, I find myself constantly on alert. When it comes to our extraordinary brain and the mind it produces, vigilance must be a constant companion.

[34] Mercier and Sperber, *The Enigma of Reason*, 333.

[35] "A camel is a horse designed by a committee," "too many cooks spoil the broth," and "herding cats" are all phrases used to disparage group decision-making.

MYSIDE AND RELATED BIASES[36]

Myside bias is the tendency to evaluate and analyze evidence and arguments in a biased manner, favoring their own side or position in a debate or discussion. This bias leads people to critically scrutinize opposing arguments more rigorously while accepting or overlooking weakness in their own arguments. Myside bias centers on distal beliefs.

Belief bias occurs when an individual's prior beliefs, attitudes, or opinions influence their evaluation of the logical validity of arguments or the credibility of information. In other words, individuals tend to judge the strength or correctness of an argument based on whether it aligns with their existing beliefs, rather than on its logical merits. Belief bias centers on testable beliefs.

Confirmation bias refers to the tendency of individuals to seek out, interpret, and remember information in a way that confirms their preexisting beliefs, opinions, or hypotheses. It leads to individuals unconsciously filtering information to focus on things that align with what they already believe while ignoring or downplaying contradictory information.

Motivated reasoning refers to the tendency to seek out and interpret information in a manner that supports their existing beliefs and to dismiss information that contradicts them. It shows up when individuals have a vested interest in a particular outcome. A current example is when people discount evidence of climate change because it contradicts with the beliefs of their social group or political ideology.

[36] Sourced and adapted from ChatGPT 3.5.

Stanovich believes there is an important distinction to make with all three biases. "Belief bias occurs when our real-world knowledge interferes with our reasoning performance, whereas myside bias occurs when we search for and interpret evidence in a manner that tends to favor the hypothesis we want to be true."[37] Confirmation bias is more widely known and is more general than the first two. The scientists mentioned in this chapter prefer the first two, as they more specifically describe and explain flaws in human reasoning.

Like myside bias, belief bias has evolutionary roots. While myside bias is understood in a social context, belief bias can be understood in the way our ancestors engaged the natural world. Early humans needed to quickly make sense of their surroundings, detect patterns, and predict potential threats. Having beliefs about the behavior of animals, the properties of plants, the behavior of other humans, and the outcomes of various actions was crucial for decision-making and survival. The inclination to form and hold beliefs conserved cognitive energy and allowed for quick action. This preference for explanations that aligned with existing beliefs worked well for hunter-gatherers. But it is an evolutionary mismatch in our complex modern world of concepts and ideas.

At the risk of overwhelming any small amount of confidence you may still have regarding your ability to reason, I will end this chapter by introducing the concept of the "knowledge illusion." Cognitive scientists Steven Sloman and Philip Fernbach document hundreds of examples of people overestimating their understanding

[37] Stanovich, *The Bias That Divides Us*, 7.

of the world and their own knowledge. They started their research asking people about everyday things such as the toilet. When asked how many people understand how a toilet works, most people raise their hand. But when pushed to explain the basic physics of the toilet, very few are successful. Most of us know very little about the workings of many of the things that make our lives easier.

In a complex world, we all have specialized knowledge in a certain area, and we rely on others for their knowledge of different domains. But we have the illusion that we know more than we do. Sloman and Fernbach exposed this illusion in dozens of simple experiments. "Most people can't tell you how a coffeemaker works, how glue holds paper together, or how the focus works on a camera, let alone something as complex as love. Our point is not that people are ignorant. It's that people are more ignorant than they think they are."[38]

During the debate over health care during President Obama's presidency, I was involved in several community discussions on health care. I facilitated one session and asked a group of about a hundred people if they had a view on Obamacare. Almost everyone raised their hands. I then asked them how confident they were that their view was correct and almost all the same hands went up. At the time, people were forming two camps in the country. One thought it was a monumental achievement. The other, the beginning of the end of civilization! (Well, maybe not quite that bad.) Eventually, I showed the audience a slide with ten questions that were fundamental to understanding how health care operated in the country. (What is the percentage of

[38] Steven Sloman and Philip Fernbach, *The Knowledge Illusion: Why We Never Think Alone* (Riverhead Books, 2017), 8.

health care paid for by the federal government? What is the role of pharmacy benefit managers [PBMs]? How many citizens are uninsured? What percentage of health-care costs are covered by employers?) I asked the audience to take a few minutes to reflect on how many of the questions they could answer with a high degree of confidence.

After a period of silence, I asked the group about their response to the questions and then I walked through the answers. The group seemed to understand that the information was critical to understanding the US health-care system and why that knowledge was important in deciding about Obamacare. What followed was a dialogue that felt less intense than at the start when emotions seemed to be high. At the end of the session, I asked the opening question again about the confidence they had in their view about Obamacare. Only a small percentage of hands went up. My role was not to sell the benefits of Obamacare but to help people understand how the health-care system works. The exercise seemed to open participants' views about health-care policy.

This example shows multiple phenomena at work. People develop strong views about complex subjects based on the views of their tribe (social group belief formation). They develop a belief that their views are the result of conscious effort and that they are highly knowledgeable about the subject based on their personal experience (the knowledge illusion). They see and hear information that is aligned with their view (confirmation bias), which solidifies their beliefs. People are not designed to be primarily rational thinkers. We operate in system one and work under the illusion that we know more than we do. In the physical world of everyday life, we get instantaneous feedback on our behavior. Touch a hot stove and you get burned. Jump into water on a cold day and you shiver. In the social world beliefs are not easily testable. What *is* immediate is negative feedback from a member of your tribe if you disagree with the prevailing view.

As Steven Pinker has pointed out, adopting a false belief because members of our group share that belief is a rational act. Evolution shaped our brains to stay connected to our group and to act quickly in response to threats. Too much information slows decision-making and burns lots of cognitive energy, so we simplify complex information to make it more manageable. But this contributes to the illusion that we understand more than we do. We can boil down Sloman and Fernbach's research into some key points: There is too much for any one individual to know. Knowledge exists in the community, and we are not conscious of the border between what we know and the knowledge that exists in the community. Thus, we think we know more than we do.

Friedrich Hayek based his economic and political philosophy in part on this illusion of human knowledge. "Compared with the totality of knowledge which is continually utilized in the evolution of a dynamic civilization, the difference between the knowledge that the wisest and that which the most ignorant individual can deliberately employ is comparatively insignificant."[39]

Hayek was arguing in favor of free markets and against central planning and socialism because of its inevitable limits to individual freedom. He preaches humility to the political class. That same quality is essential for us to avoid the knowledge illusion.

....

[39] Friedrich Hayek, *The Constitution of Liberty* (University of Chicago Press, 1960).

Ideas and Applications

- Awareness of cognitive biases is the best inoculation against succumbing to them. The first cognitive bias I learned was the halo effect. At the time, I was a recruiter. I immediately recognized that I had favored those who had backgrounds or experiences like my own. After the training, I checked myself when I noticed the halo effect kicking in.

- Remember ice cream thinking. Intuitions come easily to us, so if you find yourself jumping to a conclusion, stop and reflect. Consider the reasons for the conclusions you hold. Test them with others.

- Encourage "devil's advocacy." The concept originates from within the Catholic Church during the canonization of saints. In this context, a person called the devil's advocate was appointed to challenge the evidence and arguments in favor of canonization, ensuring a thorough examination was conducted before declaring someone a saint. It means you actively challenge yourself by taking the opposing point of view or appointing someone to do the same.

- Be open to new evidence. Train your mind to resist quick conclusions.

- Recognize the benefits of group decision-making. Research shows that diverse groups make better decisions, so enlist people with diverse backgrounds and viewpoints. Myside bias evolved to enable us to generate arguments in our favor in a conversation or debate. The coming together of conflicting ideas and beliefs often results in integration and/or adaptation, which can lead to better ideas than an individual thinking alone.

- Be humble. Remember Stanovich's research, which shows that intellect does not attenuate myside bias and, in some cases, actually strengthens it. Respect the experience, knowledge, and views of everyone. I have often been surprised by the great ideas that came from someone I least expected to contribute.
- Be even more humble. Remember that we think we know more than we do and much of what we think we know is wrong. "We experience genuine pleasure (in the form of a rush of dopamine) when processing information that supports our beliefs. Weirdly, it feels good to stick to our guns, even if we are wrong."[40]

[40] Elizabeth Kolbert, "Why Facts Don't Change Our Minds," *New Yorker*, February 27, 2017, a review of Sara Gorman and Jack Gorman, *Denying to the Grave: Why We Ignore the Facts That Will Save Us* (Oxford University Press, 2016).

chapter 12

Personality: Turtles Can't Fly

There are three things extremely hard,
Steel, a Diamond, and to know one's self.

—Benjamin Franklin

Not My Style

I was excited as I entered the training room. The session was my first as a member of Mellon's management training program and the topic was something like "getting to know you." I was somewhat of an anomaly as the only internal candidate to be admitted to the prestigious program. Most of the trainees were nonemployees recruited from top schools. Most had degrees in accounting, finance, economics, or business. I had been working at the bank for five years in several entry-level roles. I was a political science major. Some of the topics to be covered in the program, such as accounting and finance, concerned me because I had no formal training in the subjects. But I imagined I could handle this first session just fine.

As I entered the room, I noticed the floor was marked by masking tape to create four squares. After a brief welcome, the overly enthusiastic facilitator introduced the concept of social styles. He proclaimed that all of us have a predominate style and that each of us would discover ours in the session. After completing a brief survey that asked us to make a choice between sets of adjectives, we tabulated our scores and, voila, I learned

I was an "expressive," an outgoing, relationship-oriented, big-picture type. That sounded about right. The facilitator then asked us to gather inside the four boxes, so I soon found myself in the company of five other Expressives. It didn't take long for us to distinguish ourselves—true to type, we were the loudest group in the room.

We were then asked to work together as a group to come up with a consensus list of positive adjectives to describe us. The list flowed out of our mouths fast and furious, causing the scribe to ask us to slow down. We completed our list first: positive, enthusiastic, persuasive, fast-paced . . . We heard the Drivers debating intensely next to us. The Amiables and Analyticals took longer, and we learned why when the facilitator debriefed the session. The Amiables took a few minutes to get to know one another while the Analyticals carefully parsed each suggestion for their list. The debrief was lively and engaging with lots of laughter. Looking back, a little us-them dynamic had emerged. Just giving our groups labels created a minimal group dynamic. Then came the most insightful part of the session, the list of weaknesses of each style.

This part of the exercise took longer, and we had a more difficult time coming up with the list. One member of the group suggested he didn't like digging into the details of a project. After a brief discussion, we agreed we were more "big picture." That positive juxtaposition seemed to ease the pain of admitting a weakness. The facilitator pressed us on time and suggested we use the word *sometimes* before each adjective. That suggestion worked and we quickly agreed to add impulsive, impatient, and unorganized to the list. I agreed with the first two, but thought the last one was off the mark for me. The conversation on weaknesses, like the overall session, was incredibly enlightening. I was often impatient, and I did get myself in trouble on projects by not paying sufficient attention to details. Social styles training contributed to my self-awareness and was an accelerator in my long journey to better understand human behavior.

The social styles model was developed by two industrial psychologists, David Merrill and Roger Reid, in the 1960s. Using factor analysis,[1] Merrill and Reid were able to identify two scales that could be used to measure personality, assertiveness, and responsiveness.

By plotting these two dimensions on a two-by-two matrix, a model is created of four archetypal personality types that all people fall into as shown below.

Figure 6:

SOCIAL STYLES MODEL

RESPONSIVENESS: the measure of how outwardly emotional we appear to be.
ASSERTIVENESS: the measure of how outwardly we try to influence others.

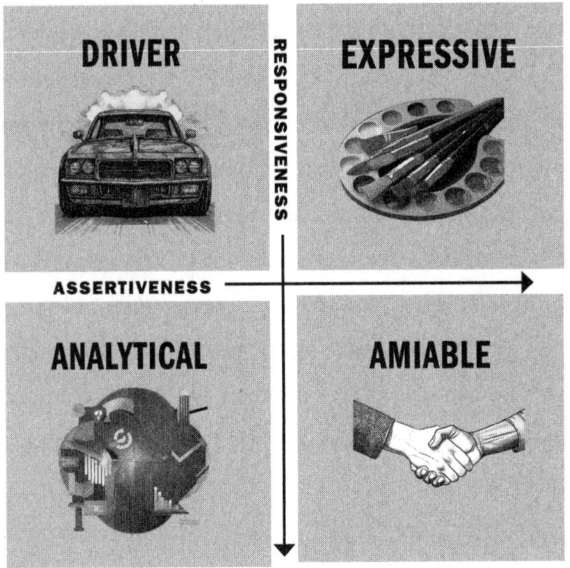

[1] Factor analysis is a statistical technique in the field of data analysis that uncovers patterns and relationships within a set of variables. The technique was also used by psychologists in the development of trait theory. Using the power of computers, psychologists were able to identify correlations between descriptive words and then organize those words into clusters called domains. The Big Five (to be discussed later in the chapter) were developed using factor analysis.

The model proved to be an insightful tool for self-awareness and even more so for understanding others. Each style has a different way of engaging with others, making decisions, and using time. The model's authors stress that no style is better than the others and that success in dealing with others comes by accepting and adjusting to differences. The latter is called versatility, the act of moderating one's behavior to make the other person feel more comfortable by aligning it to that person's behavioral preferences.

I enjoyed and was fascinated by the social styles training. I didn't know it at the time, but the session was the start of a lifelong study of personality and human behavior. I eventually became certified as a social styles trainer and was later certified in or developed in-depth knowledge of many personality typologies, including MBTI, Enneagram, DISC, Hogan Personality Inventory, Predictive Index, and several others. My study of personality and typologies raised my own level of self-awareness and helped me appreciate the many ways people interpret and respond in the social world. As a facilitator of personality training, I saw how teaching people styles seemed to improve teamwork as team members learned to appreciate differences and develop some versatility in engaging with others.

But I also learned there was a dark side to personality testing and teaching personality styles. In every session, I cautioned participants not to put people in boxes. I tried to emphasize that the types were useful tools for provoking questions, not for defining people in rigid ways. Unfortunately, all too often teaching personality types reinforced extant perceptions. As an example, after leading one of my new leadership teams through a personality style training session, one of my team members met with me to suggest that another team member be fired from the team. I knew the two did not have a great relationship and I had hoped our session would encourage them to see the strengths of each other. Instead, my visitor focused on and recited all the negative aspects of her colleague's type. I had hoped she would see the value her colleague brought with her thoughtful, cautious, analytical style. All she could see was her coworker being indecisive, inflexible, and lacking a sense of urgency.

Personality testing in workplaces is now ubiquitous and has become a $2 billion industry. In a recent book, psychologist Benjamin Hardy echoed the thoughts of many in his field—that personality tests are about as scientific as horoscopes.[2] Scientists use two concepts to measure something. Validity refers to the accuracy of a measure, whether it reflects the reality of the phenomenon you are studying. Reliability refers to the consistency of a measure over time. A reliable test, for example, will give the same result later and under different circumstances. Many well-known personality tests lack both validity and reliability.[3] The Myers-Briggs Type Indicator (MBTI) comes under the harshest criticism by scientists. MBTI, which has been taken by over fifty million people, was developed by a mother and daughter in 1943 and was first published in 1962. Neither Katharine Briggs nor her daughter, Isabel Myers, were psychologists, nor were they trained in assessment methodologies. MBTI, while hugely successful, has been called junk science and criticized for "creating the illusion of expertise about psychology."[4]

The second problem with personality testing, and perhaps

---

[2] Benjamin Hardy, *Personality Isn't Permanent: Break Free from Self-Limiting Beliefs and Rewrite Your Story* (Penguin Publishing Group, 2020).

[3] A test that lacks validity and reliability is not useful for making predictions or drawing conclusions.

[4] Benjamin Hardy, "Two Reasons Personality Tests like Myers-Briggs Could Be Harmful," *Psychology Today*, April 6, 2020.

more significant, is how people interpret and use personality tests, as in my example. Personality typologies categorize individuals and oversimplify the complexity of human personality. This leads to stereotyping and an assumption that an individual with a particular type will behave or perform in a certain way. Stereotyping, particularly by a leader, can lead to poor decision-making. I once challenged a manager who did not want to promote one of her employees to a leadership role because of his type. Her conclusion was based on her reading of the descriptive overview of the employee's type, which described the type as tending toward introversion. The manager was a high extrovert and believed that all good leaders were more like her. I helped her overcome her bias by listing several admired leaders in the company who also tended lower on the extroversion scale. Sometime later, that manager thanked me for pushing back on her first decision. Her employee turned out to be a soft-spoken but highly effective leader.

So where did I land on personality testing and personality typologies? I have participated in and led hundreds of teambuilding sessions during which I used the assessments I've mentioned. The sessions were engaging and entertaining. People find the subject of personality and human behavior fascinating and interesting. There are almost always moments of insight as participants reflect on who they are and how they see the world. The sessions are also valuable for discussing the power of diversity in teams. There is solid research that shows that diverse teams outperform less diverse teams in many situations. Properly facilitated, these sessions break down barriers and allow participants to be open about their strengths and weaknesses. But like many tools, personality testing should come with a warning label, which might look something like the following:

Personality typologies can provide useful insight into employees' minds, behaviors, and preferences. They can provide a quick and easy way to initiate a conversation about the team and its strengths and weaknesses. For individuals, identifying our type can improve our self-awareness by giving us insight into how others might experience us. A type is most useful not as an exact description of who we are but as a tool for providing us with the right questions to ask about ourselves.

Be careful not to label people based on their predominate type. Human behavior is highly contextual, and it is difficult to predict how a person will behave in situations based on their type.

Remember there is no good or bad type. Use another's type to frame questions rather than come to a conclusion about his or her unique strengths and preferences.

Don't use an individual's type as a sole or primary criterion in a high-stakes decision such as promotion or fitness for a role.[5]

Finally, see personality testing as an exercise, an icebreaker rather than a scientific tool that provides profound or hidden information. Remember, the results come from self-reported questionnaires to create a framework for conversation and discovery.

[5] Many well-known personality assessments are not predictive of job performance or success in a specific role. Industrial psychologists have developed assessments of cognitive ability, personality, emotional intelligence, and other qualities that are both scientifically valid and reliable. *Valid* means that the assessment accurately measures what it claims to measure. *Reliable* means the assessment consistently produces the same results under consistent conditions and over time.

I recognize that my warning label may look like the ones you see on the bottom of a pharmaceutical advertisement. Personality testing won't give participants a headache, upset stomach, backache, sudden loss of hearing, or the runs. But a discussion about the reality of personality testing will go a long way in avoiding or minimizing the risks of misunderstanding and misuse.[6]

Diversity of Personalities

In this book I have made the case that there is a universal human nature, that all of us have characteristics, behaviors, and tendencies that are the result of evolution. Natural selection shaped our brains as it did our bodies, to survive and pass on our genes to the next generation. Most of that selection occurred during our existence as hunter-gatherers. Our brain's negative bias, social nature, need for predictability, attention to status, fairness, and so on were selected because of their adaptive advantages. Yet in this chapter I have described human beings as having unique types, behaviors, and preferences that can be categorized and show a wide variability in our nature. How do we explain the paradox of a universal human nature yet a wide diversity of personalities? Why didn't natural selection weed out differences so that there was only one type, the one best at adapting to our ancestral environment? Or did diversity have an adaptive advantage?

Before proposing some answers to this question, we should

[6] There are psychometric assessments, developed by trained industrial psychologists, that have been proven to be valid and reliable for promotion and hiring decisions. These assessments have been developed under the US Equal Employment Opportunity Commission's Employment Tests and Selection Procedures. Some are assessments of cognitive ability, but many include personality dimensions.

review how most psychologists think about personality. The word *personality* stems from the Latin *persona*, which referred to the masks worn by actors in early plays.[7] Think of the iconic tragedy and comedy masks that are found at theatres. The masks denote the temperament of the character. Today the term *personality* refers to the combination of characteristics or qualities that defines a person's distinctive character. The most significant aspects of personality are one's psychological traits—patterns of thoughts, feelings, and behaviors in response to circumstances. Measuring traits is how personality typologies are developed. As pointed out, personality typing can be a useful shortcut to gaining insight about ourselves and others, but they oversimplify, lack empirical rigor, and are thus difficult for scientists to validate.

Interest in personality temperaments has been around since the early Greeks. Hippocrates, the ancient physician best known for his oath, believed that a person's physical and mental health were influenced by the balance of bodily fluids known as humors. These humors were associated with specific temperaments. He identified four:

- Sanguine, associated with an excess of blood. People with a sanguine temperament were believed to be cheerful and warm.
- Choleric, associated with an excess of yellow bile. People with a choleric temperament were believed to be assertive and quick-tempered.
- Melancholic, associated with an excess of black bile. People with a melancholic temperament were seen as introspective, analytical, and thoughtful yet prone to moodiness.

[7] Pierce Howard, *The Owner's Manual for the Brain: Everyday Applications from Mind-Brain Research* (Bard Press, 2006), 736.

- Phlegmatic, associated with an excess of phlegm. People with a phlegmatic temperament were believed to be calm, patient, and easygoing.

Hippocrates was highly influential for his early expression of medical ethics. His theory of humors missed the mark, but his description of temperaments was insightful. Notice how it aligns well with the social styles expressive, driver, analytical, and amiable. His use of terms for bodily fluids survives to this day in multiple languages. In English, *sanguine* means optimistic or positive, *choleric* means bad tempered or irritable, *melancholic* means feeling pensive or sad, and *phlegmatic* means having a calm disposition.

Another ancient personality typology is the Enneagram. While its origins are somewhat obscure, it may have roots in early Islamic religious practice. *Ennea* comes from the Greek word for nine, and the Enneagram model contains nine personality types. The typology gained popularity in the US in the 1970s and has a wide following of devoted believers. I was first exposed to the typology in another early leadership development program at Mellon Bank. The training was fascinating, and I experienced a moment of insight about my personality that was helpful in accelerating my development as a leader. I read deeply on the typology and began using it in leadership training and team building. Many class participants had their own moments of insight that reinforced its value in developing self-awareness. Over time I saw that the Enneagram was not very helpful in predicting behavior. While it can be a helpful tool for personal development and team building, I cautioned learners to be careful about labeling people and never to use it to make important decisions. Like the typologies mentioned earlier, the blurred lines between types make the typology difficult to use in scientific studies. There is also weakness in the various instruments used to identify type in both validity and reliability.

A more scientifically accepted way to describe personality was set in motion by Harvard psychologist Gordon Allport in the 1930s. Allport believed that something as complex as personality had to be broken down into component parts. This led him to focus on traits: the enduring pattern of thoughts, feelings, and behaviors as defined in this section. Allport faced a huge hurdle in boiling personality down into a set of meaningful and measurable traits. He and his colleagues started by making a list of words about personality from *Webster's Unabridged Dictionary*. Once the list was complete, it totaled an astonishing 17,953 entries. After a thorough review of the list to eliminate ambiguous words or psychological states (rather than enduring dispositions), they were able to narrow the list to 4,500. This was still too many to build a useful model of personality, so Allport threw out a challenge to the scientific community: find the synonym clusters that would build the desired model. Over the next forty years, many tried, but success finally came with the availability of personal computers and the factor analysis programs designed to calculate the massive number correlational relationships. By the early 1980s the results were finally in.

Personality traits can be boiled down to just five large domains. Psychologist Lewis Goldberg, a well-known personality researcher, named them the Big Five. The Big Five—also known in academic circles as the five-factor model (FFM) of personality—has become widely accepted as a comprehensive framework for understanding the dimensions of human personality. Each dimension or cluster has been given a descriptive name, and most readers will recognize a few of them. They are as follows (many use the acronyms OCEAN or CANOE for quicker recall of the five traits):

- **O**penness to Experience (sometimes just Openness): the tendency to explore new ideas and experiences. People high in openness to experience tend to be curious, imaginative, and open-minded, and enjoy novelty and variety.
- **C**onscientiousness: the tendency to control impulses and to tenaciously pursue goals. People high in conscientiousness are organized, reliable, disciplined, and responsible.
- **E**xtraversion: the tendency to actively reach out to others. People high in extraversion are stimulated by the social world, like to seek out new experiences, often take charge, and tend to experience positive emotions.
- **A**greeableness: the tendency to be altruistic, cooperative, and good-natured. People high in agreeableness are generally warm, empathetic, and considerate. They value harmony and are willing to compromise.

- **N**euroticism (More recently psychologists have used the label Emotional Stability as a more positive framing of the neuroticism continuum): the tendency to have negative feelings, particularly in reaction to perceived social threats. People high in neuroticism are anxious, have more mood swings, and more frequently experience negative emotions such as anger or sadness.[8]

....

[8] Samuel Barondes, *Making Sense of People: Decoding the Mysteries of Personality* (Pearson Education, 2012).

Each of the five factors framework is a continuum rather than a type.

A person is not simply assigned to the category of, for example, extravert or introvert, but rather is given a score on this dimension. Each dimension is orthogonal to the others, which means that the score on one factor is not correlated with the score on any other factor when sampled across many individuals. Therefore, a person's extraversion score cannot be used to predict his or her score on any of the other factors.[9]

The most important thing to keep in mind is that scoring shouldn't be evaluated as positive or negative. In other words, someone high in neuroticism may seem to have a generally negative disposition, and one could think of that as less desirable. But a team led by a manager high in openness and extraversion may avoid running off a metaphorical cliff if they wisely take the advice of a more cautious team member who happens to be high in neuroticism. The Big Five is best seen as a descriptive model of human behavior that can be helpful in predicting how others will think, act, and feel. Unlike personality types, the Big Five model is considered highly reliable and valid.

One of the more fascinating findings since the Big Five was identified is that all five traits show high levels of heritability. Research on the personalities of twins, both those raised together and apart, and on adopted individuals show heritability coefficients between 0.3 and 0.5.[10] "This means that between 30 and 50

....

[9] Workman and Reader, *Evolutionary Psychology*, 358.

[10] The study of twins, particularly twins raised apart, has contributed significant data and insight into the nature vs. nurture debate. The most extensive twin studies, the Minnesota Study of Twins Raised Apart (MISTRA), began in the 1970s. Among the most fascinating findings of MISTRA were the details on how personality traits, quirks, and tendencies of twins separated at birth and raised apart were nonetheless shared by the twins, thus proving the role of heredity.

percent of the variation among people in personality is accounted for by genetic differences between them. This therefore means that between 50 and 70 percent of the variation is down to non-genetic factors."[11] The high heritability of personality suggests the role of natural selection. Theories that explain universal human traits, such as those detailed in this book, have been developed and supported by many evolutionary psychologists. The explanation for personality differences is still the subject of much debate, but there is general agreement that personality differences have an adaptive value.

One widely accepted explanation is that variation is an adaptive strategy because individuals with different traits can take advantage of niches not filled by other members of the group. For example, thinking of the modern-day example I've described, a group of all sensation-seeking, high-introvert hunter-gatherers may push a group to explore dangerous territory. This can lead to group success as new places of safety or sources of food advance the interests of the group. But if the group is all sensation thinking and there are too many dangerous adventures, the group could walk off a genetic cliff. A group of safety-seeking, high-neurotic hunter-gatherers might be able to urge caution and slow the group down. Too many of the first are not so good for surviving—but too many of the latter, if left to their own devices, may never find new sources of food or secure places to live. I have mentioned multiple times how groups often perform better than individuals. The reason is diversity, which seems to have aided the survival of our ancient ancestors.

[11] Workman and Reader, *Evolutionary Psychology*, 359.

Parental Investment

Another widely accepted theory of evolutionary scientists is called parental investment theory. It explains differences in personality between males and females. Parental investment refers to the time, energy, and resources that a parent invests in raising and nurturing their offspring. For hunter-gatherer women, this investment was much more significant than men, as it involved long gestation, lactation, protection, feeding, teaching, and emotional support. While hunter-gatherer males contributed much more to child-raising than did their ape cousins, the differences between male and female investment were significant. Parental investment theory provides a useful framework to explain population-wide personality differences between men and women that still hold true today. Multiple studies and meta-analyses have shown that women tend to score higher in neuroticism, conscientiousness, and agreeableness than men. There does not appear to be a significant difference between men and women in extraversion or openness to experience. Men score higher on aggression and risk-taking, which are subsets of the Big Five, while women score higher in empathy.

Parental investment theory was a source of great controversy when it was first presented. It raised objections as it seemed to indicate that some behaviors were biologically determined and excluded environmental and cultural factors. Some critics thought the theory could be used to justify gender inequalities or rationalize gender discrimination. One important point to make is that the differences in the Big Five noted here are averages across wide populations. Within the general population, there are males who are highly empathic listeners and women who are high risk takers.

It is incorrect to say that men are taller than women. It is correct to say that *on average* men are taller than women. The same holds true for measuring personality traits. It is important to see these trait differences as tendencies in the same way we have described many of the universal human traits in this book.

Another reason different personality traits exist in a population may be due to what evolutionary biologists call sexual selection. First proposed by Charles Darwin in 1871, it filled a gap in explaining some traits that didn't seem to make sense using the framework of natural selection. For example, Darwin couldn't understand why peacocks had extravagant tail feathers. Natural selection couldn't explain why so much energy was expended on tails that did not seem to provide an evolutionary advantage. Sexual selection was the answer. Some traits evolve because they provide advantages in attracting or competing for mates. Sexual selection explains the intricate songs of male songbirds and may explain blond hair in humans. Blond hair is the result of a genetic mutation in early northern European populations. It became an advantage when women outnumbered males and heads were covered due to the cold. Women with blonde hair stood out and were thus able to attract male suiters. Their success led to the gene being passed on—an example of sexual selection. Sexual selection also explains personality trait differences, as some women may be attracted to men who are bold, confident, and high in extraversion. These traits may be markers for status. In hundreds of studies and surveys, women (on average) prefer men who are high in status.[12]

That's a lot of focus on personality traits. Some psychologists

[12] For a fascinating discussion of differences in sexual selection see chapter 3 of Stewart-Williams, *The Ape That Understood the Universe.*

see a focus on traits as overly reductionist and value a more complex view of personality. There are three additional elements that are worthy of discussion as we try to understand and influence others.

Self-Esteem

The first is self-esteem, which is defined as the extent to which an individual likes, values, and accepts themself. Studies show that people with high self-esteem tend to live happier and healthier lives, cope better with stress, and are more likely to persist at difficult tasks.[13] People with low self-esteem experience more negative emotions. One interesting study showed that people with low self-esteem perceived rejection in ambiguous feedback from others. Self-esteem seems to arise primarily from being accepted and valued by significant others. Relative comparison is also important in establishing and building self-esteem. Think back to the chapter on status. We are wired to pay attention to status, but a preoccupation with status can undermine feelings of self-esteem. Think of the dejected look of the silver medal winner at the Olympics. Second best *in the world*, but not good enough. Recent studies on the impact of social media show that significant negative emotions result from comparisons to the perceived better lives of others, even though a post shows only a sliver of a poster's real life.

Self-esteem may have evolutionary roots. As we have seen, belonging to a group is adaptive. Being able to maintain good relations with others helped our ancestors to survive and pass on their genes. Evolutionary psychologists believe self-esteem may be

....

[13] Daniel Schacter et. al., *Psychology*, 5th ed. (Worth Publishers, 2020), 492.

a sort of "sociometer," an "inner gauge of how much a person feels included by others at any given moment."[14] High self-esteem indicates that we are being accepted by our others. Low self-esteem, like loneliness, triggers an alarm in our brain that something is not right and needs to be corrected. The alarm is the negative emotions we feel when our self-esteem is low. Self-esteem plays a large role in what is called the "above-average effect," a cognitive bias that refers to the tendency of individuals to overestimate their own abilities, qualities, and attributes relative to others. This bias has been documented in multiple studies, including among students who overestimate their academic abilities, drivers who overrate their driving skills,[15] and employees who rate themselves as better than their peers in job performance (this last one usually being out of alignment with manager evaluations). People also consistently rate themselves higher on intelligence, attractiveness, and social skills. These "useful delusions" may be adaptive. As Shankar Vedantam points out, these delusions help us stay in love, sustain relationships, and even live longer.[16] People who do not engage in these delusions to boost their self-esteem tend to be more at risk for depression, anxiety, and other related health problems.

In my career in human resources, I ran into the related phenomenon of "self-serving bias" often. Self-serving bias refers to the tendency for people to take credit for their successes but downplay responsibility for their failures. On the many occasions when I

---

[14] Schacter, *Psychology*, 493.

[15] The AAA released a study that showed that eight in ten men think they are above-average drivers, yet traffic safety data show that 90 percent of accidents are caused by human error.

[16] Shankar Vedantam, *Useful Delusions: The Power and Paradox of the Self-Deceiving Brain*, (W. W. Norton & Company, 2021).

met with an employee to confront them with performance or behavioral problems, it was extremely rare for the employee to acknowledge ownership and accountability, even as I presented convincing evidence that the issue rested with them and them alone. Many employees blamed the manager, their colleagues, or the difficulty of the job. All of these are often real causes of job performance issues, but in the cases I am referencing, these had already been ruled out. Initially, I approached these employees with a matter-of-fact attitude. Later, I realized that through questioning I could trigger self-reflection and, in some cases, get the employee to acknowledge their role in the problem. In any event, I tried to honor the person and treat them with dignity and respect while keeping the conversation on the problem. Despite my best efforts, I am sure my face is front and center on a few dart boards!

One extreme form of positive self-esteem is a trait called narcissism. Narcissists have a grandiose view of themselves and tend to seek the admiration of others while also (at times) exploiting them. Because of their high levels of self-confidence and social skills, narcissists are often found in leadership roles in large organizations. Senior leaders often misjudge confidence for competence. This bias toward confidence also tends to reinforce gender bias since "the rate of narcissism is almost 40 percent higher in men than in women."[17] Various studies show the rate of narcissism in the general population is about 1 percent, but among CEOs, largely men, it is 5 percent.[18] In one meta-analysis of trait differences that shows very small or no differences between men and women, narcissism is one of the few

[17] Tomas Chamorro-Premuzic, *Why Do So Many Incompetent Men Become Leaders? (And How to Fix It)* (Harvard Business Review Press, 2019), 42.

[18] Chamorro-Premuzic, *Why Do So Many Incompetent Men Become Leaders?*, 42.

traits that has a significantly higher representation in men. While they can be successful in some individual contributor roles, narcissists will wreak havoc on the culture of a company in leadership roles. Spotting them is critical when deciding on leadership roles, but be aware—they are often great at interviewing. One of the worst hires I ever made was an executive who turned out to be extremely narcissistic. I asked a half dozen leaders in the company to participate in the interview process, but we all seemed to miss her narcissism. Research on narcissists shows they can be charming and convincing in an interview. It only took a few months for all of us to realize our mistake. Hate is a strong word, but it is one I heard a lot about our new team member from her peers.

Self-Awareness

Self-awareness is the second of the three additional parts of personality that are important for those wanting to influence others. Self-awareness refers to the "ability to reflect on, think about, and know things about ourselves, including how we remember, perceive, decide, think and feel."[19] Stephen Fleming is a cognitive neuroscientist who has devoted his academic life to the science of self-awareness, better known to psychologists as metacognition. The term comes from the Greek *meta* meaning after or beyond and is thus an apt name for this uniquely human trait. Fleming describes metacognition on two levels. Implicit metacognition is the self-monitoring that proceeds automatically in the brain, keeping all that is built in and learned moving toward what we intend. "Explicit metacognition refers to

---

[19] Stephen Fleming, *Know Thyself: The Science of Self-Awareness* (Basic Books, 2021), 2.

those aspects of metacognition of which we are consciously aware."[20] The neuroscientist compares these two mechanisms to the interaction between the pilots and autopilot of a modern airliner.

> The aircraft has an electronic "brain" in the form of its autopilot, which provides fine-grain self-monitoring of the plane's altitude, speed, and so on. The pilots, in turn, perceive and monitor the workings of the plane's autopilot, and such monitoring is governed by the workings of their (biological) brains. The interaction between the pilot and autopilot is a rudimentary form of "aircraft awareness"—the pilots are tasked with being aware of what the plane's autopilot is doing and intervening when necessary.[21]

The software we have wired into our brains by natural selection is our autopilot. Our metacognition is the equivalent of the pilot.

Think about negative bias (the autopilot) as we discussed in an earlier chapter. You receive the call from the boss's office and an alarm goes off in your head. Your metacognition system—self-awareness (the pilot)—recognizes the alarm as negative bias (again the autopilot that helped our hunter-gatherer ancestors survive and pass on their genes), and your labeling of the negative bias removes it from nonconsciousness to consciousness. You are now able to use the power of rational thought to turn down the alarm and think about the reasons why the boss might want to see you. Perhaps he just

[20] Fleming, *Know Thyself*, 52.

[21] Fleming, *Know Thyself*, 53.

needs an update on your most recent project. Our metacognition system allows us to recognize and tune into our emotions, enabling self-awareness. Instead of fretting about the meeting, you might call the office to learn the topic of the meeting so that you can be better prepared; the key point is that you have been "thinking about your thinking," which is another way of describing metacognition.

Fleming believes that there is a strong link between the brain systems that help us with mindreading—the ability to infer or predict the thoughts, feelings, and intentions of others—and metacognition. Evolution equipped us with mindreading, as covered earlier, to enhance our ability to cooperate with others. His research shows that self-awareness and mindreading run off the same neuro systems in the brain. Mindreading accelerated our ability to cooperate, and it is easy to see how self-awareness played a similar role. Self-awareness allows us to reflect on our thinking and behavior. If the latter results in a negative impact on someone, we are likely to receive instant feedback. The feedback gives us the opportunity to adjust or correct our behavior. I once gave a talk that started ten minutes late. I felt pressure to get all my points in, so I talked very fast. At one point I could see tension on the faces of my listeners, and I realized I needed to slow down. By paying attention to my audience and not just driving through the talk, I was able to adjust. Examples like this play out repeatedly in our social life.

Daniel Goleman is a renowned psychologist and author best known for his significant contribution to the field of emotional intelligence. Goleman describes self-awareness as foundational to having strong emotional intelligence (EQ), which he argues is more important for success in life than general intelligence (IQ). Goleman describes self-awareness as being aware of our moods, thoughts about our moods, the impact of those moods on others, and the ability to adjust.[22] The latter is key to maintaining our ability to work well with others. Goleman and other researchers found that self-awareness is a critical trait of effective leaders. Almost all leadership training now starts with building self-awareness. Personality assessments and 360-degree feedback surveys are primary tools in leadership development. I have personally benefited from the feedback provided by these tools, and in my role as a facilitator of leadership training I have seen others grow in their ability. I have also seen many leaders who never seem to make progress in either their self-awareness or their ability to lead others effectively. I have found myself frustrated and perplexed by the wide variability of results in our leadership training. After reading Stephen Fleming's research, I think I better understand the gap.

Fleming shows that self-awareness is traitlike. As pointed out above, traits have a strong genetic influence. As he writes, "a genetic starter kit may enable the implicit self-monitoring that is in place early in life."[23] Then our parents finish the job. I appreciate how my son and daughter-in-law teach my grandson, Robbie, to label his emotions, rather than just yell "you stop it or else," as many parents and grandparents of my generation did when a child had a meltdown. Don't mistake this for not holding Robbie accountable for the behaviors that sometimes result from his emotions. As an example, Robbie was once upset when he lost a game of UNO. He threw the cards and started to cry. His mom acknowledged his frustration, talked about why he might feel that way, and then made him

[22] Daniel Goleman, *Emotional Intelligence: Why It Can Matter More Than IQ* (Bantam Books, 1995).

[23] Fleming, *Know Thyself*, 91.

aware that throwing cards was unacceptable and if he did it again, he wouldn't be able to play again. I am confident my son and daughter-in-law's parenting will make him a more self-aware child.

Since metacognition is influenced by genes, some people will have a higher capacity for self-awareness than others. And if their socialization does not foster its development, the capacity will be even lower. I once had a colleague, Bill, who consistently demonstrated a lack of self-awareness. He was loud, talked over people, regularly made inappropriate comments, and seemed oblivious to the nonverbal signals of the rest of the staff. He even ignored direct feedback. When one of our team, pushed to frustration, shouted at him for making sexist comments, he did change his behavior a bit. When she was around, he would start by saying, "I know I shouldn't say this . . ." and then proceed with some unseemly remark. Bill was good at his job as long as we didn't allow him to talk to customers, but he was annoying to be around. After about a year of working with him, I ran into Bill and his father at a community event. After a brief introduction, Bill's dad started talking and he didn't stop for what seemed like an eternity. I kept looking at my watch and mentioned that I needed to head out, but Bill's dad didn't catch the hint. Whether it was more genes or more environment—and in this case it was definitely a combination of the two—Bill and his dad had low wattage in the metacognition part of their brains.

Another challenge with metacognition is that sometimes the system is susceptible to illusions and distortions. When we touch a hot stove, the burning sensation we feel is our brain's way of saying not to do that again. In the social arena, the feedback loops are less direct. "The consequences of illusions about ourselves are less obvious. If we are lacking in self-awareness, we might get quizzical looks at committee meetings"[24] and not know how to interpret them. Unlike a burn, which is clear about its message, quizzical looks require an additional level of interpretation. This additional step is subject to misinterpretation. Think of Bill, who may have thought the looks of our team were encouraging him to keep telling his story while the listeners were thinking, *Please stop.* As we learned earlier in the book, our brains receive data from the outside world, and we use that data to make predictions. Our brain is regularly filling in blanks and making predictions and inferences to make sense of our reality. Misperceptions, errors, and illusions are a regular part of our sensory processing; the same is true for our metacognitive system. This can lead to a failure of self-awareness.

Early in my career as a leader, I was asked by one of my employees for advice on a work problem. I shared my thoughts, and she responded that my comments were helpful. Over the next several months, I gave her unsolicited feedback on multiple occasions. I imagine I was expecting the positive feedback I heard the first time. She was always polite and thanked me. I inferred that she valued my advice. But that was not the case. Not long after one unsolicited advice-giving moment, she came to see me. She asked if I trusted her, and I was surprised by the question. In the conversation that followed I learned that my advice-giving sessions were demoralizing. As you recall from our chapter on status, giving advice can reduce status and create a threat state. My advice-giving did just that, as she didn't see me engaging in the same way with other members of the team. My inference that she wanted and valued my advice led to a misperception and a gap in my

[24] Fleming, *Know Thyself*, 103.

self-awareness. I learned to stop giving advice and to start conversations by asking questions about how things are going, which often leads to a two-way dialogue and insights from both parties, while unsolicited advice-giving often misses the mark.

Metacognition can be misleading for another reason, something psychologists call fluency. When we learn something quickly and easily, our brain oddly increases our confidence that what we have learned is correct. This may have been an adaptive process of our hunter-gatherer ancestors who needed to learn and respond quickly in the physical world. As Daniel Kahneman points out:

> Subjective confidence in a judgement is not a reasoned evaluation of the probability that this judgment is correct. Confidence is a feeling which reflects the coherence of the information and the cognitive ease of processing it. It is wise to take admissions of uncertainty seriously, but declarations of high confidence mainly tell you that an individual has constructed a coherent story in his mind, not necessarily that the story is true.[25]

As we try to make sense of our social world, we put together pieces of information and create a narrative that constructs a world that makes sense to us. Due to confirmation bias we then look for information that supports what we already believe. The same applies to self-awareness. We create an identity and image of ourselves based on incoming data. We then look for information

[25] Fleming, *Know Thyself*, 104.

that supports this self-perception. In the case of self-awareness, we also have protective mechanisms that cause us not to seek out contradictory information. (Negative feedback hurts both emotionally and physically, as we saw in our discussion of social pain.) Self-awareness suffers.

Artificial intelligence improves by correcting mistakes gained through feedback. Learning is an iterative system of processing data, gathering feedback, and refining its internal model. Humans play an oversight role by monitoring, reviewing, and correcting AI errors. Humans learn in similar ways, but the learning process is complicated by some of our evolutionary wiring. Human information processing is subject to multiple biases, many of them explained in this book. These biases, such as self-serving bias and confirmation bias, can block our self-awareness. We are not designed like AI—to constantly process data and correct errors—we are "designed" by natural selection to adapt and survive in a complex social world. To enhance self-awareness, we can benefit from human oversight too. In our case, feedback from family and friends is important in ensuring we have an accurate perception of ourselves.

Unlike AI, our design makes it difficult for us to seek and receive feedback, even from people we trust. Many people report that they dislike performance reviews and other forms of feedback. We fear criticism and dislike judgment. Feedback challenges the illusions we have of ourselves and our abilities. Negative feedback implies the need for change, which can cause stress as we are forced to step out of our comfort zones. Feedback can also be perceived as a threat to our status, our autonomy, and our much-needed predictability. Our emotional reactions tend to be more negative when we receive feedback, and those emotions can cloud our thinking. All this to say, seeking, receiving, and processing feedback is not the same for us as it is for AI. High levels of self-awareness increase our emotional intelligence and make us more successful in navigating our physical and social worlds. But it does not come naturally for many of us. We must overcome our wiring, frame feedback as a positive, and develop our abilities to seek and process it. Carol Dweck refers to this as having a growth mindset, viewing feedback as an opportunity for learning rather than as a threat.[26]

In the best of worlds, feedback is delivered with empathy and with a focus on growth and development. Unfortunately, many people responsible for giving feedback don't do it very well. As an HR executive, I imagined a great organization to be one with a strong learning culture. One where people engaged in regular dialogue about what is working well and what needs improvement both at a system and an individual level. What usually impeded our progress was the lack of leaders with the ability, experience, and training to deliver constructive feedback. At one level it seems like an achievable goal.

The principles of effective feedback are outlined below and are conceptually easy to understand. While some leaders never quite seem to get the hang of it, training on delivering feedback in leadership can provide huge payback in improving the culture of an organization.

[26] Carol Dweck, *Mindset: The New Psychology of Success* (Ballentine Books, 2007). In this book, Dweck makes the point that individuals with a growth mindset believe that abilities can be developed through hard work and resilience.

PRINCIPLES FOR DELIVERING EFFECTIVE FEEDBACK

Be constructive: Avoid criticism or blame and emphasize that the purpose of the feedback is improvement and growth.

Focus on behavior: Feedback on personality isn't helpful since personality isn't easily changeable. Address the specific behavior that needs to change.

Be timely and specific: Avoid generalized feedback and try to deliver the feedback as close to the observed behavior as possible. Use recent examples to bring clarity to the behavior that is at issue.

Engage in a discussion rather than a lecture: Ask for the person's perspective and make sure they play back the message so you can confirm they heard what you intended.

Manage emotions: Stay calm and empathetic. If the recipient becomes highly emotional agree to meet again later and follow up in a timely and supportive manner.

Be balanced: Acknowledge the person's strengths and provide assurance of your belief in a positive outcome.

Resilience

We have covered self-esteem and self-awareness as components of personality in addition to traits. The final component of our trio is resilience. I remember early in my career, after several work setbacks, I turned up my performance by digging more deeply into the role and working even harder. I was thrown into a job I was neither trained nor prepared for, and the early results showed. But I refused to accept failure. Eventually I turned the corner and things started to fall into place. I will never forget a meeting I had with my boss. She complimented me on my progress. She then said that I was "the most resilient person she had ever met." The word *resilient* resonated with me. Later in my adult life, I felt the pain of the loss of my first love to cancer—a brutal battle that took its toll on me and our three sons. I have experienced the loss of a job I loved because of a merger, two open-heart surgeries, a heart transplant, and many other challenges. I have been complimented often on my ability to bounce back from whatever it was that I faced. After my transplant, I began to wonder about the roots of my resiliency. My research and reflection led me to deliver a TED Talk on the subject, "Everything Will Be Alright."[27]

I credit my mom for her role modeling. Mom was the most independent and determined person I have ever met. Mary Louise Coyne, better known to everyone as Mary Lou, ran away from an abusive home at the age of seventeen to marry my father, who had just turned twenty-one. Bud, as she affectionately called him, had served two years in the Navy. They had been a couple since she was thirteen and they corresponded while he was away in the military. Dad left the Navy with few job skills and one unfortunate

[27] John Daniel, "Everything Will Be Alright," TEDx Memphis, February 2, 2019.

habit: alcohol. Alcohol abuse would flare up throughout their marriage. But the young couple was determined to make a go of life together and raise a big family. The babies came quickly, nine in total, one almost every two years. Our early life was tough. We moved often, and Dad had trouble keeping a job until he became a policeman, the first time in over a decade of marriage they had a steady paycheck. Through all the trials and tribulations of battling alcoholism, uneven paychecks, and raising children with an endless stream of needs, I never saw her buckle under pressure. Whatever the challenge, she would face it, figure it out, and keep the family moving forward.

All the Daniel children started working early. As you will recall, I had a paper route at thirteen with over a hundred customers. Through rain, sleet, or snow, like the mailman, my brother Marty and I delivered newspapers. Mom would accept no excuses. If Mom received a call from a customer saying that they had not gotten their newspaper, I'd get that look. And then off I'd go to deliver that paper, no matter how cold or how late. I started working a job on weekends and after school at the age of fifteen. And long hours were no excuse for poor grades. Mom was tough when I went to her with the minor setbacks of teenage life. While all I wanted was a little TLC, her message was consistent: "Life is tough, but you need to pick yourself up and keep it moving."

Until my boss used that label on me, I never thought about resilience as a personal quality—it was just what one does. In my research I learned that resilience is not an innate fixed trait but rather a set of skills and behaviors that one learns over time. It is a key element of personality, as it determines success or failure in navigating life's ups and downs.

Angela Duckworth is a psychologist, author, and speaker known for her research on what she calls grit, a sister quality to resilience. The latter is about bouncing back or adapting positively to adversity and trauma. Grit, as defined by Duckworth, is a combination of passion and perseverance in working toward long-term goals. Her research suggests that grit is a significant predictor of success in multiple domains. In her studies—ranging from cadets who passed the United States Military Academy intensive seven-week training program to spelling bee winners—Duckworth shows that grit, as she defined and measured it, was more important than talent. In her chapter "Effort Counts Twice," she lays out her theory. Effort is not only a contributor to skill but also a contributor to achievement.

> What this theory says is that when you consider two individuals in identical circumstances, what each achieves depends on two things, talent and effort. Talent—how fast we improve skill—absolutely matters. But effort factors into the occasion *twice*, not once. Effort builds skill. At the very same time, effort makes skill productive.[28]

Critics of Duckworth's work suggest that grit is no more than an offshoot of psychological trait conscientiousness, one of the Big Five I've discussed earlier. I will let the academics battle this one out, but in my long career observing and evaluating the qualities and personalities of thousands of people, I see resiliency and grit accompanying each other alongside self-esteem and self-awareness.

....

[28] Angela Duckworth, *GRIT: The Power of Passion and Perseverance* (Scribner, 2016), 42.

The Power of Storytelling

I close this chapter on personality by highlighting the work of psychologist Dan McAdams and the role of storytelling in shaping our personal identity. McAdams believes that a comprehensive understanding of personality includes traits, our experiences (socialization, which provides our values and beliefs), and the stories we tell ourselves. Creating stories is one of the basic functions of our brain. Our ancestors learned through experiences and then converted those experiences into stories. The stories, often told around the campfire, were a way of sharing knowledge. As Samuel Barondes writes, stories are a natural way of "organizing sequences of experiences by inferring cause-and-effect relationships that can help us predict future events. In sizing up people, we use this process to create stories about how they got to be the way they are."[29] Composing, sharing, and listening to stories comes easily to us. It is an adaptation, as it allowed our ancestors to learn and make sense of the world.

Stories are also how we make sense of ourselves. David Brooks, author and *New York Times* columnist, described this phenomenon when writing about Elon Musk: "I believe most of us tell a story about our lives and then come to live within that story. You can't know who you are unless you know how to tell a coherent story about yourself. You can know what to do next only if you know what story you are a part of."

Brooks believes that Musk's extreme ambition and values are a product of his difficult childhood in South Africa. Musk survived by diving into science fiction, games, and comics. He became enamored by the stories of heroes who emerged in his sci-fi fantasy world to

[29] Barondes, *Making Sense of People*, 123.

save doomed people. As an adult, Musk is living out his life attached to this same hero myth. Musk's self-narrative role is that he is a hero building great companies to save the world. It is this narrative that is steering the course of his life.

Most of us create some sort of narrative in the same way as Elon Musk. My TED Talk is a story about my experience as a heart transplant recipient. But it is also a telling of my life narrative. I, too, had a challenging childhood, though certainly less bleak than Musk's. Those challenges forged my grit and resiliency. I survive, I bounce back. It's what Mom did; it's what I do. It's my story. It guides me, defines me. Oprah Winfrey and I share the same birth year, 1954. Oprah was born to a teenage mother and faced poverty, sexual abuse, and a teenage pregnancy. But she also had big plans for herself—to be a successful entertainer—and she was determined not to allow anything to get in her way. Early success in telling stories in church and as a teen and working part-time at a radio station fed her narrative. In her own retelling, she always knew she would be a star. Oprah's story is well known, one of overcoming adversity through talent, hard work, and determination. It is also a story that defines who she is and guides her going forward.

By the way, it doesn't matter if all the details are exactly as they happened. Our stories are as much myth as truth. When I give talks about human behavior and personality, members of my audience are often fascinated by this notion of our personal story and how it creates our unique identity. Their comments usually go something like a recent account with one of my session participants.

> My sister is only eighteen months younger than me. We grew up in the same house, with the same parents. My parents were tough but loving. I have a very positive memory of my childhood and teen years. I made a bunch of dumb decisions as a teen but remember mom and dad being fair and reasonable. But my sister tells a completely different story. In her story we were poor and miserable, and mom and dad were tyrants. She couldn't wait to get out of the house. She did get an apartment with a girlfriend right after high school despite my parents' disapproval. She seems to be doing OK today but her memories are so different than mine.

As I often do, I asked a few follow-up questions to learn more about the lives of her and her sister. My session participant is happily married with two children, a good job, and by her accounting has a nice life. Her sister has struggled through relationships and jobs and is generally not happy with her life. There are no clear answers about how we become who we are; traits and environment play major roles, and so do the stories we create about ourselves and our lives. Stories can motivate us, and they can also become rationalizations for our circumstances.

All stories are made up of memories and interpretations of the reality we experience. We add meaning to them in our own way, and memories are altered to fit our story. Our traits play a huge role in how we interpret events. One sibling could be high in neuroticism and extra sensitive. Critical comments from a parent might cut them deeply while the same comment would roll off the back of a sibling. Our childhood friends and peer groups play a huge role in the development of our story. They play back to us how they see us, and we incorporate that view into our self-narrative. There is research from Judith Rich Harris that shows peers play a more important role in shaping personality development and personal narratives than parents.[30]

Our stories can evolve and change as we navigate through life. Personality traits, on the other hand, like the Big Five, "tend to stabilize in young adulthood and become even more stable by middle age."[31] I learned the truth of this early in my HR career, as time and again I saw managers trying to put square people into jobs that were round holes. Put simply, if someone is high in extraversion, they are unlikely to find satisfaction in a desk job. By the same token, you can't take someone low in extraversion and agreeableness and high in neuroticism and make them great at customer service. I was influenced by the work of Marcus Buckingham, who emphasizes (through many books and talks) the importance of recognizing talents and strengths and matching them to the task or job at hand.[32] The idea of development focused on improving weaknesses is often misguided, as it leads to managers trying to change behavior linked to personality traits.

The good news is that personal growth and development are possible. While traits are stable, we can change ingrained behavior patterns. Clinical psychologists use cognitive behavior therapy (CBT) as a structured process to change unhelpful or problematic

---

[30] Howard, *The Owner's Manual for the Brain*, 103–104.

[31] Barondes, *Making Sense of People*, 145.

[32] Marcus Buckingham is a bestselling author and speaker on strengths, human performance, and work. His first book, *First, Break All the Rules*, debunked several myths about developing people.

behaviors. As an HR leader, I have used some of the principles of CBT in my coaching and mentoring. The process starts with goal setting, then moves through reviewing past behavior patterns and identifying cognitive distortions, then moves to action planning. Leaders should never try to be therapists or attempt any form of psychoanalysis. Coaching should not be a deep dive into the past; it should be primarily focused on the future. The benefit of CBT and similar methods is that they are highly collaborative with an action orientation. The coach's role is to act as a listener, questioner, and guide. CBT should only be used by a trained practitioner, but the principles can be successfully applied by leaders in many situations. One well-known and popular coaching model using similar principles is called Co-Active Coaching.[33]

In one case, a talented young professional at our company wanted to be more comfortable and engaged at our company's many social events. She was envious of some of her trainee peers who seemed natural at conversation while she was held back by her shyness. I let her know that I felt awkward at social events early in my career until I learned about the conversation stack[34] in a Dale Carnegie course on improving speaking and human relations. I taught her the method and suggested she set a goal to try it with a few people at the next event. I also spent a few minutes disabusing

[33] Co-Active is the brand of the Co-Active Training Institute, which has licensed a model for training leaders on how to effectively coach others. *Co-Active Coaching* is in its fourth edition.

[34] Stacking is a technique using vivid mental pictures that refer to a concept to be memorized. Our hunter-gatherer brains remember pictures much better than words. The conversation stack includes the following: nameplate, house, work glove, jet, tennis racket, and light bulb. The vivid pictures of each of these items are a way to remember questions one can ask when meeting someone for the first time. What is your name? Where do you live? Where do you work? Have you traveled recently? How do you spend your free time? What do you think about X?

her of the notion that some people are just natural at socializing and that she never would be. While I agreed that some people have a natural inclination, I showed her that socializing is a skill that can be easily learned. I used myself as a successful example. I also shared some success stories of people like her that overcame their own dread and fear of bank social events.

At our next meeting, she reported enthusiastically that her use of the conversation stack, while a bit awkward at first, was a big hit. She talked about the big insight, that the key to good conversation is focusing on the other person and not on herself. After more tries using the questions queued up by the model, it started to feel very natural to her. I ran into her many years later and she told me she still remembers the stack and still uses it regularly. Over forty years after I first learned it, I still find it helpful when I enter a room of new people as well. As you can see in the example, successful coaching and change comes with the principles mentioned above, collaborative goal setting, listening, correcting distortions (if they show up), and action planning with a little encouragement added in.

One of my favorite children's books is titled *Why Can't You Teach a Turtle to Fly?*[35] It's about trying and succeeding at what might seem impossible. It's about the naysayers you meet along the way. It's about trying and failing at first. Sure, turtles can't fly, but the story aligns with my own life story and with my belief that personal change is possible and inspiring. The book cover shows the turtle smiling as he sails upward in a large colorful hot air balloon.

....

[35] Jeffrey Browning, ill. Elisabetta Corraro, *Why Can't You Teach a Turtle to Fly?*, 2016.

Ideas and Applications

- Don't try to change people. Traits have high levels of heritability, become somewhat set in early adulthood, and remain stable throughout a person's life. Success and even happiness come with matching people to the right role.

- Focus and build on strengths. A successful NBA coach would not take a pure three-point shooter who is not a great passer and assign him to be the point guard. I have seen managers push extraverted, creative people into routine jobs and then criticize them for poor results. The failure in this case is not with the employee but with the manager.

- Be careful not to confuse personality traits with learnable skills. In this example, my introverted mentee didn't feel natural in social situations. While many high extraverts take to socializing naturally, it is a learnable skill. The same is true for presentation skills. Some people have natural-born storytelling skills, but everyone can learn to be an effective presenter. Resilience is another quality that can be learned and developed. Some of us have natural gifts that allow us to bounce back, but research has shown that everyone can learn to be more resilient.

- Our personality is largely a product of our traits, but we also create a self-narrative, a story that defines us and drives our lives. Our sense of self is developed through our autobiographical memories and our interpretations of our experiences. Research shows that our memories are flawed and subject to favorable editing. Just as there are cognitive biases that affect information processing and decision-making, there is a large set of documented cognitive biases that tell us constantly that we are right and good. It pays to be reflective about ourselves, to keep our self-esteem in check, and to make sure we are not overestimating our knowledge, skills, and abilities.

- Remember that our metacognitive system is vulnerable. Our beliefs and our views are constructed, as is our confidence in them. As noted in the previous paragraph, our self-awareness is subject to occasional failure. Regular feedback from people we trust will help maintain an accurate picture of self. Openness to new ideas will keep us learning and humble. And knowing about our own biases and breakdowns in self-awareness should help us have a more compassionate stance toward the occasional self-awareness failures and biases we see in others.

chapter 13
Everything Will Be Alright

The experience of awe is about finding your place in the larger scheme of things. It is about quieting the press of self-interest. It is about folding into social collectives. It is about feeling reverential towards participating in some expansive process that unites us all and that ennobles our life's endeavors.

—Dacher Keltner

It was four-thirty in the morning, and I was wide awake. As I sat up in my hospital bed my mood was lifted by the soft glow of the street-lights below and the shadows that danced across the hospital room ceiling. I hadn't slept at all that night as the nursing staff prepared me for surgery. My mind bounced around through thoughts and memories. I reflected on the good and bad of my life like an accountant auditing financial results. The penchant for reflection is traitlike—it has its roots in our genes and some of us do it more than others. I reflect a lot. It can be a strength but also a curse. At that moment it was a blessing. When I summed it all up the result gave me hope. I had learned a lot. I had much to give. I was determined to live and to make the rest of my life meaningful. The opportunities would be abundant; I just had to make it through the day.

At the time, I was living with a left ventricular assist device, better known as the LVAD. The LVAD helps pump blood from the lower chambers of the heart to the rest of the body. It was designed for people with failing hearts, to keep them alive long enough to receive a donor heart. The pump is implanted inside the heart's left ventricle. A tube runs from the pump through the body and connects to a control system and battery that is carried on a belt or strap. Leslie, my wife, was my caregiver, and part of her responsibility was to help clean and rebandage the area where the tube exited my side.

When I first learned that I would need the LVAD to stay alive, I dreaded the thought. The surgery to implant the device was brutal and there were a few moments during recovery when I felt like giving up. But once the pain medications were reduced and my head cleared, my determination returned.

Life with the LVAD proved to be interesting. I quickly adjusted to carrying around my "manbag" with the control system and batteries. It did prove somewhat challenging on my first trip to the airport. The TSA agent insisted that my bag had to be loaded onto the conveyor belt for luggage screening. He relented when I lifted my shirt and showed the thin tube coming through my side. From then on, I carried a card that indicated I needed to go through an individual screening process. The LVAD batteries carried a charge for about ten to twelve hours. In the evening, I placed the batteries in a charging station and attached the wires of the control system to an outlet. Comfortable sleep was a challenge, and as to lovemaking . . . well let's just say cold wires and little machines can dampen a mood but not completely snuff out the spirit of two people in love. Yes, the LVAD was no walk in the park, but I lived life as fully as I could. I returned to work a few months after my surgery, traveled to Disney

World and the Bahamas, and even went bowling as I did every year in support of Junior Achievement.

A few months after having the LVAD installed in November 2014, Leslie and I went on our first date post-surgery to see the live version of *The Lion King* at the local Orpheum Theatre. I was excited about the date and was a bit absentminded when getting ready. After my shower, which involved a long process of wrapping and taping the machine and batteries in waterproof plastic, I dressed myself and loaded the equipment in my bag. Given that we live downtown, only a few minutes from the theatre, I didn't take my backup batteries, which was a regular practice when I went to work. We were enjoying the show when about an hour in I heard a soft beep. Leslie, who had a finely tuned ear when it came to matters of the LVAD, whispered a question. "Did you change your batteries after work?" Oops! In my excitement and rush to get ready I had not replaced the batteries that I had installed at seven that morning. I didn't have to answer; she could see the look on my face.

We never learned what would happen if the batteries completely died. We knew that the control unit had a small amount of backup power, but the beeping sound called for quick action. Luckily, we had found a parking spot right near the front door of the theatre. I did not want Leslie, who had done so much for me over those many months, to miss the play, so I decided to return home on my own. I raced home (the LVAD does not impede driving ability), replaced the drained batteries with the recently charged ones, and drove back to the theatre. The parking spot I left was vacant, so I was able to get back just as intermission was ending. We both loved the show and now have our own story to tell about the harried adventure of the soft beep, drained batteries, and driving way beyond the speed limit.

Prior to having the LVAD installed, I spent a few months in the hospital waiting for a donor heart. I remember hoping and praying for a donor because the thought of the LVAD frightened me. The doctors warned that the surgery would take four or more hours and that recovery would be demanding. The doctors also laid out the risks: internal bleeding, infection, blood clots, device problems, right heart failure, and more. I did have some post-surgery internal bleeding and developed an infection. While the doctors pulled me through, the whole process was exhausting. I remember one of the doctors advising me that a recent recipient had received a new heart only two months after his LVAD surgery. I think he was trying to cheer me up. But all I could think about was not wanting to go through open-heart surgery anytime soon.

As the summer months neared, I began to feel myself again. I adapted to life with the LVAD while also finding it a tremendous nuisance. I was not ready yet, but I was beginning to look forward to living without carrying around a machine to keep me alive. I was also a little more anxious when I learned one of my new LVAD social media support group friends had died of a blood clot. During one of my checkups, I asked one of the transplant center staff when I should pull my 1A status. That refers to a transplant protocol. Heart patients waiting for a donor and doing well on the LVAD are considered lower status. But LVAD patients get a thirty-day window when they can request a move to the highest status. In response to my question, the staff member said it was best to request a status upgrade during long holiday weekends. The sad truth is that young people take risks and die in accidents more frequently on holiday weekends, thus increasing the supply of donors. I was taken aback by the sobering reminder that I would live only if someone else died.

I decided that I would work to get stronger, enjoy the summer, and hope for a donor in the fall. I had lost thirty pounds and a lot of muscle while going through the surgery and recovery, so even after six months, I still felt weak. Work was also part of my calculation. I was back at work full-time and fully engaged even with the LVAD by my side. I had just missed four months of work for the first time in my career. I loved my job, and being an executive is like being an entrepreneur. An executive sets the vision, selects and motivates the team, and facilitates team decision-making. While my CEO was gracious and very supportive, no one can really step in and be a temporary CHRO. I never held any illusion that I was irreplaceable, but I hoped to return to my job after the transplant. I felt a deep pride of ownership over my department and my responsibilities. While I was at the mercy of donor availability, to the extent I had any control I could handle a few months more on the LVAD. I waited to pull the trigger on my thirty-day window.

I will always remember the phone call. Psychologists call those moments flash-bulb memories, vivid, long-lasting events burned into the psyche.

I was having lunch with a colleague from the bank. Anne and I didn't work closely or for very long, but her smiling, supporting face will stay with me forever. I ordered a cheeseburger and fries, a rare order for me. Then I said to Anne that I was going to enjoy that cheeseburger to the fullest. What the heck, my heart was already done for, and I would soon be trading it in for a new one. I might as well enjoy it while I can. Then my phone rang, and I could see it was Baptist Hospital. I answered and it was Amanda with the transplant team.

"Mr. Daniel, we have a heart for you. If you give me your authorization, we can trigger your thirty-day window. You need to gather your things and head to the hospital."

Leslie and I had rehearsed this moment repeatedly. What would be our answer if the donor was in Nashville, where we were also listed? How would we get there within the three-hour window? What if the donor heart was from an older patient or one who smoked? My mind was racing, but Anne was calming company. There would be no cheeseburger that day. My answer to Amanda was yes.

Leslie was away on a trip, and my multiple calls to her went unanswered. She was in an area with bad cell service. Once back at the office, my assistant gathered my colleagues and staff to share the news. Several people offered to drive me home and to the hospital, but I decided I would be fine on my own. Once I gathered my belongings and LVAD supplies at home, I headed for the hospital. It was a trip I had made dozens of times, but I took a few wrong turns and it took forty-five minutes, almost twice as long as usual. I was in a bit of a daze. Worry and excitement are emotions that have a lot in common. They both activate the sympathetic nervous system, which serves us well in fight-or-flight situations, but not when you must make important decisions. Once I arrived at the hospital, the staff took blood samples and ran multiple tests. The results confirmed an almost perfect match.

I learned that the donor had been on mechanical support after suffering a catastrophic brain injury in a motorcycle accident. A breathing machine kept the donor heart provided with oxygen, which allowed the hospital to schedule surgery for early the next morning. There would be no urgent drill, as is often the case with transplantation. The ideal transplant team was arranged, and surgery was scheduled. Meanwhile, multiple colleagues and friends were attempting to contact Leslie. She often tells the story about how she felt bad being away at such an important moment and of her ninety-mile-per-hour, three-hour drive from the Nashville area, loaded with students from the school where she worked. I often think there was more than one miracle that day, as they all made it safely back to Memphis. Since the surgery was scheduled for the morning, Leslie was there to send me off.

Finally, around 5 a.m. I heard the phone ring at the nurse's station and then the words I had been waiting for: "They're ready for you." I hugged Les and my sons and began my journey to the operating room. The ten-minute trip seemed longer. I was in better health than I had been on my previous trip just ten months earlier. Despite the challenges of living with the LVAD, I had done well. I was less anxious—so much so that I didn't need a sedative and my head was clear. More time to think and reflect. One of the ways I kept my spirits up during the long process of recovery from LVAD surgery was dreaming of taking a long bicycle ride in the mountains of Colorado. I had taken such a trip years before and it was one of my favorite memories. I pictured blue skies and felt the feelings of fresh air and what one friend calls being "good tired." That vision got me through some down days, and it came back to me now. I was determined to get through this second open-heart surgery and make that trip again. I felt confident, and I couldn't wait to wake up without the LVAD tethered to my side.

As I rolled into the operating room, I was struck by the scene. Heart transplantation surgery is a team sport. There are usually two surgeons, an anesthesiologist, a perfusionist who runs the heart-lung machine, surgical nurses, and other technicians. My stretcher bed was propped up so I could survey the room. The surgical team were all dressed in blue-and-white surgical clothes. Their faces were covered in masks, and their shoes wrapped in disposable blue bags. The room was filled with TV screens, a vast array of technology, surgical lights, booms, and multiple operating tables. The staff were busy and focused. A thought formed in my head: this must be what it's like when a special forces ops team is preparing for a mission. For a few moments I felt alone amid all the buzz around me. And then one of the operating team members put her hand over my hand. In a calming voice she said, "Hello, Mr. Daniel, everything is going to be alright." Then I felt a cold fluid flow through my veins. My next memory was waking up a day later and seeing the beautiful smile of my loving wife.

On Awe

I have a sense of awe about the whole experience. At times, it feels like I watched someone else go through it, like it was all a movie with someone else as its protagonist. One day the doctors took out the heart I was born with and put in a new one. As I write this several years later, everything did turn out alright. There is not a day that goes by that I don't think about my new heart. The experience changed me in profound ways. Little things that once troubled me trouble me less. I have a deeper appreciation for life. I feel more humble, less important, but even more motivated to do something meaningful with my life. I feel a responsibility to make the extra time I have more meaningful. Leslie, who is a breast cancer survivor, shares some of these same thoughts and emotions. We have dedicated our retirement life to serving our community. We have learned what the research on happiness shows, that a life with meaning and purpose is the key to a joyful and satisfactory one. And even though we are retired, our busy schedule has us cherish our weekends as much as when we were both working.

The Grand Canyon, the Sistine Chapel, the birth of a baby, a towering redwood have all been reported to induce a deep feeling of awe. Dacher Keltner is a professor of psychology who has spent fifteen years on the science of awe and has charted its transformational power. Professor Keltner describes awe as the feeling of being in the presence of something vast that transcends our understanding of the world. He studies how people are impacted by the vastness of Yosemite, a grove of tall eucalyptus trees, and the giant T-Rex replica, all near his Berkeley campus. In a series of experiments, he found that after experiencing awe people were more helpful to a person who had stumbled. His research also showed that people reported feeling less entitled and self-important than other study participants if they had an awe-inspiring experience. While awe rises in the presence of the extraordinary, like natural phenomena and magnificent works of art or culture, people also report feeling awe in basic acts of human skill and virtue.

Early in my career, I worked in a banking office as an assistant manager. One of our staff was an unassuming loan officer. Dave was friendly but quiet and for most of the day he kept his focus on work. His two distinguishing characteristics were his ill-fitting suits and combed-over hair. His appearance made him the victim of covert but rude comments from the rest of the staff, most notably the office manager, who was somewhat of a bully. One day an elderly customer passed out while waiting in the teller line. I looked up from my desk after I heard a loud gasp from the tellers and then I saw Dave jump into action. He laid the customer on his back, checked his pulse, and then began performing CPR. He then shouted for someone to call

911. Soon the ambulance arrived, and after attending to the man the EMTs carted him off on a stretcher. We learned later that the customer had suffered a heart attack and that Dave had saved the man's life. One of the senior executives came to the office a week later and presented Dave with a commendation after a little ceremony. We talked about the incident for months. As for Dave, his reputation was greatly enhanced. I never heard another negative comment about him, and our manager started treating him with new respect and even included him in our weekly management meetings.

Awe-inspiring experiences are emotionally intense and are associated with changes in brain activity. The release of neurochemicals such as dopamine and norepinephrine influence how we process. The emotional impact solidifies a memory of the event, but it can also change a person's perspective. Studies show that people in a state of awe are more sociable and more open. All of us in the branch that day were impacted by Dave's kindness and courage to act. Dave gained new respect, but the rest of us gained something too. Workplaces always have their share of drama, and our branch was no different. But after the incident, at least for a while, there seemed to be more respect for each other and an overall improvement in office teamwork. In retrospect, the incident also gives me a clue as to the evolutionary roots of awe.

We have seen that the foundation of human success is our capacity for cooperation and collective action. Evolutionary psychologists suggest that awe played an important role in reinforcing social bonds and group dynamics.

> This thinking assumes that for groups to work well, and for humans to survive and reproduce, we must often

> subordinate self-interest in the service of the collective. The collective must often supersede the concerns, needs and demands of the self. Awe evolved to meet this demand of human sociality.[1]

Our ancestors faced extraordinary challenges from predators, other groups, and the environment. We can imagine how individual acts of bravery in fighting off a ferocious saber-toothed tiger, battling an enemy warrior, or leading the group in the face of a powerful storm inspired awe. These acts synchronized the group like some invisible force. People are pulled together by a unifying common purpose when awe acts to suppress individual self-interest in favor of group action. Every sports fan has a memory of a great team, inspired by the spectacular play of one member and pulled to victory by an almost supernatural force. Our capacity for awe is woven into our psyche for its adaptive value in creating connectedness and curbing selfishness.

I remember the sensation of awe the first time I visited Niagara Falls. I feel awe when I reflect on my survival of heart transplantation. I have also had repeated feelings of awe over the same event. In 2012, President Obama paid tribute to the band Led Zeppelin at the annual Kennedy Center Honors. Led Zeppelin was my favorite band in high school and the first major act I saw perform in person, at Three Rivers Stadium in Pittsburgh. My favorite song is "Stairway to Heaven," and luckily that was the song chosen for the live Kennedy Center audience. The lead singer was Ann Wilson, the powerful lead singer of Heart, backed up

---

[1] Dacher Keltner, *Born to Be Good: The Science of a Meaningful Life* (W. W. Norton & Company, 2009), 259.

by her sister Nancy, a full chorus, and a full symphony orchestra. Playing drums was Jason Bonham, the son of deceased drummer John Bonham. In the audience were the three surviving members of Led Zeppelin. The performance was transcendent. Near the end of the song, the cameras zoomed in on lead singer Robert Plant and guitarist Jimmy Page. They both had tears in their eyes. I remember feeling goosebumps, and a tear welled up in my eyes as well. I felt an immediate sense of joy, and I was not alone—the audience rose in an extended standing ovation.

On occasion I will watch the performance to experience the joy again. I am not alone in that either. There are multiple versions on YouTube and combined they have over forty million views. Every time I see it and hear the music, I get goose bumps. The latter are scientifically known as piloerection, "the activation of minute muscles that surround hair follicles distributed throughout the body but in particular in the back of the neck and back."[2] In primates (and probably with our ancient ancestors) piloerection plays a role in adversarial encounters. Piloerection creates the perception of size expansion by having the hair stand on end. Keltner points out that piloerection shifted its use with modern humans.

> In humans, piloerection shifted in its use, coming to occur regularly when we ourselves feel expanded beyond the boundaries of our skin, and feel connected to other group members. We feel goose bumps when listening to an elevating symphony, when chanting in common

---

[2] Keltner, *Born to Be Good*, 263.

> cause at a political rally, when hearing a brilliant mind-expanding lecture, because our self is expanding beyond our physical boundaries to fold into a collective. Piloerection shifted from an association with adversarial defense to connection to the collective.[3]

Political leaders often use awe as a psychological and strategic tool to captivate and influence their followers. When you see the major political party conventions every four years during the presidential election cycle, you can see attempts to provoke awe. The convention stages are adorned with grand multimedia displays. The meetings are filled with emotional stories and testimonials. Videos are used to mark the party's historic victories, past glories, and famous former party leaders. The conventions are intended to sway some voters, but they are mostly used to build enthusiasm for the candidate and the party platform. Conventions usually give a political party a post-convention bounce in the polls. Attendees report leaving with higher levels of commitment and loyalty to the candidate and to their fellow party members. History is filled with autocrats and authoritarian leaders who used awe to win over followers and maintain their power. Documentaries of Nazi Germany show how Hitler used mass rallies, symbols, fiery speeches, and grand displays to build his following. More recently, Kim Jong Un of North Korea and President Xi of China use mass rallies and awe-inspiring displays of military might to maintain a personality cult of leadership. They both foster a sense of us-against-them that reinforces collective loyalty to the party.

[3] Keltner, *Born to Be Good*, 263.

Delivering Awe through Story

The sensation of awe can be created by stories. Our brains love stories, as they are the most efficient means of transmitting information. "As human culture evolved in complexity, storytelling became more than a vital cultural adaptation—our brains evolved with reflexive use of narrative as part of our cognition. Stories shaped our minds, our societies, and our interaction with the environment. Stories save our lives."[4] They do this by embedding critical information in our collective memory.

Through most of human history there was no other way to transmit information, so our brains got very good at recording and telling stories. A list of facts uses only one part of the brain; stories generate activity in multiple parts. Research shows that information gained through stories is twenty-two times more memorable than that gained through other methods.[5]

Brain scans show that the act of storytelling actually synchronizes brains. A storyteller can implant not only information and ideas but emotions. Storytelling binds people together as if they are experiencing an event as one in real time. Oxytocin facilitates this bonding experience. As we have seen in previous chapters, oxytocin is often referred to as the love hormone. As a neurotransmitter, it motivates connection and cooperation. Paul Zak has studied how the oxytocin system can be hacked and used as a motivational tool. Zak measured oxytocin levels in the blood of study subjects. He then showed them videos of character-driven narratives. He found that the stories raised oxytocin levels. He also found that the amount of

[4] Vince, *Transcendence*, 82.

[5] Vince, *Transcendence*, 85.

oxytocin predicted how much people were willing to help others—for example, donating money to a charity associated with the narrative.[6] Stories that create a sense of awe are even more powerful, particularly when they draw attention to a transcendent purpose, like a story that highlights an extraordinary project that helps an organization meet its core mission and purpose.

One fascinating example of the power of storytelling comes from a company that was struggling with declining customer service scores. The CEO had the marketing department deliver multiple presentations to the executive management team about customer satisfaction, but nothing changed. After probing the marketing department about what was happening on the front lines, they suggested he watch some videos of customer focus groups. The customer stories shared in the focus groups were filled with specific details, and the CEO could see the frustration and disappointment on the faces of the customers. He asked the chief marketing officer to share the videos at the next executive meeting and ditch the PowerPoints filled with customer data. In an interview years later, the CEO reported that the stories had a profound impact on his executives. It brought them together in a common purpose. There was no more finger-pointing at who was responsible. The videos created a powerful call to action. Eventually the customer satisfaction scores began to rise again.

We think of business as a place of reason, logic, and data, but storytelling and the sensation of awe have their place as well. Here's Paul Zak talking about his research on oxytocin and its application to business:

---

[6] Zak, "Why Your Brain Loves Good Storytelling," 2.

> These findings on the neurobiology of storytelling are relevant to business settings. For example, my experiments show that character-driven stories with emotional content result in a better understanding of the key points a speaker wishes to make and enable a better recall of these points weeks later. In terms of making an impact, this blows the standard PowerPoint presentation to bits. I advise businesspeople to begin every presentation with a compelling, human-scale story. Why should customers care about the project you are proposing? How does it change the world or improve lives? How will people feel when it is completed? These are the components that make information persuasible and memorable.[7]

I have found that leaders underuse storytelling and are uncomfortable with emotion. Yet the research is compelling about the power of emotional, awe-inspiring stories to motivate and inspire people. These same leaders pay significant sums to have motivational speakers at their annual leadership meetings and offsites, then fail to use storytelling as part of their own leadership toolkit.

Ideas and Applications

- Leaders should develop their storytelling skills and set the tone by incorporating storytelling into their own communication style. Share personal anecdotes, experiences, and examples. Personal storytelling makes a leader's messages

7 Zak, "Why Your Brain Loves Good Storytelling," 3.

more relatable and engaging. It has the added benefit of building trust, particularly if the leaders show vulnerability. For example, leaders who share stories of their setbacks and mistakes create a safe place for others to learn and grow.

- Organizations should provide training and workshops on storytelling. Some people have a natural ability to tell stories, yet everyone can learn the techniques and principles of great storytelling. Stories that work have a clear beginning, middle, and end, lead to an ultimate triumph or lesson learned, and evoke emotions such as empathy, determination, or hope.
- Build an inventory of stories about the organization and share them frequently. Culture is partially the product of the stories that are shared widely among employees. Stories are the best way to communicate the vision and values of the organization. I once worked for a CEO who often talked about how much he valued employees. During a visit to one of the bank's out-of-town locations, he learned that a team of employees had been working long hours for days on an important project. Several of the employees needed to get home, but their commercial flight had been canceled. The CEO stayed behind and had the employees fly back home on the corporate jet. That story became the stuff of legend in the company and spoke more about his and the company's values than many speeches and emails ever could.
- Leaders should find ways to create the sensation of awe through offsite visits to awe-inspiring places. Visits to the Grand Canyon, Yosemite, or Niagara Falls may not be

practical, but brief offsite visits to art and natural history museums, grand cathedrals, or local architectural marvels may evoke awe while reinforcing team identity. The most widely used technique is the use of inspirational speakers or videos that showcase extraordinary accomplishments, art, or innovation. Many companies use motivational speakers, but a prerequisite should be the speaker's ability to evoke the sensation of awe because of its power to reduce the self and reinforce group identity.

chapter 14

Thinking as One Brain

Leadership is always a relationship,
and truly successful leadership thrives
in a culture of high openness and trust.
Leadership and culture can be seen as two sides
of the same coin, and culture is quintessentially
as group phenomenon.

—EDGAR SCHEIN

Team Spirit and Power Density

I HAVE FORMED and led many teams in my life. All had some important purpose and mission, but none could compare to the importance of the purpose of that surgical team on the day I was wheeled into the operating room. Their goal was to save a life—mine! Heart transplantation is a well-established surgical procedure with a high success rate. But it is a complex and time-consuming operation. Look at a depiction of a human heart with all its valves and veins. Prior to my transplant I would look away from the pictures in the cardiologist's office. The thought of the surgeons sewing in all those connections in my chest stressed me out!

My curiosity was about the surgical team and their environment. How were the team members selected? What was the leadership style of the lead surgeon? Was there a strict hierarchy of decision-making? How well do the surgical team members work together? Can a surgical nurse challenge a lead surgeon during the procedure if he sees something amiss?

These are clearly the questions of a former human resources executive. In that role I thought a great deal about how our company got our ten thousand people to do what we wanted them to do, such as serve our customers and make them satisfied, live by our values, collaborate effectively, take the initiative to solve problems, and innovate. I developed a strongly held hypothesis about management and leadership—management cannot hover over every moment and interaction, but culture can. Thus, my question on that momentous day was this: What is the culture of this surgical team? With heart transplantation, mistakes can be catastrophic.

On August 5, 1997, Korean Air Flight 801 crashed into a mountain, killing 228 of the 254 people on board. Malcom Gladwell tells the story of 801 in *Outliers,* his book about human performance and success. In the case of flight 801, Gladwell highlights how cultural factors, specifically the high power distance index (PDI) in Korean culture, may have influenced the communication dynamics in the cockpit. The copilot and crew members were hesitant to question or challenge the decisions of the captain, contributing to the tragic miscommunication that led to the crash.

PDI refers to a dimension of culture discovered by Geert Hofstede in his study of global cultures. "Power distance is concerned with attitudes toward hierarchy, specifically with how much a particular culture values and respects authority."[1] Research shows that

[1] Gladwell, *Outliers*, 205.

Korea has one of the highest PDIs by country, which means people lower in the hierarchy are more likely to defer to higher-ups and less likely to challenge those in positions of authority. Research on team performance shows that high PDI can significantly undermine team performance.

In *Outliers*, Gladwell documents the research on the causes of plane crashes. In surveys, most people assume that plane crashes are caused by weather or mechanical failure. In fact, most crashes are caused by human error.

> The typical accident involves seven consecutive human errors. One of the pilots does something wrong that itself is not the problem. Then one of them makes another error on top of that, which combined with the first error does not amount to catastrophe. But then they make a third error on top of that, and then another and another and another.[2]

In Gladwell's telling, you quickly get the point. If one member of that cockpit sees the captain make a mistake and then fails to question or challenge it, disaster results. At the time of the crash of flight 801, Korean Air had one of the worst loss rates in the airline industry. Evidence suggests that the culture of the cockpit was a significant contributing factor. Korean Air eventually improved its performance, but only after it acknowledged the importance of culture and its influence on communication and collaboration.

....

[2] Gladwell, *Outliers*, 184.

Psychological Safety

Amy Edmondson might describe the old Korean Air cockpit culture as one that lacked psychological safety. Edmondson, a professor at Harvard Business School, is renowned for her extensive research on the concept of psychological safety. She defines psychological safety as "a climate where people feel safe enough to take interpersonal risks by speaking up and sharing concerns, questions, and ideas."[3] Her research highlights the connection between psychological safety and team performance. Teams with an elevated level of psychological safety tend to be more innovative and better at problem-solving. They also share information and collaborate more effectively. Korean Air took significant steps to improve its safety following the crash of flight 801 and several other high-profile accidents. While some improvements were made in aircraft and safety equipment, most of the effort involved cultural reforms and communication training. A key area of focus was breaking down the traditional hierarchical culture of the cockpit and teaching team members how to be more assertive and showing leaders how to foster an environment of openness and challenge.

The health-care industry continuously works to improve patient outcomes. Yet after decades of work and huge investments in technology and training, gaps in quality remained significant. In health care these gaps lead to sick patients failing to recover or, worse, patient mortality. Professor Jody Hoffer Gittell began to study organization performance in health care after earning her doctorate and delivering her first baby. Her first-hand experience with the

[3] Amy Edmondson, *The Fearless Organization: Creating Psychological Safety in the Workplace for Learning, Innovation, and Growth*, (Wiley, 2018), 22.

health-care system led her to begin a nine-hospital study with a focus on surgeries. At the time, she was armed with a theory she had developed working with airlines and the coordination of flight departures. Gittell saw that the quality and nature of relationships was a key factor in organizational performance. This led to the development of Relational Coordination Theory. Simply put, this theory proposes that highly interdependent work is most effectively coordinated through relationships of shared goals, shared knowledge, and mutual respect. The latter overlaps with Edmondson's notion of psychological safety. As Gittell learned, "mutual respect increases the likelihood that participants will be receptive to input from their colleagues in other functions, irrespective of their relative status."[4]

Like the operating team at my transplant, most work in hospitals requires high levels of teamwork and collaboration. Effective collaboration and communication among doctors, nurses, technicians, and support staff are crucial for providing high-quality patient care. Yet in many hospitals, the ideal levels of collaboration and communication are undermined by status, hierarchy, tightly defined roles, and the corresponding lack of psychological safety. Reviews show that many failed surgeries could have been salvaged if only team members had spoken up and challenged or questioned surgeons during a procedure. Like the copilot who failed to question the captain and allowed their jet to crash into a mountain, nurses and support staff often fail to point out errors or share valuable information out of fear of retribution from the higher-status surgeon. The organizational characteristics that undermine performance are legacies of the industrial era. Bureaucracy, hierarchical

[4] Jody Gittell, *Transforming Relationships for High Performance: The Power of Relational Coordination* (Stanford Business Books, 2016), 14.

planning and decision-making, and following orders are remnants of a model that served organizations well during the industrial era with its focus on minimizing complexity and maximizing efficiency. In our modern era of technology and the knowledge worker, most work is highly interdependent. High levels of interdependency require an emphasis on relationships, coordination, trust, psychological safety, and mutual respect.

Along with mutual respect, Gittell's research shows the importance of shared knowledge and shared goals. The inherited bureaucracy that defines most organizations is antithetical to all three. Here is a description of the typical bureaucracy:

- There is a formal hierarchy.
- Power is invested in positions.
- Authority trickles down.
- Big leaders appoint little leaders.
- Strategies and budgets are set at the top.
- Central staff groups make policy and ensure compliance.
- Job roles are tightly defined.
- Control is achieved through oversight, rules, and sanctions.
- Managers assign tasks and assess performance.
- Compensation correlates with rank.
- Everyone competes for promotion.[5]

Many organizations are more complex than the industrial assembly line but retain the characteristics of the industrial era model. In that model, work is largely task dependent and sequential.

[5] Gary Hamel and Michele Zanini, *Humanocracy: Creating Organizations as Amazing as the People Inside Them* (Harvard Business Review Press, 2020), 17.

Worker A does his task and then passes it on to Worker B to do her part. Directions come from the boss and are not to be questioned. Goals are assigned to the worker and focus is on the task at hand. There is less focus on the team and the big picture. This model was great for efficiency and standardization. But as technology has automated many simple tasks, most work has become more complex and highly interdependent. The world has become more complex, and it is rapidly changing. The modern workplace demands workers who are innovative problem-solvers. Most work today requires teams to accomplish organizational goals. Teamwork requires that teams start with the same goals and the same knowledge base and understanding of the current state. The conversations required in the modern workplace need to be built on a foundation of strong personal relationships.

Gittell's concept of relational coordination also expands beyond the social-emotional to unbureaucratic operating structures. Job descriptions and reward systems are redesigned to focus on shared responsibilities and shared rewards. Meetings are transformed from top-down goal dissemination and business updates to team goal setting and getting everyone on the same page. Conflict is actively managed as a process to bring together opposing perspectives and generate new insights and innovative solutions. Shared protocols to guide the work are developed collaboratively by all who have a role therein. Checklists become a tool for group communication and preparation. All relevant information is accessible to all participants and becomes a tool for group performance management. In the hierarchical structure of bureaucratic organizations, information was controlled at the top and flowed downward alongside goals, orders, and performance reviews. A pictorial representation of bureaucracy is the triangle with arrows pointing downward. An organization steeped in relational coordination would look like a circle with arrows pointing back and forth in multiple directions as evidence of the flow of knowledge and information.

Even in an organization practiced in relational coordination, one key to success is team member courage and the confidence to speak their mind. Edmondson frames this as an issue of personal risk.

> Most people in organizations are being evaluated—whether infrequently, overtly, or implicitly—in an ongoing way. The presence of others with more power or status makes the threat of evaluation especially salient, but it by no means disappears in the presence of peers and subordinates.

She describes four specific risks that will make sense to readers based on our description of our evolved social brain.

1. People don't speak up for fear of being seen as ignorant.
2. People don't ask for help, particularly from those of higher status.
3. People often fail to make critical comments because they don't want to appear to be negative or disruptive.
4. People don't speak up "to avoid disrupting or imposing on others' time and goodwill."[6]

[6] Amy Edmondson, "Managing the Risk of Learning: Psychological Safety in Work Teams," in eds. Michael A. West, Dean Tjosvold, and Ken G. Smith, *The International Handbook of Organizational Teamwork* (Wiley, 2003), 255–75.

Sometimes we don't ask for feedback for fear of what we will hear. In meetings we sometimes don't speak up out of a belief that what we have to offer is not important and that we may be wasting others' time. As Edmondson points out, the risk to the individual is far greater in proportion than the lost value of an idea or insight might be to the organization. In an individual's silent calculation, speaking up and saying the wrong thing may damage her reputation and career. But the thousands of unspoken but valuable ideas, insights, and helpful criticisms add up to a massive value loss for the organization.[7]

How a Group Thinks

For our hunter-gather ancestors, all knowledge and learning came from the group. The accumulation of that knowledge is what we call culture. Our brains are wired for culture because, as we saw in an earlier chapter, culture is our survival vehicle,[8] our species's biological strategy. Compared to other large mammals we are neither fast nor strong, but we dominated the ecosystem because of our ability to cooperate and share knowledge that existed at the level of culture, not in any single brain. Belonging may be the most powerful force in our human nature.

In his insightful book *The Culture Code*, Daniel Coyle builds a compelling case for the importance of culture and belonging. Once you get more than two people together to complete a task or solve a problem and keep them together for

[7] Edmondson, *The Fearless Organization*, 34, Table 2.2.

[8] Pagel, *Wired for Culture*, 66.

an extended period, something emerges—a group identity, a way of doing things, a set of beliefs about the way things are, a set of norms about behavior. That is culture. We are wired for culture; it comes naturally to us. Belonging is the connective tissue of culture. As Coyle points out, our brains are constantly searching for belonging cues.

> Belonging cues are behaviors that create safe connection in groups. They include, among others, eye contact, proximity, energy, mimicry, turn taking, body language, vocal pitch, consistency of emphasis, and whether everyone talks to everyone else in the group. Like any language, belonging cues cannot be reduced to an isolated moment but rather consist of a steady pulse of interactions within a social relationship. Their function is to answer the ancient ever-present questions glowing in our brains: *Are we safe here? What's our future with these people? Are there dangers lurking?*[9]

Those questions make sense to those who understand how our brains were shaped by natural selection during thousands of years as hunter-gatherers. Coyle quotes Amy Edmondson when emphasizing the importance of the question of personal safety and our strong propensity for paying attention to cues that relay information about our interpersonal relationships.

[9] Daniel Coyle, *The Culture Code: The Secrets of Highly Successful Groups* (Bantam, 2018), 10.

> We have a place in our brain that's always worried about what other people think of us, especially higher-ups. As far as our brain is concerned, if our social system rejects us, we could die. Given that our sense of danger is so natural and automatic, organizations have to do some pretty special things to overcome that natural trigger.[10]

Safety from the Top Down

Here we can shift into the implications of this understanding to a description of the role of leadership and its role in maximizing individual and organizational performance. At one time, in the industrial era's bureaucratic workplace, leaders sat at the top of the hierarchy, decided on the right strategy, set long-term goals, designed highly structured organizations, relayed orders, and pushed for standardization and efficiency. Leadership was top down, communication one way, following orders and fulfilling tightly defined roles valued over innovation and problem-solving. In the age of the knowledge worker, every worker is valued for their intellectual capital. In other words, not their bodies but their brains. The key question for leaders then is this: What are the conditions that will allow these brains to work best?

Remember that our brains are constantly monitoring the environment for threats and rewards. The goal of leaders should be to create environments that produce reward states and to eliminate behaviors that trigger threat states. Early in my career and in my first job at the family gas station, I saw how threats and

---

[10] Coyle, *The Culture Code*, 12.

shouting produced short-term results but undermined motivation, cooperation, and commitment. This is not to suggest, as a behaviorist might, that leaders simply replace threats, shouting, and other negative behaviors with positive behaviors. As one leadership trainer once suggested to me, a carrot is just another form of a stick.

Creating a genuinely positive environment means creating a workplace where people have a sense of belonging, where they feel psychologically safe, where they have a strong sense of autonomy, and where they feel that what they do matters. This is an important shift in framing about the role of leadership. Leadership theorists often focus on the leader's relationship with followers. Treat people with respect. Practice servant leadership. Be a good listener. These ideas and suggestions are valuable. But a better way to think about it is to think in terms of culture. As Edgar and Peter Schein declared, "The only thing of real importance that leaders do is create and manage culture."

The Scheins describe "traditional twentieth-century leadership" as transactional, which unwittingly creates conditions of low openness and trust. In their view, leadership and culture can be seen as "two sides of the same coin" with "culture quintessentially a group phenomenon."[11] They suggest that we reframe our thinking about leadership training from a focus on improving leadership skills to a focus on developing a deeper understanding about how to improve group performance. In *Humble Leadership: The Power of Relationships, Openness, and Trust*, the Scheins lay out the key principles of humble leadership.

[11] Edgar Schein and Peter Schein, *Humble Leadership: The Power of Relationships, Openness, and Trust* (Berrett-Koehler, 2018), ix.

Relationships: Leaders should focus on building strong relationships with their team members. Schein and Schein describe four levels of relationships (see the following figure on page 310) and suggest that Level 2 is the minimum for creating a culture of high performance, as this is the level that encourages team members to question, challenge, explore, and contribute their insights.

Shared Inquiry: Instead of providing all the answers, leaders engage in shared inquiry with their teams. They facilitate group process rather than decide and communicate their version of truth and action plan. Leaders should promote a learning culture where individuals are encouraged to question and contribute their knowledge and insights.

Cocreation of Meaning: Humble leadership involves a collective effort to create meaning and make sense of challenges and opportunities faced by the organization. It acknowledges that insights and solutions can come from various levels.

Group Identity: Leaders should work toward creating a shared identity and sense of belonging within the team or organization. This helps foster a collaborative spirit and commitment to common goals.

Schein and Schein's humble leadership model challenges traditional top-down leadership structures and encourages a more inclusive and participative approach. Readers of this book will appreciate the reasons why this approach is so powerful as it meets the most basic needs of our human nature—our need for belonging, identity, autonomy, learning, and growth and our desire for meaning and purpose.

SCHEIN'S FOUR LEVELS OF RELATIONSHIPS

Level Minus 1: total impersonal domination and coercion

Level 1: transactional role and rule-based supervision, service, and most forms of "professional" helping relationships

Level 2: personal cooperation and trusting relationships, as in friendships and in effective teams

Level 3: emotionally intimate and total mutual commitment[12]

Figure 7: Schein Leadership Model

Check Your Ego, Make Way for Awe

I eventually did get answers to my questions about the culture of at least one transplant surgical team. Dr. John Craig is a cardiothoracic surgeon who has performed hundreds of open-heart surgeries, including transplants. I interviewed Dr. Craig before I started writing this book. I was most interested in how he creates the right culture for a high-performance team. Like the pilots in the cockpit of a 747, in heart transplantation there is little room for error. I was not surprised when he started his discussion by describing how he fosters positive relationships with the surgical team members. He works to get to know the hospital staff, and he asserted that little things matter like saying hello, checking in on people through visits and texts, and being open about himself and his nonwork life.

[12] Schein and Schein, *Humble Leadership*, 3.

"I found that it was most important that I check my ego at the door," he said.

This assures that team members feel comfortable speaking up and even challenging him during surgery.

Heart transplantation requires extremely high levels of cooperation, coordination, and speed. As Dr. Craig described it to me, "Despite my years of experience, I can't see all that is going on and I need the eyes and ears of everyone on the surgical team." He contrasted his approach with lead surgeons he has worked with who were products of an earlier generation. Their identities were wrapped up in their title and years of experience. They were definitive in their direction, always barking orders, and uninterested in hearing what others in the operating room had to say. As we learned from Dr. Jody Kittel's research, hospital cultures like that were unsafe and often led to judgment errors, mistakes, and poor patient outcomes.

"I want us all thinking as one brain," said Dr. Craig.[13]

While his description of his leadership style was enlightening, I was most struck by Dr. Craig's comments on the sense of awe generated every time a transplanted heart starts beating. He described it as "a front row seat in witnessing a miracle."[14] Talk about team building. Heart transplantation can involve exhausting, four- to six-hour surgeries. Yet Dr. Craig described the emotional reward that accrues to the whole team with a successful surgery. Awe is humbling and renewing both for him and the team.

The workplace has changed dramatically over the last two decades, but some organizational models of leadership are stuck in

....

[13] Interview with Dr. John Michael Craig, cardiothoracic surgeon, January 25, 2021.

[14] Craig interview.

the past. Organizations need to be less hierarchical, less bureaucratic, and more focused on creating a culture that fosters flexibility, change, speed, and innovation. Humans' social brains are naturally wired to operate in the complex web of relationships that make up a culture. When they form, cultures naturally evolve the norms, values, and rules of engagement that guide behavior. But cultures need to be intentionally designed in the same way that organizational structure is designed.

Edgar Schein warned, "If you don't manage culture, your culture will manage you." A leader does this by creating clarity around mission, purpose, and values. Rules of engagement must be clear and clearly aligned with organizational values. Words are important, but actions matter much more. Take an organization that states that one of its values is to "treat everyone with dignity and respect," yet its managers are permitted to shout and emotionally abuse people. The stated values will be ignored, and the culture will become accepting of abusive behavior.

One of the toughest decisions a leader makes is to terminate an employee. Yet it is one of the most important actions for leaders who want to "manage" their culture. People who do not accept and live by the organization's values must go.

One of my favorite managers was one who encouraged people to challenge him if we disagreed. He repeatedly asked for feedback on his decisions and management style. He followed a leader who was tyrannical and dismissive, so it took time for people to trust him. But eventually we all learned that it was acceptable to take contrary positions and speak our minds about issues that concerned us. He thanked people for their feedback and ideas, and I never saw anyone face repercussions for expressing their views. Eventually, this behavior became the new norm for our department. In his first days, this new manager spoke about his values of openness and trust, but it was his role modeling that "managed" the culture. I remember it as one of the best periods of my career.

Bryan Jordan, the CEO of First Horizon, my boss and partner for over fifteen years, led our company with the same values of openness and trust. Bryan believes that the best ideas for serving customers and improving work processes come from the people doing the work. He values a steady upward flow of information and ideas. He also values open dialogue and a steady flow of feedback. As CEO, Bryan has sponsored several employee councils, one focused on creating a positive work environment, one focused on improving quality, and another focused on diversity, equity, and inclusion. All these groups were made up of employees who applied or were appointed to speak for themselves and their colleagues. The conversations in these meetings were documented and presented to executive leadership as a guide for making changes in the organization. The company also sponsored an annual employee engagement survey and a process to provide upward feedback to leaders. These processes managed culture by institutionalizing the values of openness and trust.

Some level of structure is still necessary to run a modern organization. Organization charts and hierarchies of authority and decision-making still make sense. Jobs will still exist (although less tightly defined than in the past) even as work becomes more fluid and employees constantly move from team to team. Change mostly occurs through how organizations operationalize relationships, such as pushing decisions down to the appropriate level, thus delinking knowledge from formal hierarchies and allowing everyone access to information. It assumes that everyone, regardless of level, has some knowledge, ideas, or experience that will be of value.

Another way to think about culture is as the sum of all the relationships in an organization. Imagine for a moment that you had technology to record every conversation that occurred within the company and that those conversations could be tagged as either positive or negative. Using this kind of dichotomy and drawing on Confucius, Dacher Keltner created the jen ratio.

> The jen ratio is a lens into the balance of good and bad in your life. In the denominator of the jen ratio, place recent actions in which someone has brought the bad in others to completion. . . . Above this, in the numerator of the ratio, tally up the actions that bring good in others to completion.[15]

The higher the jen ratio, the higher the "humanity" of the culture. In some organizations, the negativity, distrust, and lack of empowerment and ownership can be picked up in elevator and hallway conversations ("nothing ever changes around here," "the people in charge are out to screw the little guys," "you can't trust the people in the xyz department," and so forth). In others, the jen ratio is high; people feel empowered and that their voices are heard, conflicts are managed productively, and employees feel seen, recognized, and rewarded. One way to think about "managing" culture is to think about how leadership can improve the quality of every conversation. The ideas are endless—teach conflict management skills, foster the

[15] Keltner, *Born to Be Good*, 4.

development of relationships across work silos, hold frequent team-building sessions to enhance trust in teams, and invest in leadership training that teaches leaders how to facilitate productive Level 2 and 3 relationships as described by Schein.

Building and maintaining a culture of positive and productive relationships among team members should be emphasized as one of the most important responsibilities of leaders.

Ideas and Applications

- My leadership style evolved over the years, influenced most by the Scheins' earlier writings on organizational culture and leadership. Over the years, I tried to deepen my relationships with my team members and focused my efforts on creating a culture of openness and trust. These practices served me well.
- Hire for cultural fit over competencies. I looked for people who were collaborators and had a temperament and orientation toward team success versus individual success. I surprised and frustrated some members of my leadership team on occasion when I suggested we hire people light in HR experience. Later, my colleagues acknowledged that the new hires fit well with the team and were significant contributors to team comradery and performance. On a few occasions I let go of highly competent team members who were prima donnas. While good at their job, their focus on individual success undermined team culture.[16]

[16] I acknowledge a few bad hires along the way. It's hard to have 100 percent success when it comes to predicting human behavior and performance, no matter the level of your assessment skills and the rigor of your hiring process.

- Build a leadership team that can operate in a humble leadership model. When assuming leadership of a new team, I always started with an assessment period of my leadership team members. Unfortunately, I often found that some were steeped in traditional hierarchical organizational models. They wanted tightly defined jobs, did not like to share information, wanted direction, and preferred not to take the initiative on solving problems or, more importantly, on changing processes and innovating. I tried my best to be respectful and compassionate, but I had to remove these people from the team. I had learned from experience that some people don't have the personal confidence, the ability to make decisions, and the comfort to operate within a vision and broad team goals without day-to-day direction.

- Develop the team. When taking over a new team there is almost always a need to move quickly. That is why changes to the leadership team are necessary. Once the team is in place and the vision set, team development must be among the goals. A major part of team development is building the skills of team members to work in an environment where they are empowered and know how to use group processes to drive change.

- Build team identity and shared goals. Vision and team goals were always developed through group conversation. Instead of spelling it out myself, I used offsite meetings to develop a shared understanding of the current state. I would present data gathered in advance from surveys and interviews about how the department was viewed by key clients. We also developed a shared view of the challenges faced by the company, the department, and the workforce. This shared understanding made the next step, goal setting, easier. I prefer to have a free-wheeling discussion of all potential goals and then use the group process to narrow the list to five to eight of the most important and urgent. Individual team member goals then flowed from the group goals. As most of us have learned, and as research supports, people who participate in goal setting have higher levels of commitment to achieving those goals.

- Keep team meetings unstructured but highly engaging. I found leadership team meetings to be more valuable with a free-flowing agenda and lots of conversation. I often used the first part of the meeting to give team members an update on the company's financials, CEO and executive priorities, and general company happenings. But the most valuable part of the meetings was the discussion about what was happening in the department. What were the urgent challenges? What was the status of key projects, focusing less on successes and more on significant exceptions to desired results? The key to a good meeting was me listening, guiding the conversation, and team members doing most of the talking. The purpose of meetings should be to build alignment, solve group problems, and to allow team members to hold one another accountable for their part in meeting the team's work projects and goals.

- Focus on the soft stuff. The primary role of a leader is to create culture. The socially oriented brains of our team members work best when they feel psychologically safe, empowered (a sense of autonomy), connected to one another and to the team, and certain that they and the work they do matter. Modern leaders need to be skilled in icebreakers, team-building exercises, conflict management and team assessment tools, personality inventories, and all the other techniques of organizational development.[17]

- Be humble and vulnerable. Brené Brown has been a leading voice in pointing out the power of vulnerability in the modern workplace. She defines vulnerability as "the emotion that we experience during times of uncertainty, risk, and emotional exposure."[18] Schein shows how trust is the key to relationships; Brown's research shows that the key to building trust is vulnerability, and that vulnerability is the foundation of meaningful human connection. Vulnerability is not over-sharing. It is not opening to the world all our past failures and deepest thoughts. Vulnerability is the willingness and the courage to admit that I don't know everything. I don't have all the answers. I have made mistakes. I need help. Leaders who share personal stories about their past failures and what they learned from them often create an immediate bond of trust with their followers. This in turn begins the process of creating a psychologically safe workplace and culture. Early in my career I worked for leaders who would never show vulnerability. They saw it as a weakness. They believed they were paid to have all the answers and that they should never admit to ignorance. The workplaces they created were not conducive to

[17] A business partner-oriented HR department should have professionals who act as independent facilitators and teach OD principles and methodologies.

[18] Brené Brown, *Dare to Lead: Brave Work. Tough Conversations. Whole Hearts.* (Random House, 2018), 19.

innovation, change, or learning. I saw my first company, filled with such leaders, fail to change with the environment—it nearly failed altogether. It was eventually sold to a larger bank, as it could never develop a nimble and responsive culture in a changing industry.

Conclusion

The history of human evolution goes back six or seven million years, when a common ancestor of humans and chimpanzees left the trees of the tropical rainforest for the vast savanna of Africa. These early hominins displayed a mix of apelike and human characteristics.

The demands of the savanna changed our ancestors' biology. Among the first species were the Australopiths, who were bipedal and evolved over two to four million years to become the first members of the genus *Homo*. About 2.5 million years ago, the earliest species of genus *Homo* developed larger brains, lost their fur, and gained the capacity to sweat to cool their bodies. This new body allowed them to travel long distances. Bigger brains led to more sophisticated tool use and a new social structure. That hunter-gatherer lifestyle would go on to shape the final surviving species of genus *Homo, Homo sapiens.*

The secret to our success in dominating the planet is not primarily in our powers of rationality, our problem-solving abilities, or our raw intellect. Our success is due to our culturally oriented social brain. We have deeply embedded mechanisms in our brain that allow us to learn and share knowledge, to promote social interactions and social relationships, and to accept distinct roles that contribute to the greater culture. Individually, we are each one node in a system. Knowledge exists in that network of connected brains. When an individual in the system dies, culture still exists in all the other minds. Individual brains are replaceable.

Culture is a highly complex adaptation. Like other biological adaptations—standing upright, opposable thumbs, and furless bodies—culture allowed us to survive and thrive. Mark Pagel, in *Wired for Culture*, uses the term *culture survival vehicles* to "capture the idea that our species evolved to build, in the form of their societies, tribes or cultures, a second body or vehicle to go along with the vehicle that is their physical body. Like our physical bodies, this cultural body wraps us in a protective layer, not of muscles and skin but of knowledge and technologies . . . it gives us our language, cooperation and shared identity."[1]

Because we are wrapped in this cultural survival vehicle, we can survive and flourish in a wide variety of environments. Individual smartness matters, but our ancestors' success as a species came from their abilities to accumulate knowledge, constantly build upon what they learned, and share those innovations with others in the population. The others in turn built upon those innovations and spread what they learned (the ratchet effect). Among the many mechanisms built into our brains is the ability to learn by watching others. We don't have to figure out everything for ourselves. We have a predilection to pay attention to those who have knowledge so we can learn from them.

The environment shaped our bodies and our brains, but the new social structure would have even more profound impacts on the

[1] Pagel, *Wired for Culture*, 12–13.

way we think and behave today. A human child's brain is not a blank slate. As we have learned, it comes with a bunch of stuff already built in. While it does not have the level of instinctive knowledge as do its primate cousins, the young brain is built to learn new things. Scientists estimate that between birth and age three a child's brain makes one million connections per second. Learning language is the first order of business for the young brain as this knowledge is the foundation for participating in culture. It is estimated that by age two a toddler is learning between two to three new words per day. If a child lives in a German household, it will first learn to speak German.

Similarly, cultural learning will vary widely based on the cultural environment. In the past, an Inuit child would learn how to survive in the cold and eventually how to build kayaks and ice fish. A child born in the tropics would learn how to conserve energy during the hottest time of the day, how to find water, and the intricacies of tracking and hunting. This built-in ability for observational learning is how a toddler learns to connect to a culture. The young brain is an imitation machine, as any new parent quickly learns.

Our ancestors moved from central Africa and learned to adapt and survive in every habitat on the planet through culture and eventually through gene-culture coevolution. An individual, despite the great capacity of the human intellect, is unlikely to have survived alone in unfamiliar surroundings. But united with others, humans incrementally learned, innovated, and accumulated knowledge and technologies as they expanded to new territories. They then passed that knowledge on to their offspring. Over tens of thousands of years, knowledge grew and natural selection did its work, building the basic structure of human brains that are with us today.

Culture—the shared values, knowledge, and practices of a group—is itself an adaptation like the many biological adaptations that allowed our species to become unique and dominant. While other primates show evidence of culture, none approach the scale of human culture. It likely started with the Australopiths, who left the rainforest for the savanna. Those who survived did so in groups. They learned and adapted. Natural selection did its work. At some point, their ancestors learned to start and control fire, cook food, and expand beyond a diet of seeds and tubers to one of large animals. Calories became more abundant, and brains got bigger. Culture got more complex.

Culture is the origin of our values, beliefs, and norms. Culture creates social structures, guides our behavior, and gives us meaning. A "bad" culture, like a dysfunctional family, produces disordered people. A "good" culture can lead to the creation of a civilization that nourishes not only our bodies but also our souls.

Enter gene-culture coevolution. Natural selection favored brains that not only had higher levels of reasoning, problem-solving, and memory, but brains that worked well in groups, that sought the benefits of observational learning and cooperation. Natural selection further refined the human brain to produce behaviors we still see today: socializing and connecting, obeying norms, responding emotionally to tribal symbols, paying close attention to fairness and cheating, respecting status and hierarchy, experiencing guilt and shame, and separating *us* from *them*. All these behaviors and many more can be explored and understood in a deeper way through the lens of evolutionary theory.

We have seen that our brains were shaped by the forces of evolution through natural selection to survive and thrive in a particular environment. As we close this book, I hope you will leave it seeing that our social brains work best—i.e., they are more collaborative, more innovative, better problem-solvers—when they feel safety, belonging, and fairness, have their status and autonomy affirmed, and are given a sense of meaning and purpose.

Our human nature faces some powerful, conflicting centripetal forces. One is a concern for our own interests; the other is the recognition that our greatest achievements, in fact our historical survival, are possible only through our ability to cooperate and collaborate with others. The key to leading and influencing is to understand and master the balance of appealing to individual needs and concerns while reinforcing the power and benefits of group membership.

appendix 1
More Thoughts on Leadership

Originally published in an earlier form as "Dancing in Harvard Yard 11: Of Leaves, Leadership, and the Power of Culture," LinkedIn, October 6, 2022

Where are the leaders who can lead us from the challenging place we find ourselves? Do we have a negative recency bias that causes us to evaluate today's leaders poorly compared to the leaders in our history books? Has the nature of leadership changed? How do we find the next generation of leaders? Big questions for us all to contemplate.

In 2022, the *Wall Street Journal* ran an article titled "Great Leadership, Redefined."[1] The authors, from the Drucker Institute, combined a study of best-run companies (using thirty-four effectiveness metrics) with the results of thousands of psychometric assessments of traits and competencies to identify the profile of a "great leader." While cautious in their wording, the authors suggest an ideal set of traits and competencies for leading in turbulent times. I found the results interesting and generally in line with the profiles of successful leaders I have seen in action in recent years. I must repeat what I have heard at least a hundred times since I started my educational journey at Harvard: correlation is not causation! Has this research revealed the secret to successful leadership—leaders

[1] Rick Wartzman and Kelly Tang, "Great Leadership, Redefined," *Wall Street Journal*, September 19, 2022.

only need to show more openness, more trust, more adaptability, and then all will be fine? If only it were that simple.

The quixotic search for the perfect traits of a successful leader has been attempted for over a century. The fundamental assumption is that effective leaders have certain qualities or competencies that differentiate them from less-successful leaders. The key is to find those unique qualities and use them to select or train leaders. There are several problems with this approach. For one, traits are highly influenced by heredity and very difficult to change beyond a narrow range. A leader can build competencies through learning and experience, but leaders never act alone; by definition, leaders have followers, and their engagement is the real stuff of leadership. By focusing on the traits and competencies of the leader, a researcher misses more than half of the equation, the people being led and the culture that emerges around them.

At a more basic level, the so-named "effective company" data is a snapshot. There are lots of factors that lead to company success: market factors, timing, and often serendipity. Many books touting successful leaders or companies have eventually turned out to be flawed, as many of the sampled companies succumbed to market factors or internal dysfunctions, and their leaders found themselves on a path to early retirement. A better approach would be to find successful companies that thrived over multiple generations. No one leader can be given complete credit for long-term success. Culture is often found to be the real differentiator.

This trait-based approach to understanding leadership is unidimensional. Leadership is a complex social phenomenon that takes place in a specific context with a set of unique people called followers. More recent approaches to studying leadership have considered elements beyond the makeup of the individual in the leadership role. Situational leadership suggests that leaders should change their behavior based on the skill and motivation of the people they are leading. Servant leadership suggests that the main role of a leader is not to exercise power over others but to serve, share power, and foster leadersnip in others. Both these approaches make sense.

I have come to believe that the leader's main role is to build culture. Humans are deeply wired to live and thrive within culture. Harvard professor Joseph Henrich, in *The Secret of Our Success*, describes us as a primarily "cultural species" and says that natural selection has built into our brains a multitude of mechanisms that help us operate better as a group. Research has demonstrated that in certain situations, there is "wisdom in the crowd"—that is, groups often come up with better ideas or solutions than individuals acting alone. The key to leadership is learning how to tap that wisdom. Early in my career I supervised just one or two people. My acts of leadership were primarily engaging in one-to-one relationships with those I led. Once I started managing larger groups, I noticed that an additional phenomenon emerged—what we now know as culture.

Humans are wired with social brains. We care deeply about what others think about us, and we pay close attention to social cues. These socially oriented brains allow us to work together closely, to form group bonds and a group identity. Working together we gain additional strengths and abilities. As individuals, our hunter-gatherer ancestors were easily outmatched by stronger and faster carnivores. But by working together, our ancestors became predators and chased after the beasts until they lay exhausted from the hunt. The planning, coordination, and communication required for a successful hunt allowed us to survive for thousands of years, and the skills we acquired are deeply embedded in our nature.

So, if we are social and cultural creatures, what are the implications for leadership? What should leaders do? Here are a few thoughts. First, build a group identity, one that has purpose and meaning beyond meeting work objectives. In the latter part of my career, all my teams built a vision statement that included an aspirational goal. For example, we set in place the idea that we would be recognized as a thought leader in our field, that others would come to us for best practices and ideas. People want to be part of something special and unique, and I believe that our vision helped meet that need. Eventually, our team did win several recognition awards for local and regional HR professional organizations that validated our sense that we were moving closer to our aspirational goal. Team members felt they were part of something special, not just in a job, collecting paychecks.

Leaders also need to be engaged in managing the relationships between team members. I once fired a highly competent leader from our leadership team because she had difficulty working well with others. She was a prima donna who had a toxic need for recognition and attention, and her behavior was upsetting and disruptive to the team. I also ensured that our team had time to build relationships of trust. At our quarterly off-sites, we checked in on our goals, spent time on alignment building and problem solving, but also took time to do team building and have fun.

I once worked for a very capable leader who disliked engaging with team members who were stuck in a dispute about how to proceed on a project or solve a team problem. His belief was that we should be "adult enough" to work it out. But that is difficult when two team members share equal power and strong but differing views about how to move ahead. A leader must step in and act as a guide and facilitator. I tried not to frame it as breaking a tie or using my power to make the final decision; I tried to use my experience, knowledge, and influence to guide the decision-making process. Things didn't always work out to everyone's complete satisfaction, but the process allowed the team to move forward. While with my one-time boss, there were times when decisions dragged on for months. The damage to team progress and morale was significant.

A leader needs to ensure a psychologically safe workplace. In her excellent book *The Fearless Organization: Creating Psychological Safety in the Workplace for Learning, Innovation, and Growth*, Harvard professor Amy Edmondson lays out a strong case for building a culture in which people feel free to speak up and suggest ideas without fear of ridicule, renunciation, or retaliation. As pointed out earlier, our socially wired brains are highly sensitive to how we are perceived by others, particularly higher-ups. On a nonconscious and sometimes conscious level, our brains are constantly asking an important question: Am I safe here? Employees who feel trusted and safe are more collaborative, solve problems more effectively, and are significantly more innovative. The most important person in creating a psychologically safe workplace is the leader, who by declaration and role modeling ensures that all their colleagues' brains are in a trust state and not a threat state.

As a leader, I recognized later in my career that my experience and knowledge were valuable but nowhere near as valuable as the collective knowledge and experience of my team. I came to realize that my job was not to always have the answer but to create a safe place for the best answer to emerge from the team. To create a learning culture, leaders should ask lots of questions. Research has shown that people are highly motivated when their ideas are generated from within. I saw that my team members would follow my lead because they trusted my knowledge and experience. But I also noticed that our biggest successes did not originate from my ideas but from theirs.

In summary, it is a good idea to reflect on your strengths and build on your personal competencies. But I have seen successful leaders with a wide variety of personality types, strengths, and experiences. The successful ones recognize the importance of culture and of creating team identity and purpose. They recognize the wisdom of teams and the importance of creating a psychologically safe environment. The key thing to remember is that the leader doesn't have to be the smartest person in the room—just the one who brings out the best answer through the culture they have built.

appendix 2

Are Leaders Born or Made?

Originally published in an earlier form as
"Dancing in Harvard Yard 7:
Are Leaders Born or Made?,"
LinkedIn, May 24, 2022

One of the Advanced Leadership Initiative (ALI) sessions I attended during my fellowship at Harvard was led by Professor Linda Hill of the Harvard Business School. Professor Hill is regarded as one of the top experts on leadership and innovation and has also studied leadership development. During her session, one of our ALI members raised this age-old question: Are leaders born or made? Based on my classmate's experience and a recent study of CEOs in his organization, his conclusion was that leaders were "more born than made."

Professor Hill seemed a bit startled by the conclusion. I immediately thought, *Here's a woman who has spent most of her academic life studying and teaching people how to be better leaders. If leadership ability is innate, she most likely would have selected another career path.* After gathering her thoughts, Professor Hill pointed out that covering the research, behind that question would take far more time than the ninety minutes allotted for our session, but that based on her research, leadership effectiveness is largely the result of a self-development process.

So what does the research say about this question? Let's start with twin studies that show that some people have an innate predisposition to leadership roles. These studies don't address leadership effectiveness but an individual's desire to lead. Other research points to the fact that this desire to lead also correlates with a desire to grow one's leadership effectiveness. In my thirty years as an HR executive, I observed the performance and development of thousands of leaders. The best leaders were often regular readers of leadership literature, the first to sign up for leadership development, and the most active participants in leadership training. My experience seems to confirm Professor Hill's comment. If you care about being a better leader, you will work at it.

There are major research challenges in answering this big question. One is to identify the qualities that differentiate average from high-performing leaders. Two decades ago, Daniel Goleman, Richard Boyatzis, and Annie McKee released *Primal Leadership: Realizing the Power of Emotional Intelligence*. The book became an international bestseller, and their work became the foundation of a leadership development program that has gathered data on thousands of leaders. Their finding: great leaders have high emotional intelligence. More specifically, they exhibit qualities such as empathy, self-awareness, and emotional stability.

Their research has been supported by much that followed. In *Humble Leadership*, Edgar Schein argues that leadership is primarily relational and built on the capacity of the leader to cultivate an environment of openness and trust. In a meta-analysis of research on the psychological predictors of leadership effectiveness, personality traits such as curiosity, extroversion, and emotional stability explain around 40 percent of the variability between leaders' performance. The Center for Creative Leadership has identified empathy, courage, self-awareness, and the ability to influence among the ten key qualities for effective leadership.

Now back to the debate about born versus made. The key qualities of leadership as documented above are largely trait based; based on decades of research, primarily twin studies, we now know that personality traits have high levels of heritability. For example, according to studies of the Big Five personality traits (extroversion, agreeableness, openness, conscientiousness, and neuroticism—based on the most widely accepted theory of personality) about 40 to 60 percent of variance can be explained by heredity. So does this mean leaders are born? Not so fast.

I like Jonathan Haidt's analogy about the brain being like a book. The first draft is written by the genes during fetal development. No chapters are complete at birth, just rough outlines waiting to be filled in by experience. It seems some of us have some natural wiring that drives us to leadership roles and some traits that serve us well in creating an environment that people want to work in. Genes matter. But the good news is they aren't destiny. We do have agency, and all of us have the capacity to be effective leaders.

Some of us are naturally more people oriented, some of us have a greater need to influence, and some of us have better awareness and control of our mood states. But many years of research on leadership development shows that people can increase their emotional intelligence, can learn to communicate more effectively, and can develop the personal courage to take positions on issues, make decisions, and inspire others.

Going back to our ALI discussion, I mentioned that my classmate asked the question about born versus made relative to CEOs. We can add another dimension to this debate: general mental ability

(GMA), better known as IQ. It is well established that GMA is the single best predictor of job performance for almost every level of job from processor to professional to senior executive. As an HR executive, I used GMA testing for many jobs and almost always for senior-level roles. The more complex the role, the stronger the relationship between GMA and performance.

Like personality traits, GMA is highly heritable. In fact, using statistical analysis of populations, researchers have found heritability of intelligence between 57 and 73 percent. One study showed that Fortune 500 CEOs are cognitively highly gifted and often in the top 3 percent in IQ scores. While a relationship exists, it doesn't mean the smarter you are the more likely you are to be a successful CEO. The evidence seems to suggest a baseline intelligence is needed to manage the complexities and challenges of being a CEO. But being a little bit smarter doesn't mean a little bit better, particularly in leading others. CEOs also need high levels of experience, resiliency, and emotional intelligence.

We all enter life with a repertoire of innate abilities, proclivities, and aptitudes (the born stuff). I can see why my colleague saw evidence for the great leaders are born argument. There is much to support the case. But it is our life experience, the skills we develop, the knowledge we gain that make us who we are. Back to Haidt, our brain is a book in draft—the chapters are outlined, but our unfolding lives fill in the rest of the story. The answer to the big question then . . . leaders are both born and made.

I once coached a leader who did not have the empathy and emotional intelligence to be a good leader. He loved the status and pay of the role, but he didn't seem to care about the feelings of others. When I told him I was ready to give up on him, he asked me for one piece of advice that would help him be a better leader. I pointed to a sign he had recently hung on his office wall for all his employees to see. It read, "My door is always open . . . hopefully you'll leave." I suggested he remove it.

appendix 3

The Power of Dreams

Originally published in an earlier form as
"Dancing in Harvard Yard 8: Dreams,
a Miracle, and the *Blue Baron*,"
LinkedIn, June 5, 2022

I HAVE WRITTEN a great deal about stories and why leaders should use more to connect with the people they lead. I used stories in my role as an executive. The best stories come from our life experiences. The one I shared that seemed to touch people the most was a story written long ago by my mom, titled "The Adventures of the Blue Baron: How to Take a Vacation with a Family of Eleven When You Own a Five-Passenger Car." Here's the backstory and my version.

Mom and Dad secretly married at a tender age; she was only seventeen, and he just short of twenty-one. Mom's marriage caused a rift with her father that never healed. Except for the few words that would come with the passing of the phone, they never spoke again. Their first home was an extra bedroom at Grandpa Daniel's house. They both worked in local retail stores. She had just graduated high school. Dad had quit school at sixteen and later joined the Navy. He returned home from duty with few job skills. And so, with only a few dollars in their pockets but lots of love in their hearts, their life together began.

Mom said she always wanted a large family. The babies came in a steady stream, with Maureen arriving in February 1952, followed by the rest of us in '53, '54 (me), '56, '57, '60, '61, '65, and '66. Facing life largely on their own, Mom and Dad struggled. In the first decade together, Dad had difficulty finding steady work and paying the rent. We were forced to move ten times before Mom found a kind real estate agent who helped her secure the house that would become our family home. It is still in the family today.

I remember regularly helping Mom and Dad clean the agent's local office and cutting grass at his house. I learned later that that was how they paid the mortgage when times were tight. How Mom managed to buy a house with bad credit, no money down, and Dad working irregularly is a small miracle, one I'll save for another story.

While finances were tight and Dad struggled with his demons, I remember a largely happy childhood. The home Mom found was right across the street from a large city park. We had one another, lots of friends, and Mom's steely determination to provide us a good life.

But there was one thing our family never had a chance to experience together—a family vacation. Dad was a big talker and a dreamer. He often rattled on about his plans for a fancy family vacation, among other things, that never came to pass. As my older sisters came to the end of their high school years, Dad must have felt pressure to deliver. Then one cold January day, Dad's big dream began to take shape.

My brothers and I were watching a game on TV when we heard some commotion outside. As we peeked through the window, we saw Dad on his police motorcycle (Dad became a policeman in 1966, and for the first time the Daniel family had a steady paycheck) and behind him was a tow truck. On the back of the truck was an old, beat-up half-bus. I'll let Mom take over the story.

A banged up red railroad crew bus, forlorn and unwanted, sat in a lot on the North Side. Something inside wasn't working, and after ten years of faithful service, the powers that be decided it was ready for the junkyard.

Then one day, one of Pittsburgh's finest pulled up in the lot on his motorcycle.

"Hey fella," he said. "What's wrong with that bus? How much is it?"

After much discussing of the problems the bus had acquired on its journey through life and the possibilities of its future, the two men parted with an agreement, and that bus could go home with the policeman after a small money transaction had taken place.

As we walked outside, Dad's excitement was palpable. He looked over to us and said, "Boys, I bought this bus. We are going to fix it up, paint it, and we're going to Disney World in it!" We were teenage boys in a working-class neighborhood. We were horrified. What would our friends think of Dad's latest scheme?

But Dad had a dream, and dreams can be powerful. The old bus was towed to the alley behind our house. The rough Pittsburgh winter seemed to make it look even worse. And my friends did get a good laugh out of it. "What's your crazy dad going to do with that old bus?" I played down his plans to my friends, but secretly I was excited about it. Could this old hunk of junk make it to Disney World?

Over the years, I have learned a lot about big dreams. At first many people are skeptical, even belittling about another's big dreams. Most times they mean well. "Do you really want to take that risk?"

"Are you sure that old bus is safe?" But Dad was undaunted. He had a dream, and most of his dreams hadn't quite worked out. This one was for his family.

As spring rolled around, on most mornings you could find Dad, who worked the late shift, working on the bus. Our neighbor, an old handyman himself, would often be found with him. And after school and on weekends you could find the younger neighborhood kids rallying around Mr. Daniel and his old bus. Little kids have imaginations not yet crushed by the inner critic of adolescence.

In the meantime, Mom was making plans behind the scenes. She wasn't quite sure about that bus, but she knew her Bud, as she affectionately called him. This dream was for his kids. It had done something to him. He was determined, and she would not be caught flat-footed. Calls to campsites, tourist spots, and even Disney were made. A target date was set: August 1972.

Dad's plans were probably ignited by word that Walt Disney had opened the Magic Kingdom in Orlando, Florida, in October 1971. Dad had been to Florida in the Navy; he had a map in his mind. He knew his kids faithfully watched Walt Disney's TV show every Sunday night. But how could he get eleven people to cover almost two thousand miles on a shoestring budget? Then he saw that bus.

As spring transitioned to summer, the number of believers multiplied. That's the funny thing about big dreams. When you are determined and you dig in, people start signing on. As the August date got closer, on any summer morning you could find a half dozen or more people working on Mr. Daniel's old bus.

In those days there was still separation of labor by gender. The boys scraped, sanded, and painted outside while the girls made seat covers and curtains for the windows. The bus would not only serve as transportation but as a live-in camper. A rack was welded on the top of the bus and painted white. This would hold the tents, cots, grills, and other camping necessities.

In July the old bus was painted a bright blue color with leftover paint from one of Dad's friends. Much to my dismay, Dad found someone to paint our name on the bus.

The Daniel Family shone in white lettering on the driver's side of the bus. And my sisters came up with a name, largely due to the paint and a well-known song of the era. *The Blue Baron* was painted on the top front of the bus above the windshield.

It took months of work and a new battery to get the engine to run after many failed tries to turn it. I remember a bunch of us bus workers standing by and hearing the engine grind and grind. Other than the *grrrr* of the pistons churning, there was a quiet tension, and then *vroom* followed by a big cheer. Dad, bursting with pride, called for all of us to jump on board as he rode around the neighborhood loudly honking the bus's odd-sounding horn. I was on the bus for that first ride. I was seventeen. I was horrified!

As the day of departure got closer, Mr. Daniel, his old bus, and his big dream became the talk of the neighborhood. As final preparations were made the bus was parked in front of the house. Every day people would walk by and wish us well. Now back to Mom's version of the story of that eventful day.

> *The sun was just beginning to shine brightly that August morning. The cop, his wife, and the nine kids scurried around locking doors and windows, grabbing forgotten shoes and sweaters. And then they all piled into the Baron. Everyone picked their seat, settled down, sat breathlessly, and waited. Close the door, fix the seat, adjust the mirror, and the cop, finally comfortable in the driver's seat, said, "Ok, roll call! Everyone here? Do we have everything? Florida, here we come!"*

Dad had a dream, and dreams can be powerful. As he pulled away from the house, I remember him saying, "I am not sure we will make it to Florida, but wherever we end up, we are going to pitch the tents and stay for two weeks."

About one hour outside of Pittsburgh, a Good Samaritan driver waved us over to alert Dad that an inner tire had gone flat. I could see the concern on his face. He had stashed $200 above the budget for emergencies, and a new tire would eat up half of it. After a quick tire change, we were off again. There would never be another emergency. The *Blue Baron* would hold.

The rest of the trip went largely as planned. First stop, Washington, DC, our nation's capital and a great place for a family looking for free stuff to do. After our history lesson, we next arrived at Virginia Beach and my first view of the ocean. Next came Myrtle Beach, where we set up camp right on the sand.

As the first of two weeks unfolded there were stops in Jekyll Island, Georgia, and Jacksonville and Daytona Beach, Florida. And then finally the highlight of the trip, the Magic Kingdom. In the first year of operation, there was only one park in what is now Walt Disney World. The Magic Kingdom had only twenty-two attractions, but we loved it. Besides, one day was all our budget could afford.

After a few days of rest at a campsite in Florida, we started the one-thousand-mile journey back home. Our crazy father had done it! Along the way a bonding occurred that often happens with families after sharing meaningful events. It seemed all the conflicts and sibling rivalries were pushed to the back of our minds as we cherished that remarkable journey.

Our trip south to Disney followed a route along the East Coast. Our return trip took us through the deep and mid-South. We visited lakes and parks and a few relatives along the way. We passed through the beautiful bluegrass of Kentucky, through the flat turnpikes in Ohio, and then on to the hills of western Pennsylvania. We started counting the miles out loud as we got closer to home.

We prayed as the bus made noises and jerked about on a few steep climbs. And we prayed that we would make it home in time to see our friends to tell them about our adventure. As we climbed over the last hill at the top of our home street, we cheered. Many of our friends in the nearby park saw us coming. They raced to the bus and cheered, "The Daniels have made it home!" "They did it! They made it to Disney and back!"

Dad beamed with pride as he stood outside the bus and received all the welcoming cheers. This time it had really mattered, and he had done it! And as for that old bus . . . well, after one additional short trip, its life gave out. It sat behind our house for a while before it met its inevitable fate, a last resting place at the junkyard.

And as for me, I wasn't horrified anymore.

In 1996, Mom and Dad heard that Disney was planning a big twenty-fifth anniversary celebration of the opening of Disney World. They called a family meeting—with grandchildren, the family now numbered over thirty-five—to plan our own anniversary celebration. We reminisced about the adventures of the *Blue Baron*, as we often do, and enthusiastically embraced the idea. Sadly, both Mom and Dad died within a month of each other in May and June of 1997. Our anniversary trip was delayed a bit. But we all made it back later that year.

Mom and Dad had purchased a brick outside the Magic Kingdom commemorating our 1972 trip. On the return trip we fanned out across the front of the Magic Kingdom to find that piece of family history. There was a lot of ground to cover, but with over thirty people we found it. We gathered around the brick in a circle, hugged, and prayed for Mom and Dad—all in our Daniel Family T-shirts. It was one of those special moments in life.

Dreams can be powerful. They can lead to miracles, and sometimes the stories that are left behind can inspire for generations.

Acknowledgments

I OWE A HUGE debt of gratitude to Leslie. You supported me through two open-heart surgeries including my heart transplant. During the months of living on the Left Ventricular Assist Device and the recovery from both surgeries, your patience and optimism never wavered. Thank you for your enthusiastic support of my one-year appointment as a Fellow at Harvard. I know the time away from each other and the travel was challenging, but you never complained. I will never forget how you walked over a mile in the snow in Cambridge so you didn't miss your morning exercise class. And lastly, thank you for your support while writing this book and for your partnership in building Bluff City Pickleball, our social enterprise. During those early months you never lost faith in me or the grand idea of providing a place for people to connect and improve their health and wellbeing.

I want to acknowledge the role played by the women in the early part of my life. Mom was a role model for strength and resilience. She raised nine children with only the most modest of financial means and all my siblings grew to be loving parents, supportive aunts and uncles, and productive engaged citizens. Mom always challenged me to think about others and to see the world through the lens of critical thinking. This book could not have happened if my young mind hadn't flourished under her early mentorship. Thank you to my five sisters who still provide encouragement and thoughtful advice and, on a few occasions, hard messages I need to hear. I will also never forget my first love, Janet, whom cancer took from us in 2011. She fell in love with an awkward, working-class kid with not much going for him but an associate's degree from the local community college and some big dreams. If you can read from heaven, thank you for believing in me.

Thank you to my three sons, John, Jason, and Jeff. I can see the strength and resilience of our family passed on to you. Jason and Jeff, you are amazing dads with the way you love and invest in your children. All three of you exhibit qualities I value most of all, the ability to think critically and to care about others. Our many conversations over the time I was researching and writing this book helped me in countless ways. I add my thanks to Lindsey and Teresa, the mothers of my grandchildren. We are blessed by your brilliance and your kindness.

I am also deeply grateful to all my managers, peers, and those I was fortunate to lead. You helped shape me as a partner and a leader over my forty-seven years in banking. One deserves special mention, Bryan Jordan, at first my colleague and then my boss. I can't imagine that there could have been a better partnership than ours. I always admired the thoughtful way you made decisions while also caring deeply about how those decisions impacted the lives of people. Our many conversations about work, people, politics, and life in general challenged and stretched my thinking. Your support during the loss of my first love and during my recovery from open-heart surgeries was critical in helping me get back on my feet.

Special thanks to my colleagues on the executive management team at First Horizon during the decade we worked to restore a struggling company to its former glory. My years at First Horizon were the most satisfying of my career. Here's a tip of my hat to Yousef Valine, David Popwell, Charlie Tuggle, BJ Losch, Vernon Stafford, Susan Springfield, Mike Kisber, Mike Waddell, and Bruce Lievsay. And finally, thank you to those who followed and believed in me as a leader. Most of what I share in this book came from learning from and with you. Special mention to Angela Moss, Ken Bottoms, Tanya Hart, Gardiner Gruenewald, Kevin Nieman, Mario Brown, Kristi Morgan, Markita Jack, Karen Sones, Cindy Cleveland, Carl Potenza, Doug Edwards, Kevin Rodgers, Jill Hidaji, Maggie Laureano, Barbara Blyth, Audrey Fox Bonnet, and the best colleague of all time, Linda Jones.

Thank you to the Harvard Advanced Leadership Initiative class of 2022. My year in Cambridge was the most rewarding development experience of my life. I cherish the many hours of dialogue, debate, and learning with some of the finest people in the world, all there to make our planet a better place to live. And finally, thank you to my dear friend Mark Sullivan. Our friendship has spanned four decades. When your number lights up on my phone, I know the time that follows will include updates on life, interesting ideas, and kind words.